TRUE NATURE

Copyright © 2022 by David Smart

All rights reserved. No portion of this book may be reproduced mechanically, electronically, or by any other means including photocopying without the written consent of the publisher.

ISBN: 978-1-7349842-2-4

Also available in electronic format.

Cover by Kett McKenna
www.Instagram.com/kettdoesart

Edited by Ben Wolf
https://benwolf.com

Typesetting by Jo Roderick
www.BookCover.biz

If you would like to read more of my work, my thru-hiking memoir The Trail Provides is available on Amazon and Audible today. I also keep a blog, which you can follow at
www.ThinkingWithDavid.com

Send inquiries to **smartdavid@mac.com**.

For you—the dreamer, seeker, and lover.

"As a mighty flood sweeps away the sleeping village, so death carries away the person of distracted mind who only plucks the flowers of pleasure."

–Dhammapada, Verse 47

True Nature

TRUE NATURE

The Wise Woman in Nepal and Searching the Himalayas for Enlightenment

DAVID SMART

2022

True Nature

CHAPTER 1
ARRIVAL

Her eyes, like whirlpools, pull me into her. We kiss. I melt into her. Warm sensations flood my body as our lips touch. I run my hands across her breasts. Her skin is soft and smooth and real, as if nothing had ever split us apart.

After, I collapse into her arms. Raindrops pelt the windowpane, and winds sweep through the city streets. I hold her and tell her I love her. She smiles and whispers to me.

"What?" I ask.

I can't hear anything. Not the sound of my own voice. Not the rain. Not the thunder. Her lips move again, her eyebrows knit together, and her face twists into a grimace. And then the floor crumbles beneath me.

I reach out for her, but it's too late. Down I go, further and further into a deep dark abyss. All the way to the bottom.

The cabin shakes as our plane touches down, and I wake up covered in sweat. I exhale deeply, grab my daypack, and lift myself up. After twenty-four hours in coach, my mind feels like a blur and my legs feel like wooden planks. But I shake them out and follow Bradley toward the exit.

It's an early spring day, and a thick humidity washes over me as I make my way down onto the tarmac. *Why's it so hot here?*

I imagined Kathmandu as sharing the Himalaya's cold mountaintop climate. A crisp, magical snowfall blanketing the ground. Instead, I gaze up to an overcast sky shrouding the sun and a fog covering the horizon. The Himalayas must be out there somewhere. I blink hard, trying to shake myself from the dream, but everything remains the same.

I look over at Bradley and manage a smile. "We made it."

Bradley squeezes my shoulder and grins. "We sure did, brother."

Bradley at the Kathmandu airport

We follow the crowd of passengers into the brick building then shuffle through the airport's hallways like zombies.

"Next!"

Bradley and I hand our passports to the immigration officer, a man with a blue cap, matching uniform, and bushy eyebrows.

"How long you stay?" His gaze bears down on us, his bushy-brows reaching out to grab me.

Chapter 1

"Ninety days," Bradley replies.

The officer's eyes narrow. "Long time..."

Ninety days does seem like a long time to travel abroad in some sense, but it's only half the time we spent on the trail. I can't help but think we're in a race against time.

"Trekking?" the officer asks.

"Yes, sir," Bradley says. "And living with a spiritual teacher. We're here for enlightenment."

The man stares at us blankly, and his mind seems to weigh the importance of this information. Then he stamps our visas and waves us through unceremoniously.

"Next!"

As we take the hallway to security, Bradley turns to me and shrugs. "Hey, not everyone's going to get it."

Yeah, I guess not. Few people seem to care about enlightenment these days. My interest only developed within the last three years, shortly after the trail.

The Pacific Crest Trail, also known as the PCT or what I now call "the trail," changed my life forever. Four years ago, I hiked for six months across the United States from Mexico to Canada through California, Oregon, and Washington. I made that trek with Bradley—my former college fraternity brother turned lifelong friend.

It was the journey of a lifetime. Together, we struggled through harsh deserts, pristine forests, and desolate wilderness. We hiked an average of twenty miles a day from April to October through heat, hail, sleet, and snow. We met fascinating people, slept beneath the stars, overcame near-death situations, and pushed beyond our imagined capabilities. The trail brought us together and seeded the desire for yet another adventure.

After pushing past security, Bradley and I glimpse our backpacks beside the carousel. *Thank God.* I've put more money into my backpack and its contents than any other material possession in my life. Not to mention an envelope holding a thousand dollars cash. My budget for the entire trip.

It's not much, but Bradley says we're living rent-free with the wise woman. All I need to worry about is covering the cost of trekking permits, meals, and hostels for the other ninety days. Avoiding unplanned expenses and living on a shoestring budget is mission critical. We've got to stretch the dough as long as possible.

Also, maybe it's flawed logic, but I figure the cash is safer in my backpack than in my fanny pack where it could easily fall out if I'm not careful. The odds of me losing my backpack seem far less likely. If that happens, I'm already screwed. Might as well put all my eggs in one basket.

I throw my backpack over my shoulder and give it a few good shakes with my knees. It's heavy, nearly twice the base weight of my backpack from the trail. *Did I pack more just than the essentials?*

My gear for the next three months

Chapter 1

I take mental stock of my belongings: A twenty-degree sleeping bag, a one-person tent, and a twenty-liter titanium cookpot. Two hard-shell plastic water bottles. A toothbrush, a bottle of toothpaste, and a headlamp. A small knife, a titanium spoon. I've got the clothes on my back, the sandals on my feet, a rain jacket, down jacket, three changes of clothes, and a brand-new pair of trail runners. Bradley and I started hiking the PCT barefoot, and I'm not making *that* mistake again.

It doesn't seem like much, but the little things add up. The added weight must be from thinking international travel necessitates a larger wardrobe, a decision I'm already regretting.

After stopping by the currency exchange, we walk outside. A familiar humid air descends upon us, as does a swarm of tour guides, hoteliers, and taxi drivers.

"Taxi! Hotel! Taxi!"

"I'll handle this," Bradley says to me. "Mind seeing what that hostel was called?"

"Sure thing."

I shrug off my backpack, slide down a brick wall, and connect my phone to the airport's Wi-Fi. An old friend from the trail had recently visited Kathmandu. *Where did he recommend we stay, again?*

As I search for his message, I wonder: *why didn't Bradley and I book a hostel in advance?* Come to think of it, we don't have any concrete plans for this trip. I suppose it's because we've been through hell and back together. We'd hiked across the United States, escaped blizzards, nearly died of dehydration in the middle of the desert, and pushed for thirty-mile days to finish the trail—accomplishments I never thought possible for myself in this lifetime.

Ultimately, walking across the country in the face of such challenges reinforced our confidence to problem-solve, brought greater meaning to our hike, and brought us closer together.

By this point, we're like brothers. The need for plans or itineraries is trivial compared to our previous challenges and even takes away the opportunity for potentially magical scenarios. We know what's important. The details are superficial.

As the thought completes itself, I find my answer.

Check out Zostel, my hiker friend had messaged me.

Zostel. That's the one. A bit of a ridiculous name, though. *Hostel Zostel.* Sounds less like a hostel and more like a Dr. Seuss allegory about a hippie's utopian commune.

I shoulder my backpack and join Bradley in the street as he tosses his own backpack into the trunk of a yellow cab. For being such a tall guy, he must figure he can carry a heavier pack because his is nearly twice the size of mine and takes up nearly the entire trunk. I begin the process of shoving mine in, too.

"This is our guy," Bradley says. "Did you find us a place?"

"Yeah. How much for the ride?"

"Cheapest I could get him was fifty rupees."

"Isn't that less than a dollar?"

Bradley smiles and slaps me on the back. "I told you I'd handle it, didn't I?"

I slam the trunk closed then nod. I guess our money might last in a place like this after all.

The moment we hop into the backseat, a man wearing sunglasses slides into the front passenger's seat and introduces himself as our guide. We didn't ask for this service, but he speaks decent English. Maybe he knows something we don't.

The man drops his sunglasses to the bridge of his nose and gazes through the rearview. "Where you want to go?"

"Zostel," I say. "Hostel Zostel."

The guide relays the request to our driver and the two discuss in Nepali. When we pull out from the parking lot, I scramble for my non-existent seatbelt.

"Don't worry," the guide says. "Driving is no problem."

Chapter 1

I'll soon realize he's lied to me. But for now, the ride isn't too bad.

A long stretch of highway carries us over a hill, revealing a city sprawling across a wide valley beneath a hazy sky. Kathmandu Valley. The hive of civilization appears unending. Building after building stretches over an uneven landscape, settled in a smog like the bottom of a murky pool.

We dip into the valley, passing worn-down buildings, shanties, and under-construction shops lining the dirt road. Where the road widens, we're thrust into the throng of downtown traffic. I stare wide-eyed out the windshield as a flurry of motorcycles, mopeds, and scooters weave frantically around us. Beeping horns, sputtering tailpipes, and revving engines clog the streets, sounds so loud that they feel as if they're coming from inside my skull.

Kathmandu taxi ride into the city

Our driver slams the brakes, and I clench my teeth. A motorbike narrowly slides in front of our bumper then disappears into the mass of motor vehicles ahead as if nothing had even happened.

Everything is disorienting: driving on the left side of the road, the complete lack of stoplights, signals, and street signs. I have no idea if we're heading in the right direction, and if laws apply to the roads, they appear to be more like suggestions.

I roll down my window to get a grip on what's going on, but when a putrid smog pours into the vehicle, I roll it back up. My eyes sting from the foul air.

"*Po-llu-shun*," the guide says, glancing through the rear-view mirror. "In last five years, lots of *po-llu-shun*. So many of vehicles."

"Ah," I reply. That explains the hazy skies. It's the pollution, not my dream-world bleeding into reality.

Bradley shakes his head as he gazes out at the smog. "Good thing we shouldn't be here for too long. As soon as we nail down our trekking plans, we can head out and meet Sajana in Pokhara. Pokhara's supposed to be a smaller city. So hopefully less motorbikes, less pollution."

"Air much better in Pokhara," echoes the guide.

"What about the Himalayas?" Bradley asks, leaning forward and pointing into the haze. "How's that air?"

"Very pure, very fresh. No *po-llu-shun*."

Bradley falls back into his seat and grins. "I can almost smell it from here."

His sarcasm is dead-on. Even though we must be surrounded by the Himalayas, this foreign, lawless city is a purgatory between one world and the next. Kathmandu feels miles away from that pure Himalayan air.

I lose myself to staring at the passing motorbikes when our taxi turns into an alleyway and stops before a gated building with a marble façade. It looks like a hotel, and one that's way beyond our price range.

"This nice hostel!" the guide says. "You go inside and see?"

"Is this Zostel?" Bradley asks bluntly.

Chapter 1

"No, but very nice. You come and see?"

Bradley and I exchange glances.

"Nah." Bradley reaches into his fanny pack and hands over some rupees. "Which way to Zostel?"

The driver points down the street.

"Take care," Bradley says as he exits the cab and shuts the door.

The two of us haul our backpacks out of the trunk.

"What was that about?" I ask. "Why'd they bring us here?"

"Who knows. Maybe he knows the guy who owns the place. That's the thing about guides, man. You really have to find the right one if you want to get to where you're going."

Bradley slams the tailgate shut, and the cab disappears into the swarm of traffic. I guess we're our own guides now.

"Need money for the cab?" I ask.
"Nah, you can get the next one. Where to?"

I search my phone for Zostel. It's only a few miles away, the perfect distance for a couple of hikers ready to relive the good old days.

The sidewalk leading downtown is narrow like slot canyons and slick from the morning rain. I jump across puddles wading in the cracked cement and peer down the alleyways. Packs of stray dogs laying in the shadows lift their heads before returning their chins to rest against their wet paws once again.

We soon come to a congested four-way intersection where droves of motorcycles whiz by. My shoulders tense as I search for traffic lights or signs to aid our crossing.

"Now!" Bradley blurts out.

So much for that plan.

We leap off the curb and make a run for the other side, my backpack bobbing up and down and slamming against my back. My heart thunders inside my ears, drowning out the approaching honks. As I leap over the curb on the other side, a fresh wave of traffic closes in behind us.

I catch my breath as the street stretches past a traffic blockade into a flashy well-paved district, then a twisting alleyway thick with wayfaring backpackers, dingy tattoos parlors, massage joints, restaurants, and gift shops. It's an entirely different realm from the worn-down buildings at the outskirts of town. Here, the shops on either side of the alley advertise travel packages for mountain expeditions via posters tacked onto windows. Knock-off merchandise from the outdoor outfitters spills out onto the streets atop racks, blankets, and boxes. Backpacks, puffy jackets, beanies, socks, hiking boots… everything a Himalayan trekking expedition requires. Had I not wasted so much money on all my fancy gear, I could've bought everything here at a fraction of the retail price.

A crowd of hippies, nomads, and vagabonds of all ages walk by wearing zip-off pants, trail runners, and huge backpacks. Middle-aged parents hold the hands of their kids, an elderly couple spends their retirement money, the younger couples our age are probably here to seal the deal. The couple walking in front of us speaks English, but instead of sparking up conversation with them, I opt to revel in the foreign atmosphere. Even though we're among fellow tourists, I want to *feel* like I'm on an adventure. A part of me misses the shanties, slightly disturbed to have flown halfway across the world only to wander into the most touristy and inauthentic part of town.

Just past another flashy tattoo parlor, Bradley stops and stares down a dark, stone-walled alleyway.

"Hostel Yog," he says with curiosity, reading the shadowed, wood-burned signage hung up on the wall. "Let's check it out!"

I scratch my beard and study the sign's decorative peace signs, yin-yangs, and flowers. The place is undoubtedly infested with fellow hippies.

"Wait, but what about Zostel?" I ask.

"We're here, bro. Let's give it a shot."

Chapter 1

As Bradley turns down the brick-walled alleyway, I sigh. If we're here, we might as well check it out. A change of plans can't be the worst thing to happen to us. So I take-off after him, dashing down the alley and following him into the shadows.

CHAPTER 2
HOSTEL YOG

Rows of Tibetan prayer flags strung up above the red-brick alleyway flap in the wind, welcoming our entrance onto the hostel premises.

Nearing Hostel Yog

We pass through an iron gate into a small courtyard where a young brunette woman with glasses sits behind an outdoor

Chapter 2

reception desk. Her green eyes match her floral sundress. Beside her sits a young man with long blond hair typing away at his laptop. Both look to be tourists around my age, likely in a work-for-stay exchange at the hostel.

The young brunette, once lost in the pages of her book, looks up and flashes a smile. If I hadn't seen her previous relaxed expression, I would've thought the smile was permanently painted onto her face.

"Welcome," she says in clear English. She must American or Canadian.

The young man's fingers continue clicking away at his laptop.

Bradley leans across the desk. "How much for a bed in this joint?"

The girl pushes her oversized glasses higher up the bridge of her button nose then slides a brochure across the desk. "Depends on what you're looking for. Bunk rooms start at five USD a night, privates at fifteen. You guys need some privacy?"

Bradley and I roll our eyes and laugh.

"We'll take a bunkroom," I say.

"Sure thing."

As she turns to her laptop, I pretend to read the brochure, stealing occasional glances her way. *Is she with this other guy working the desk?* It wouldn't surprise me. His tanned figure, Hawaiian T-shirt, and sundried blonde hair look like just her type. For some reason, everyone my age has a soulmate but me.

"Looks like we've got plenty of bunkrooms available," she says, finally. "Cash or card?"

"Mind if we take a look around first?" Bradley asks.

The girl slides out of her seat and snags a key ring from beneath the desk. "I can give you a quick tour if you want. You're welcome to leave your backpacks here. Right this way, please."

We nod to the laptop guy, stash our backpacks behind the desk, then follow the brunette through the lounge toward the front door. A handful of fellow hippies scattered among the hammocks and sofas nod before returning to their smartphones.

The girl with the green sundress shows us inside. As she begins to describe the hostel's amenities that include a rooftop view, I peer down the first-floor hallway. Decorative plaques hang on each of the bunkroom doors. Written on the plaques are single words of Pali, an ancient language used in Buddhist scripture, naming the rooms after various spiritual qualities. *Effort, Gratitude, Happiness…*

"Our bunk rooms are pretty much all the same," the brunette admits as we ascend the narrow wooden stairway, which creaks ominously with each step. "Six bunks, lockers, and a shared bathroom on each floor. The showers have hot water; they just take a minute to heat up. You really must be patient with everything here. Ah, here we are. This is the one."

The brunette stops before a door labeled *Wisdom*, thumbs through her keyring, and pushes it open.

I give the room a once-over. It looks like a hostel bunk room, exactly as described. Three bunk beds section-off the room like large cubbies. Six high school-styled lockers press up against the wall. A lone window faces the alleyway. Two beds seem to be claimed and someone's stuff is spread across the floor toward one corner, but no occupants are present.

"I'll give you some time to look it over," she says.

"Looks good to me," Bradley says. "Don't you think?"

Whatever the situation at Zostel, I rid myself of the thought. This doesn't seem terrible.

We seal the deal back at the reception desk, forking over five dollars in rupees in exchange for keys and access to the Wi-Fi password.

"Have fun," she says with a wink, sliding the keys across the desk.

Chapter 2

As we grab our backpacks and hike back up the stairwell, I turn to Bradley. "What was that about?"

"What do you mean?"

"Did you get the feeling... I mean, did she think we were gay or something?"

Bradley laughs. "I guess we do spend a lot of time together. It's funny—whenever I travel with you, people either think we're gay or brothers."

I chuckle. "We don't even look anything alike. I've got brown hair, blue eyes. You've got black hair, green eyes."

Bradley points to my fanny pack and moves his hand down in a sweeping motion. We're wearing the same brand of fanny pack, hiking pants, and hand-made Jesus sandals. If Bradley hadn't cut his long hippie-hairstyle during his time at the meditation center, we'd be matching in the hair department, too.

"Could be the build," he says, flexing his bicep.

"Sickly-skinny?"

"Speak for yourself, bro!"

By the time we reach the fourth floor, Bradley stops and gestures at the *Wisdom* nameplate. "Fitting, huh?"

"Yeah... fitting," I lie. To me, the room's exactly like the others, just as the smiling brunette said. Our room could have been named *Happiness, Bliss,* or *Serenity,* and Bradley still would have considered it an omen. I can only imagine the fanfare had our room been named *Enlightenment.*

When Bradley unlocks the door, I ease my backpack onto the floor, climb to the top of one of the bunks, and let out a deep groan as my back hits the mattress. After more than twenty-four hours of flight-time and airport layovers, resting on a legitimate horizontal surface brings my eyes to a tight and instant close. Had it not been days since my last workout, I could happily pass out here and now. But if I want to keep my sickly-skinny-strong figure during these next ninety days, my spine must bend, and my body must move.

Bradley's in the bunk beneath mine, so I lean over and ask: "Wanna check out the roof?"

His eyes snap open. "Way ahead of you, brother."

We lock the door to *Wisdom* and ascend three flights of stairs, finding a door leading onto a small rooftop overlooking the entire city.

I shuffle to the edge and lean over the guardrail. My heart pumps as I gaze out at that same expansive view from the highway. The urban sprawl surrounds us on all sides, rippling towards the edges of the world beneath a hazy, sunlit sky.

"What a spot," Bradley says.

"Not too shabby." I mean it this time.

Bradley posing on the Hostel Yog rooftop

I spread my tightened body onto the brick floor and slowly attempt to reanimate and shift my bones back into place by stretching my limbs out as far as they go. My breath strains as I move through yoga asanas, leaving droplets of sweat on the dusty rooftop.

Chapter 2

I get the sense of needing to inhale twice as hard just to suck in a good breath. Must be the pollution, or maybe the altitude. Supposedly, Kathmandu is nearly a mile above sea-level. Since the Himalayas stand at least three miles above sea-level, working out in the thin and polluted air is good training for what lies ahead.

After yoga and push-ups and my never-fail stretching routine, the fog inside my head and the stiffness in my bones begins to dissipate, and I collapse with my sweat-soaked back pressed against the warm brick. Above me, a seamless unbroken curtain of smog stretches across the sky and shields us from the sun. There's not a single crack in the entire ocean of clouds.

Bradley stands, throws his shirt over his shoulder, and leans against the ledge, gazing over the city for a while. I wonder what's on his mind. Before I can talk to him about our hiking plans or ask more about the wise woman, he turns away from the city.

"I'll see you downstairs," he says off-handedly, then he disappears through the doorway.

I get the sense that the traveling is getting to him, too. He must want to be alone.

Come to think of it, from the chaos of the airport, the taxi ride, and wandering the city streets, I've hardly had any time to myself these last few days. Despite the air quality, it feels good to find some space to breathe, to have moved my body, and to find a moment's semblance of normalcy atop this roof.

I remain still and look up to the clouded skies, her shape forming into my imagination. Her whirlpool eyes, the smell of her hair, and her smooth, warm skin strikes me like waves from a sea of endless imagination. She draws me close and touches her lips to mine.

Then, a very real and pungent stench invades my nostrils and awakens me from my daydreams. I lower my nose to my chest, take a whiff, and recoil. Even though the trail was four years ago, those six months of outdoor living proved to me that

I didn't need deodorant. The same goes for body wash, soap, fragrance, or fashion unless a formal social situation required it. My body's natural pheromones were far superior to any manufactured, store-bought product. And now that I've quit my job at the smoothie shop back home, once again living out of a backpack, I'm only buying and packing the essentials.

I push myself up from the dusty brick floor, throw on my shirt, and decide to hit the showers until a chorus of laughter erupts from the downstairs lounge. It's those hippies. And maybe there's a woman there, too. Someone who's my type.

Unlikely. But whoever's down there won't mind a little stank.

CHAPTER 3
SKY DIVING

Down in the outdoor lounge, I find Bradley kicked-back in a hammock. Across from him, a couple of fellow hippies sit cozied-up next to each other on a beat-up couch. They wave as I approach, and we shake hands.

Nina from Australia and Daniel from South Africa. Two hemp T-shirt-, cargo short-, and Chaco sandal-wearing travelers. I can't tell whether they're siblings or dating, a thought which puts into perspective the predicament in which Bradley and I keep finding ourselves.

"Bradley was just telling us you guys hiked across the US," Nina says. "That's amazing!"

"Thanks," I say. "It was a lot of things. Amazing was definitely one of them."

"Are you two looking to hike while you're here?" Nina asks.

"That's the plan," Bradley says.

"What trek have you planned?" Daniel asks.

A silence fills the courtyard.

Bradley laughs. "We're still deciding. We'll head to the Tourist Center tomorrow and research our options."

"If it means anything," Nina says. "I really enjoyed the Annapurna Circuit. It's a bit touristy in places, but the views are spectacular. Whatever you decide on, with mountains like the Himalayas, you really can't go wrong."

I hope she's right. We can't go wrong, can we?

"Is that why you came to Nepal?" Daniel asks. "The trekking?"

"Partly," Bradley replies. "I've also been in touch with a wise woman."

Daniel's eyebrows rise with intrigue. "May I ask her name?"

"Sajana," Bradley says. "We plan on living with her for a while. Maybe dip into enlightenment."

"Enlightenment, huh?" Daniel asks. "Are you guys big meditators?"

Bradley nods. "I've been living at a vipassana meditation retreat center."

Nina tilts her head to the side. "Vispana?" she asks. "What's that?"

"*Vipassana*," Bradley repeats. "It's a Pali word that means seeing clearly. It's also a meditation technique taught in ten-day long courses. It's… a lot of sitting." Bradley laughs. "Ten hours a day for ten days straight. There's an oath of silence. Wake-up calls at four in the morning. No reading, writing, cell phones, listening to music, or physical exercise."

"Damn," Nina says. "And you've spent a lot of time there?"

"The last four years."

"Geez," Daniel says. "Same for you, David?"

"I've only been to a handful of courses," I reply. "Not as many as Bradley."

I wasn't going to say it out loud, but I often wondered if I should have lived full-time at a meditation center like Bradley. I could only imagine his growth. Instead, I decided to write about the trail and start a relationship. Now that those were over with, a heavy guilt took root at the heart of my very being. *If I was serious about enlightenment, wouldn't I*

Chapter 3

give up everything and let go of worldly attachments? Was I weak in pursuing material desires? Maybe, by stepping away, Bradley had progressed ahead of me on this path. And while the thought gnawed at me with a curious rage, it was in the past. I'd taken the necessary actions by coming here.

"I'm curious," Daniel says. "How'd you find out about these meditation centers?"

I glance at Bradley in deference.

"I sat my first retreat before we started the trail," Bradley says. "It was transformative, to say the least. When I told David about it, we signed up to sit a course at the retreat center in Canada following the trail. Unfortunately, all our side adventures really slowed us down. We missed the retreat by a couple weeks. But life at the center called to me. I found a retreat center in Georgia and dove in deep. I've been there until the last couple weeks."

"That's a long time," Nina says. "What made you want to do it, David?"

"Life back home wasn't the same after finishing the trail," I reply. "The trail felt so... *immersive.* Hiking for twenty miles a day beneath the elements, connecting with so many beautiful people. That same sense of adventure didn't exist in the city.

"I found purpose in writing about the trail, but I also sought something deeper. I wanted to completely transcend suffering, as crazy as that may sound. I'd never done any formal meditation before, but the trail hardened me. The meditation retreats sounded intense, but I needed insight, and if meditation was the path, then I had to give it a shot."

"Maybe I'll take the leap myself one day," Nina says. "It sounds like a great place to break down and rebuild."

"I'll bet there's a course nearby," Bradley says. "Retreat centers seem to be popping up all over the world."

Nina scratches the back of her neck. "I don't know. Ten days is such a big commitment."

"If you think about it," Bradley replies, "ten days really isn't that long in the grand scheme of things. If you could forever change your life in ten days, wouldn't you make the trade?"

Nina shrugs. "When you put it that way. Although, I'd probably have to quit my job to make it happen."

"Do you like your job?" I ask.

What a millennial thing to ask someone, I realize. Not "is your job valuable?" Or "does it contribute to society?" But "do you *like* it?"

Oh, well. The words have already left my lips.

"I have a weird relationship with my job," Nina says. "I'll be fine for a couple months, but then out of nowhere, I'll get this slimy feeling all over my skin. A gross feeling like I don't belong there. As if I'm in the wrong place, doing the wrong thing. Just another cog in the machine, stuck beneath the wheel. And for what? To keep things going? Sure, some things we need in this world, but for other things, I wonder if we'd be fine without them. I'd quit in a heartbeat if I could, but someone's got to pay the bills." Nina sighs. "I shouldn't worry about it. I'm here and really enjoying Nepal while it lasts. It's such a beautiful place. I wish I could stay forever! Say, how'd you guys end up here anyways? Do you guys not have jobs?"

"I worked a big-boy job after college," Bradley replies. "About a year later, I went on vacation. Never stepped foot in that office again and haven't looked back since." Bradley points back to his chest and grins. "This is my job now. Been working hard for at least the last eight long years."

"I feel that," Daniel says.

"What about you, David?" Nina asks.

"Pretty much the same story." I keep it intentionally vague on my end. The details are too embarrassing. No one wants to hear me go on about how I hardly earn a living from writing. How I find the cheapest rent possible wherever I go. How I live off my investment and retirement accounts,

Chapter 3

praying they go up. And how I spend months at a time living with my parents.

"David's a writer," Bradley says. "He wrote a book about our hike."

"Damn, dude," Daniel says. "You guys are living the life."

I think for a second. "Maybe. I think I'm still looking for answers."

"Makes sense," Nina says. "I'd say most people are in the same boat."

The four of us continue to chat as the sun sinks down over the hostel's brick walls, giving rise to the golden hour. The patio's festive lights illuminate a colorful glow, moths bounce to the light, and Bob Marley chants down Babylon from the overhead speakers.

I can't help but notice every little gesture shared between Nina and Daniel. Every gaze, smile, giggle, and touch sparks a pang of envy in my chest.

"Looks like it's about that time." Bradley lifts himself out of the hammock. "I'd better hit the showers, meditate, and find some food before everything shuts down."

"It was great meeting you two," Nina says. "I'm sure we'll see you around."

I'm not as certain, but I do wish her and Daniel the best on what remains of their trip. I hope they find the answers they're looking for.

Before leaving, Nina turns to us and says, "Hey, make sure you don't fall into some cult."

I scratch the back of my head and feign a smile. "I'll try."

I know she's joking, but the warning irks me and causes me to think. I really have no idea what I'm getting into, do I? I've flown around the world to live with someone I know almost nothing about. Good thing I'm well aware of the dangers of cults and their gurus. After all, I'd seen *Wild Wild Country*. If this situation turns out anything like that, I'll get out quick before the brainwashing sinks in too deep.

After a much-needed hot shower, I climb atop my bunk-bed, wedge a pillow beneath me, and set a timer for one hour. I can't afford to miss a meditation session—not after all my progress. Bradley must have the same idea because his bunk falls silent, too.

The moment before meditation feels like I'm about to jump out of a plane. Butterflies swarm my stomach. My heartbeat accelerates. My breath quickens. My only hope at a manageable free-fall is deploying my practice.

So I jump. My eyes close, the world disappears, and I plummet into a void, ready to emerge lighter on the other side.

After the trail, and after my first vipassana retreat, I began meditating religiously. Each day, I sat for one hour in the morning and one hour in the evening. After four years of practice, it became clear my endgame was enlightenment. To be free from all suffering, mental anguish, disease, and worry. A permanent state of existence that transcends the mundane aspects of life. I'd heard stories of teachers like Eckhart Tolle, Michael Taft, and rumors of others who had awoken. I decided that if they could do it, then I could, too, because if the truth could be known to one man, then it could be known to all.

Suffering might sound like a strong word to use. So far, everything in life seemed to be laid out in front of me in good order. But no matter what happened outside me, discontentment still followed me like a shadow. Walking across the country and practicing meditation hadn't alleviated me of problems. If anything, my awareness of my problems became clearer. Enlightenment was the only thing that could solve my problems at the root level.

Originally, I practiced vipassana. I would inwardly scan my body from head to toe, observing the pulsing, tingling, and throbbing sensations, doing my best to remain aware and equanimous with all phenomena. This technique brought many interesting experiences and benefits, and I began to think this technique was the best, the right, and the only technique

Chapter 3

worthy of practice. I judged those who didn't meditate and anyone who meditated differently. *Those people were ignorant, wasting time, and in store for a sad fate*—so I thought.

More recently, my perspective and practice had begun to change. I don't recall a specific moment for this shift. It happened gradually, like the blossoming of a flower. I now gave myself permission to practice methods not prescribed by any discipline. Methods that felt right for me. But I had yet to reach enlightenment and I wondered if I would ever reach my goal. Without a technique, who was my teacher? Without a path, where would I walk? Abandoning a prescribed lineage left me feeling alone, like a crab searching the ocean floor for a new shell. Something was missing, and I'd traveled here to find it.

Time drags on, and while the hour-long meditation must be close to over with, the timer still hasn't gone off. *Maybe I didn't set it right. Maybe I cancelled it accidentally.* Such thoughts tend to arrive when the pain of sitting in complete stillness takes over my body and mind, and I can't take it much longer.

When I finally hear snores erupt in the bunk below me, I think, *Screw it. That's my cue.*

I release myself from stillness, look at my timer, and sigh. Forty-five seconds remaining. What a shame. Maybe next time, I can do better.

I cancel the timer and lay down. After two dreadful nights of non-stop travel, I've got to nap before dinner.

Suddenly, she and I are lying next to each other on the Japanese futon again. Rain pelts the window. I stare into her eyes. We kiss. My blood boils. We make love.

She looks at me and says something inaudible.

The floor crumbles, and I fall into nothingness.

I go down. All the way to the bottom.

CHAPTER 4
DAL BHAT

I wake in a hot sweat atop my bunk, the dream clinging to me. It's nearing dark outside the window. Seven p.m. says my phone. A full hour had passed during my nap.

I can tell Bradley's still asleep, so I quietly descend my bunk and pull her letter from my backpack. I've read it before, but I carry it up to the top bunk, read it again, and wipe a tear suspended in the corner of my eye.

If I've moved on, why is my reaction still so strong?

My relationship with Hannah felt more real than any other —as if all my past relationships had led up to it. Hannah was short with cute brown eyes and long brown hair. She loved unconditionally with a soft touch and expressed her emotions clearly. She was intelligent, patient, and kind, connected to something beyond herself. Her calming presence slowed me down and balanced my seeking and striving.

Why would anyone give up someone like that?

Because despite all her lovely traits, I harbored this haunting feeling within me that she wasn't the one. Because I convinced myself that I would feel fulfilled when the right person came into my life. And when I wasn't yet, I questioned our relationship. But something felt better than nothing, so I held onto her, dragged her along, and used her as a source of confidence. She filled a void I imagined another woman

Chapter 4

would one day fill. I kept my thoughts hidden from her, and I kept myself from committing to our relationship.

The morning AC chills my hot sweat. My body gives a slight shiver, and I remember the feeling of falling in a dream.

I told her the truth during a long drive home after a Valentine's Day vacation. After such a wonderful weekend spent together, it was the last thing she expected. We cried, but her cry was different. I knew she suffered more because I'd ripped her heart to shreds.

After we said our final goodbyes, I began to wonder if I'd made a mistake. Had I self-sabotaged the relationship? How does anyone know if a person is the right one for them? Whatever the case, an unbearable heartbreak dug into me. I wanted to get back together but trying again would bring the same result. I wasn't ready. Instead, I sensed something much deeper first needed solving.

My body shivers again and shakes my mind out of dreams and thoughts. I set down the letter and lean over the top bunk. "Bradley, you awake?"

"Yeah."

"You hungry?"

"Famished."

We slip on our Jesus sandals, strap on our fanny packs, and take to the streets.

As the sun sets, we saunter along the tourist district's gift shops, tattoo parlors, and restaurants. The savory smells of street food waft under my nose, and my stomach rumbles. *When was the last time I ate?* Nothing comes to mind. It's not a huge deal, though. It happens often—days where I hardly eat a thing. Maybe a nice, predictable meal would help ease my mind and body.

"Keep an eye out for *dal bhat*," Bradley says.

"*Dal* what?"

"You haven't eaten *dal bhat* before?"

I shake my head. "Don't think so."

True Nature

"Oh, bro! It's a Nepalese staple! Basically, just rice, vegetables, and curry. This woman back at the meditation center made it for us a couple of times. Holy smokes, that stuff was *good*. And fun, too. I think you'll dig it."

Just as I'm pondering what could possibly be fun about a food item, a middle-aged man pops out of a nearby restaurant.

"You try?" he offers, shoving menus in our faces. "Good food! *Very good* food!"

The food seems fine and *dal bhat's* on the menu, but we're only in Kathmandu a couple nights. Instead, we forge onward to find the best possible *dal bhat* at the lowest possible price. But every restaurant seems to have the exact same menu: *momos, chapatis, khaja, roti,* and *dal bhat*. At all the same price, too. Different doors with different nameplates leading to identical rooms. Collusion of the highest order. The illusion of choice around every turn.

Tired and hungry, we turn around and settle for the original place nearest the hostel. The middle-aged man out front welcomes our return and quickly conducts us inside to a booth at the back.

I slide into the seat across from Bradley, fold my legs up beneath me, and look around at the eastern lanterns hanging from the ceiling. Soft chanting pipes in through the overhead speakers. It's a place where tourists go and eat their tourist food.

Our waiter swings by the table with menus and glasses of lemon water.

"*Dal bhat,*" Bradley says, cutting right to the chase and handing back his menu.

The waiter nods then looks at me.

"Uhm… *dal bhat*?" I repeat.

The man takes my menu, wobbles his head, then departs around the corner to the kitchen.

I raise my eyebrow. "Did I offend him?"

Chapter 4

"You mean that side-to-side head wobble?" Bradley laughs. "That's just how Nepali people say yes. It looks like indifference or disagreement, but it's meant to be affirmative. They do it in India, too. Another lesson from the meditation center. It's confusing at first, but you'll get used to it."

Bradley impersonates the gesture, and we go back and forth practicing the head wobble, laughing.

When the waiter next swings by our table, he picks up on the game and gives us an exaggerated head wobble. We laugh as he refills my water, but Bradley's glass remains untouched. He only drinks after meals, a habit he says helps digestion. I haven't researched it myself, so either I've been missing something or it's another one of Bradley's far-out beliefs. Either way, it seems strange to me to deprive myself of a perfectly good glass of water until after dinner.

With the waiter still tableside, Bradley points at his glass. "How do you say water in Nepali?"

"*Pani.*"

Good idea, I think. If we're here for three months, we should learn some of the language. I type it into my phone: *Pah-nee = water.*

"What about hello?" I ask.

"*Namaste.*"

Nah-mas-te. An obvious one, the classic salutation to any Western yoga class.

"Thank you?... You're welcome?"

Dhan-ya-bhat... Swog-a-tahm.

Our waiter seems appeased in helping us build a foundational vocabulary. He then excuses himself, returning with two large plates of food, which he sets before us.

"Dal," he says, pointing to the lentil soup. Then he points to the rice. "*Bhat.*"

Dal plus *bhat*. Makes sense.

"*Aloo, achar, saag,*" our waiter says, pointing to the potatoes, spicy pickles, and cooked greens.

When he sets silverware down onto the table, Bradley hands his set back. "No thanks. I'll eat with my hands. How do you say in Nepali?"

"*Atlehandso!*" Our waiter smiles, thrilled by this decision.

Bradley wobbles his head and repeats the word, solidifying "*at-le-handso*" into his memory. Then he looks at me. "Take notes."

At that, he pours the cup of *dal* atop the mound of rice and shoves his hands in. The goopy rice spills out from between his fingers as he squeezes together the food on his plate.

I stare at him, perplexed. *What the hell is he doing?*

Satisfied with his mixing, he begins to shovel large handfuls into his mouth. He open- mouth chews, and his eyes roll back into his head.

My first-ever plate of dal bhat

"Don't knock it 'til you try it," he says, hardly finished with the bite. "The key is a four-finger scoop and a push of the thumb. You'll look like a damned fool grabbing with all five fingers."

Chapter 4

"You learn that the hard way?"

Bradley nods. "That woman I told you about, the one at the meditation center who made *dal bhat*? The first time I tried eating it, I stuck my whole hand in my mouth. She wouldn't let me live it down for months. You can eat it however you want to. I'm just letting you know. They only offer the silverware because we're tourists."

I glance at my own dish, wobble my head, and shrug. *Screw it. When in Kathmandu.*

I pour the cup of *dal* onto the *bhat* and stick my hand in.

"Shit!" I let out, yanking away my hand from the scalding food.

Bradley points to his temple with one of his food-smothered fingers. "Mind over matter, bro."

Yeah, right. I wait a minute before dipping my hand back in. This time, the temperature's tolerable. As I shove my fingers in and stir everything together like paints on a canvas, a smile lifts across my face. I shovel a handful of *dal bhat* into my mouth and chew. The warm, delicious mush slides down my throat and causes me to reach for water.

"It's the *achar*," Bradley says. "Those spicy pickles will get you."

Right as we're about to finish, the waiter swings by our table and asks if we want more food.

"You mean like… for free?" Bradley asks.

Surprisingly, the waiter nods.

"Bring it on," Bradley says.

How could anyone pass up that offer?

By the time I clean off a second plate of *dal bhat*, my belly feels like a boulder. I lay back against the booth and breathe. Done with his third plate, Bradley licks his fingers clean and chugs half his lemon water. Two thousand rupees pays for the both of us, dirt-cheap for all the food we ate.

"I got this one," I say, laying down a crisp, rupee monopoly-money bill.

"You sure?"

"What's mine is yours, brother."

Bradley looks at me a second as if pondering my words, then he stands.

"Ready?" he asks, downing the last of his lemon water.

* * *

Neon signs, dim lanterns, and white windows illuminate the tourist district's dark alleyways. In the slim crack between the buildings hangs a dusty full moon. A cacophony of beeps and honks collide with the music blasting from the tavern doorways. Groups of tourists stroll by in both directions, laughing and smiling. The place feels happening, but I'm ready for bed.

"Psst, hashish?"

Bradley and I turn to see a man lurking behind us.

"No thanks, brother," Bradley says.

Then, we hear it again a few steps later. "Hashish?"

Fully prepared to reprimand the guy, we turn around to find an entirely different person. We laugh and wave him off. When it happens a third time, Bradley turns to me and says: "Must be something about us, huh?"

Once again, we glance down at our Jesus sandals and adjust our fanny packs. I push my hair out of my face. "I wonder what it could be."

At this point, I don't fault anyone for mistaking us for gay hippie stoner siblings.

Compared to the tourist district's symphony of noises, Hostel Yog is pleasantly quiet. Odd, though. I'd half-expected some late-night festivities or dope-smoking in the lounge, but the silence is more than welcome.

In *Wisdom*, it's even more so the case: not a noise to be heard. Only two sleeping bodies buried beneath the sheets in

Chapter 4

two of the lower bunks. Having roommates gives us even more reason to settle in soon.

Tired and ready for a full night's rest, I brush my teeth in the shared bathroom then climb into bed. The usual mix of the day's concerns swirl about my mind like a whirlpool.

"Hashish?"

"Have you decided on trekking plans?"

"Don't fall into a cult."

Usually, I'd meditate before bedtime to clear my mind of this incessant chatter, but I'm exhausted. It's a good thing I've already fulfilled my two hours.

I shut my eyes and think about the reasons for my journey to the Far East. Tomorrow, we'll secure our trekking permits to hike the Himalayas. Then we'll seek out the wise woman in a place called Pokhara. Will that be enough? Or have I made a huge mistake by coming here?

CHAPTER 5
INTO THE CITY

I open my eyes at seven a.m. the next morning to the sound of rain pulverizing the city's tin rooftops. From outside our half-cracked hostel window, the gutters overflow. Streams flood the alleyways and swirl down the streets.

No one in *Wisdom* says a word.

What's there to do in the rain? I meditate for an hour then lay down. The weather report on my phone says the rain won't let up until later this afternoon. Nothing to do, nowhere to go.

Given so much free time, the old me would write, but I have nothing to write about. After writing about the trail, my well of creativity had run dry. I have no stories which I can pour my heart into. Nothing like *those* stories. Writing that book had consumed my life and I couldn't imagine starting over. The very thought was like looking up to an ocean of black storm clouds suspended above a mountain peak. Instead, I scroll through social media, toss the phone to my side, and wait.

Six hours pass in *Wisdom*, and still the rain falls. As I find myself slipping into sleep, the unmistakable sound of kissing sails across the room. I perk up. Lips smack, a mattress creaks, and an exchange of whispers passes beneath covers.

Chapter 5

Rainy morning in my Hostel Yog bunk

"Hey," she says aloud suddenly. "Are you guys awake?"

It's Nina. I recognize her voice from yesterday's conversation in the lounge.

"It sounds like y'all are having fun over there," Bradley quips.

"Sorry guys," Daniel says.

"I promise we weren't doing anything too bad!" Nina tacks on. "There's nothing to do in the rain. Lazy day."

I imagine myself in place of Daniel, curled up beside Nina. My arms wrap around her. Our lips touch. She smells like Hannah—a misty blend of Cyprus oil, coffee beans, and warm sourdough bread.

My imagination fades with the rain, which slows to a drizzle then stops completely. Droplets slide off the rooftops and splash into street puddles. A soft birdsong drifts through the open hostel window, soon interrupted by engines, horns, and jackhammers rumbling up the alleyways.

"You guys want to grab a bite to eat with us?" Nina asks out of the blue. "I'm going crazy staying cooped up in here all day."

"Would love to," Bradley says, lifting himself out of bed. "But we've got plans to visit the Tourist Center. The sooner we can secure our trekking permits, the sooner we can get out of here and start hiking."

"Oh, one more thing," Nina says. "There's an app called maps.me. If you download the city maps ahead of time, you can access them anywhere without Wi-Fi."

"Oh, nice! Thanks." I download it on the spot.

"Ready?" Bradley asks after clicking on his fanny pack.

I check my phone, realizing it's already noon and check-out was at eleven. We really should get going. "Yeah. Are you bringing your backpack?"

"For now. Just gotta make sure they've got room for us tonight."

I roll out of bed, change into shorts and a T-shirt, pack my backpack, and walk to the doorway. I turn back briefly.

"Hey," I say. "The place around the corner has some tasty *dal bhat*. Super cheap, too."

"Man," Nina says. "I totally would, but I'm already so sick of that stuff. It's like the only thing people eat here!"

Chapter 5

* * *

The same smiling brunette with glasses greets us at the front desk. The same blond guy types away at his computer.

"Aw, are you two heading out already?" she asks, setting down her book.

"We're looking to catch a bus," Bradley explains. "Well, two separate buses to two separate places. One to the tourist center and another to Pokhara."

"City buses are easy enough." She points out the gate and says to keep walking until we hit the main drag. "You can't miss it. As for trips to Pokhara, did you say? Hm, people don't go there very often. At least not that I know of. I'm sure we can find you something, though. Babe, do you mind looking up bus times to Pokhara for these two gentlemen?"

Without a word, the guy sets his laptop on the desk and pulls out an enormous binder from a desk drawer. We wait in silence as he flips through the pages. Finally, he slides the binder in front of the brunette and places his laptop back in his lap.

"Thanks, babe," she says to him with a wink.

Jealousy and nausea seize my gut. I shoo away the desire to vomit last night's *dal bhat* all over the desk and refocus my attention.

"Pokhara," she says. "The buses from Kathmandu leave at six-thirty in the morning and two in the afternoon."

Bradley looks my direction. "What do you say we take the early bus tomorrow? That gives us time to nail down our trekking plans today and arrive with plenty of time at Sajana's."

I think it over and agree. It's hard to believe we're only a day's journey from meeting the wise woman.

"Don't worry about reservations," the smiling brunette says. "There should be plenty of room. Just show up fifteen minutes early to claim a seat and pay the driver. It's super cheap, like a thousand rupees."

Bradley places his elbows on the desk and interlocks his hands. "You guys have room for us tonight?"

"In the bunk room, I assume?" She gives us a wink.

We work out the booking details, hold onto our room keys, and stash our backpacks behind the front desk.

"They're safe here," she says. "Good luck with your trekking permits."

"Thanks," I reply.

As it turns out, we'll need all the luck we can get.

CHAPTER 6
THE UNLIKELY GUIDE

We walk the rain-slick alleyways to the city center. Despite the morning rain and oppressive humidity, life on the drag seems to have gone on as normal. A flurry of scooters, motorbikes, and cars whiz by in both directions. Their incessant beeps and honks overwhelm my eardrums.

As I search for buses, Bradley marches up the steps of a nearby shop—a much more direct means of getting things done.

The woman behind the counter wears red lipstick and a matching dot on her forehead—a *tika*, signifying the purity of her faith.

"City bus?" he asks her. "City bus to tourist center?"

The woman's dot rises from her smartphone. Then she wobbles her head and points to the street.

"And Pokhara? Pokhara bus?"

Another head wobble and point to the street.

I guess we can catch both buses in the exact same place. Sounds easy enough.

"*Dhanyabad.*" Bradley spins back around to the street and posts up on the sidewalk.

The two of us squat down and watch the river of motorbikes and scooters. I glimpse beat-up sedans, worn-down minivans, and lost cows crossing the road, but not one city bus.

Lost in thought, I find myself wondering why everything in the city seems to be falling apart or in need of repair. Everywhere I turn, there's piles of bricks, heaps of rubble, and bags of concrete. It's… unusual. More than what seems to make sense in any developing urban environment.

My mind hardly registers the young man hanging out the door of a passing minivan, raising his hand at us. What did *he* want? It takes a moment for the answer to sink in.

I raise my hand at the next young man leaning halfway out a minivan. Noticing my wave, he slaps the side of the vehicle twice, and the car pulls over down the street. It's not exactly the "city bus" we imagined, but it does the trick.

A Kathmandu city bus

Bradley and I sprint down the sidewalk and stare inside the jam-packed vehicle.

Chapter 6

The young man wearing a soccer jersey waves us inside. "*Espaysh!*"

Space? No, there doesn't appear to be any.

"Tourist Center?" Bradley asks anyway.

The motorbikes piled up behind us lay on their horns. The boy wobbles his head and waves us in even more emphatically. There's no time to waste. Bradley and I shrug and hop in.

I hunch inside the crammed minivan, the young man slaps the steel shell of the van, and we jolt forward. Bradley and I press our hands against the roof to keep from falling backward.

Despite a full vehicle, everyone keeps quiet. Nothing plays from the radio. Motorbikes honk all around us. A humid breeze from the half-rolled-down windows and the open-door rustles through the cabin and whisks across my face. At least the morning rain subdued the stench of the smog, making the air a bit more breathable.

It's a long, crowded ride across town. Every few intersections, someone slaps the outside of the minivan, and we come to a halt. People hop off, people hop on, and I somehow find the side of my face pressed up against the window. I look over at Bradley and snicker at the sight of him sitting halfway atop an old man's lap.

"Bradley," I whisper. "When do we get off?"

"Eventually."

I roll my eyes. Maybe the young slapper knows. I make my way beside him at the next stop.

"Tourist Center? Trekking permits?" I figure two questions offer more clarity compared to one.

"I tell," he replies.

A few stops later, the young slapper gives me a firm nod. I pay him his requested fifteen cents worth of rupees and we hop off onto a crowded street.

"We should have gotten off earlier," Bradley says, turning up the sidewalk.

"Why?" I ask.

"I saw the Tourist Center on the other side of the park. This way."

I check my phone to make sure, bumping into pedestrians and apologizing as we walk. To my surprise, Nina's map-app has somehow downloaded every nook and cranny of the city's streets onto my phone. It's useful, but to my disappointment, it confirms Bradley's hunch that we indeed passed the Tourist Center.

The smells of street food waft beneath my nose as I stuff my phone into my fanny and continue up the sidewalk. I haven't eaten today, but food can wait. We're on a mission. I'll just fast through it—a useful skill for a nomad with unmet needs.

We cross a pedestrian bridge over a crowded highway and arrive at the Tourist Center. A warm draft and the musty smell of stale paper that accompanies most federal buildings floats between the dusty wooden floorboards and the tall ceilings. We walk the hallway past closed office doors into a dead-quiet waiting room.

Three tourist couples about our age sit in office chairs, filling out forms, and whispering to each other like it's a library. I double-take at the smiling couples then turn to Bradley. While he's not the gender of my ideal life-long travel companion, at least he's experienced and battle-tested. I don't have to look after him, and he knows the same about me.

One of the girls wearing a jean jacket turns to me and points to the front desk.

"Trekking permits are over there," she giggles.

I must look lost.

Bradley and I trot over to the front desk and flash a smile to the woman sitting behind her computer. Her hoop earrings jiggle as she looks up.

Chapter 6

"We're looking for trail permits," Bradley says.

Her earrings wobble again as she reaches over and pats a stack of papers with her hand.

"Thanks," I reply, taking a form from each stack.

We find ourselves a table and mull over our trekking options: the Annapurna Circuit is a fourteen-day hike but seems too touristy. The Manaslu and the Tsum Valley trails are remote, but only ten and four-days respectively, and both require a guide. I scratch my beard. Nothing fits my desires.

"Do we really *need* a guide, though?" I ask Bradley.

"Nope," he says. "Let me try to work some magic. Take notes."

Bradley slides in front of the woman behind the desk and flashes a bright smile. "Hey. Do the Manaslu and Tsum Valley trails require a guide?"

"Yes, a guide," she says, nodding firmly. Her nod is a definitive up and down nod—not even the slightest side-to-side wobble, not a good start. "You need a company-sponsored guide for these trails," she continues. "There are many guide options online and in the city."

I roll my eyes. The mere thought of stepping into one of those Kathmandu tourist traps and inquiring about a "travel package" makes my head spin. Plus, who knows how many hundreds of dollars a guide would cost us?

Bradley leans across the table, raises his eyebrow, and flashes his widest and brightest grin.

"Here's the thing," he explains. "The two of us have hiked thousands of miles together. Over two thousand, in fact. Just a few years ago, we hiked across the United States! So given our unique situation, perhaps we could make one little exception here and grant us a permit without the need for a guide?"

The woman looks Bradley up and down, matches his smile, then goes back to typing. Her hoop earrings come to a standstill.

"Thanks…" Bradley says sarcastically, turning around, and plopping down into one of the chairs.

I join him and look around at the other couples filling out paperwork.

"Now what?" he asks.

"No idea." I sigh. It's a deep sigh heavy with frustration. I'm sure the Annapurna Circuit is a great hike, but achieving enlightenment is a delicate matter. Every variable has considerable importance, like a scientist conducting his prized experiment. The slightest miscalculation could throw the whole thing off.

The Himalayas, the tallest mountain range on the planet, are the perfect setting for my search for enlightenment. I'd learned that the human brain released a neurochemical at high altitudes called DMT, the same chemical produced during deep meditative states, psychedelic states, and moments before death. The altitude paired with a strong meditation practice offered the chance at a profound ego-death experience—the perfect recipe to find the understanding I sought.

Unfortunately, new and confounding variables arise before me. Tourists and guides bring too much socialization and distraction. Plus, there's no way some old-timer knows any more than we do about trekking.

Just as I'm contemplating the frustration of abandoning the mission and walking back to Hostel Yog without a trekking permit, a shadow descends upon us.

I look up.

A round-bellied man shakes his silver wristwatch higher up his thick forearm and studies the two of us.

"Who says they are looking for guide?" he asks.

"That's us," says Bradley.

"Come." Then the man turns around and waddles into one of the offices.

I glance at Bradley. "Who was that?"

Bradley rises to a stand. "Only one way to find out."

Chapter 6

We follow the man inside his office to see him sitting behind his desk.

"Please, sit," the man says.

Bradley and I slowly lower onto a leather couch. I glance around. There's really nothing to the place. No windows, pictures, or paintings hung on the walls.

Given the man's attire, he doesn't seem to belong in such an ordinary public office. But there he sits in his leather chair, tapping his pen against his desk like a clock ticking away the time.

Then he leans forward and smiles.

CHAPTER 7
GANESH

"My name is Ganesh," he says. "You two are very fortunate today. It so happens that at this moment, you are in the right place at the right time. You see, I am owner of a guide company. Best in all of Nepal. I overhear your conversation from outside. You say you need guide for trekking. I can provide this for you."

"The thing is," Bradley says. "We don't really need a guide. We're—"

"First, some questions. How many days you stay in Nepal?"

"Eighty," Bradley says.

"Long time," Ganesh nods, impressed.

We nod.

"And you are unsure of what trekking to do?"

"That's right," I say.

"And it is only the two of you, yes?"

We nod again.

"No girlfriends?"

"Nope," Bradley says.

"And you?" Ganesh asks me.

"Nope." *This guy… unbelievable.*

"I see. Not important."

Chapter 7

Ganesh looks down and rearranges the papers on his desk as if pondering something very, very important. He carefully places his pen onto the desk and exhales. Finally, he leans forward.

"In that case, here is my offer to you both. Annapurna, Manaslu, and Tsum Valley. Three trails. Twenty-one days of trekking. Yes, I feel this is good option for you."

Bradley and I glance at each other. *Hiking parts of all three trails for twenty-one days? That's an option?* It's much longer than the ten days we planned for, but it feels like something special—a mini-thru-hike! The perfect length of time to immerse myself in the mountains. Maybe there's something to this guy after all.

"There is more," Ganesh says with a grin. He walks out from behind his desk and sits in one of the chairs beside us. "For Manaslu and Tsum Valley, as you know, they are very remote trails, trails you cannot enter without a guide. Unfortunately, there is no way around this. Nothing I can do.

"So the question becomes, who has best guide for you? There are so many of trekking companies. So many of guides you can choose from in the city. Most will give good experience. You trek up, you trek down. You take picture, you go home. Everything is good and fine.

"But I see something different in you. Something special. This, I noticed when you walked in. Difficult to explain, this feeling. I see you two sitting in the hall looking like you do." He gestures at our general appearance and hippie attire. "You are looking for something more, yes? For this reason, I want to make you this offer. Here, I show you."

Bradley and I glance at each other as Ganesh runs over to his desk. We watch as he rummages madly through desk drawers, pulling out folders, and sifting through papers. Whatever this guy is cooking up, it's either a huge scam or divine intervention. My curiosity grows in every passing moment.

Bradley and Ganesh mid-negotiation

Finally, Ganesh's eyes light up. He plops back onto the chair and slides a small polaroid across the table.

"His name, Lama Dai," Ganesh says.

I lean over and study the image. It's a black-and-white photo of an old man with a clean-shaven head. He looks something like a monk. A sense of kindness and tranquility rests upon the old man's face. His eyes squint as if enduring harsh sunlight or a camera's flash, an action that has no bearing on his inner peace.

"Lama Dai is Tibetan lama. You know what is lama? Very serious meditator. Two hours meditation a day. One hour in morning, one hour in evening. He eat only vegetable. He know little English. Few word. But it *enough*. He know the mountains. He lead hundreds of trekkings for fifteen years. I could go on, but first—is this guide and trek something interesting for you?"

Bradley and I glance at each other. Our jaws are nearly separated from our faces. *Twenty-one days trekking the Himalayas*

Chapter 7

with a Buddhist lama? It's the most picture-perfect adventure. Not even the two of us could have dreamt up such a trek in our wildest imaginations.

"Ganesh," Bradley begins. He leans forward and sneaks me his trademark *let-me-handle-this* glance. "It's an interesting proposal, but I think first we need to talk about—"

"Price!" Ganesh says with a wide grin.

I let out a smirk. What can I say? The man knows business.

"Of course, of course. We will talk price. But first, there is more."

"More?" I react.

Bradley shoots me a look telling me to play it cool.

"Yes, more. As I have said, Lama Dai is very special guide. He knows different routes. Special routes. If you wish, he will take you to mountain monasteries. Holy places where many monks go to find peace in this lifetime."

I tilt my head. "Does this place have a name?"

The man shrugs. "I have never been. Very few people go. It so high in the mountains. But Lama Dai can take you. He is special like this. A very special guide with special ways of leading. Anyway, to price…"

Ganesh scrambles to his desk then returns with a calculator, pen and paper, and begins mumbling and scribbling. The numbers floating around inside his head seem to click, and he looks up at us.

"A special price, just for you. Such good deal! I lose big! But I have no worries. Why no worries? Because one tourist for trekking helps many people. One trek help the guide, porters, farmers, cooks, so many of villagers. So here is the price. Everything together, nothing else needed. Permits, food, lodging, lama… each of you, one thousand dollars US."

Bradley straightens his posture. "Ganesh, do you mind giving us time to discuss this in private?"

"Of course, of course," he says, standing and stepping out into the hallway. "Let me know when you make decision."

When Ganesh closes the door, I turn to Bradley.

"Is this for real?"

He smiles. "Seems like it. But a grand is a lot more than the two-fifty we budgeted."

"Yeah, that's my budget for the whole trip."

"Same. I'd say we could talk him down further, but it's already a hell of a deal. Twenty-one days is a lot longer than ten, don't you think? I wasn't planning on it, but I can dig deeper into my bank account if I need to. I doubt we'll get this opportunity again. It seems like divine timing."

I think on it and decide I could swing the extra money, too. There's cash in my savings I can pull from, and my retirement account is still sitting around if I really need it. Since we're living with the wise woman, I doubt I'll need much money after trekking. I'd planned on most of my expenses going toward the hike anyway. Not to mention, if I'm serious about this whole enlightenment thing, I need to start letting go of my material possessions. Money isn't making me happy as it is. I'd thrown away everything else already, and I'd go on trading away the rest of it if it meant getting closer to the goal.

"Alright," I say. "Are we doing this?"

"It's meant to be, brother. This why we came here, man. To find our true nature. First Sajana and now a Tibetan lama?"

I nod. "Let's do this"

Bradley smiles. "I'll get Ganesh."

Bradley opens the door, and Ganesh bolts into the room.

"Decision?"

"Ganesh," Bradley says, plopping back down on the couch, "you've got yourself a deal, my friend!"

A huge smile floats across Ganesh's face, and he furiously shakes Bradley's hand.

"Good! *Very* good! You will not regret!"

Ganesh's handshake consumes mine in his tight grip.

Chapter 7

"Okay, next step very important. The day of trekking will depend. I will contact lama and submit government paperwork to see best day for you to begin. Maybe as early as Monday."

Monday?! My stomach flutters.

"That's three days away," I say.

"Yes," Ganesh replies. "I can make this happen for you. You see, I have connections in Nepali government. Things happen very fast with connections. Of course, there is one last very important formality. We will go to my office and handle the final paperwork there."

With that, Ganesh throws on a black trench coat, snags a briefcase from beside his desk, and heads out the door.

"Hold on, Ganesh!" Bradley says. "This isn't your office?"

Ganesh turns around and flashes a grin. "This just for tourist. Paperwork at my home. Very close." And with that, he turns back around and disappears out the door.

Bradley looks at me, I look at Bradley. Head wobbles exchange, and we follow Ganesh down the hall.

Contrary to his large physique, Ganesh barrels down the hall like an elephant making a beeline for the nearest swimming hole. I speed-walk to keep up, expecting him to turn into a different office room at any moment, but he instead charges right out the front doors of the Tourist Center.

We trail Ganesh like cops in hot pursuit. He turns up the street, plows through a crowd of pedestrians, then flags down a taxi.

"Come," he says, jogging around to the front passenger's seat. "We go now. Very close."

I narrow my eyes. It's at this moment that the peculiarity of getting in a car with a stranger dawns on me—but we've already come this far. If we want the deal of a lifetime done, we don't have another choice.

CHAPTER 8
THE ART OF THE DEAL

I hop in the back of the taxi after Bradley and buckle up. As we accelerate into the mass of motorbikes and scooters, Ganesh and the driver converse back and forth in Nepali. Despite traffic coming to a complete standstill, our driver somehow maneuvers around the congestion and speeds up the street.

Ganesh turns around with raised eyebrows and gives a thumbs up. "Good driver! Very good!"

After a frantic ten-minute dash to the edge of town, we stop in front of a seedy, nondescript residential building.

"This way," Ganesh says, barreling out of the taxi.

As Ganesh leads us through a locked gate, I get the creeping suspicion we've pushed our luck too far this time.

"Is this your office, Ganesh?" Bradley asks.

"Yes, this way."

We step inside a dark, empty foyer and follow Ganesh up the stairwell. My sandals click against the wooden boards as we climb flight after flight, soon arriving at a beaded doorway. Ganesh slips off his shoes, pushes aside the beaded curtain, and disappears as if through a portal.

I peel off my Jesus sandals and follow Bradley through the curtain into a dark, carpeted hallway. At the end of the

Chapter 8

hall lies a small office room. A skinny young man sits behind a desk. He lifts his head and smiles.

"This is my son, Ishur," Ganesh says.

We *namaste* the young gentleman and shake his hand. He looks like a thinner, younger version of Ganesh.

"Please, sit," Ganesh says. "Make yourself comfortable."

As the two gentlemen converse in Nepali, Bradley and I plop onto opposite ends of a leather couch and study the room. Framed posters of the Himalayas, awards, and photographs cover every inch of the walls.

Ganesh must notice my wandering eyes. He plucks one of the framed photographs off the wall and hands it to me.

"This photo," he says, pointing to the image. "Very important. You see, I was once Head of Tourism Department here in Nepal. Here is current President of Nepal, and this is me."

Sure enough, Ganesh stands arm-in-arm with a man who looks like he could be the President. Is he actually? I have no idea, nor will I ever know. But who would lie about such things?

Whatever the case, Ganesh seems like a big deal. Legitimate evidence of Ganesh's authority causes my shoulders to relax. Maybe that's why he drags clients halfway across the city.

Ganesh hangs the photo back up and turns to us. "You know the three religions of Nepal, yes?"

Bradley thinks for a second. "Hinduism, Buddhism, and Islam?"

Ganesh shakes his head. "Hinduism, Buddhism, Tourism!"

A large grin spreads across his face, and I can't help but let out a chuckle.

"OK, enough joking. Ishur!" The rest of what Ganesh says is in Nepali.

Ishur proceeds to open a desk drawer and rifle through stacks of papers. Like father, like son. Completed with his search,

Ishur crosses the room and hands the contents to his father. Ganesh flips through the documents carefully, divides them into two piles, and hands us each our own stack. Then he places a fancy ballpoint pen onto the table.

"You have health insurance, yes?"

I nod.

Ganesh looks at Bradley.

"Yeah," Bradley says. "Processing."

I pinch my arm to keep from laughing. Neither of us wanted to pay for international health insurance. If Bradley hadn't recommended a sketchy, low-cost catastrophic plan at the last-minute, and if not for my caring mother's demands and offers to pay, I'd be without it. I don't like relying on my parents, but if mom wanted peace of mind, I wasn't going to argue.

Last I heard from Bradley was that despite his mother requesting the same, he insisted he didn't need it. Had he ever gotten it? Who knows. But I doubt it's a dealbreaker for Ganesh.

"Good," Ganesh says, finding a leather chair and leaning back. "Please, fill these out. If you have questions, you may ask."

As we fill out paperwork, an unsettling silence descends upon the room. Ganesh gets oddly quiet—a stark contrast to the non-stop scramble of the day thus far. I have a feeling he has something on his mind. As if he's thinking about something very, very important.

"Hold the paperwork," Ganesh says, letting out a deep sigh and leaning forward.

I set the pen down.

"What's wrong?" Bradley asks.

"Everything happens so quickly. I have not had time to think. Now, I've slowed down and I'm thinking. I gave a good deal, you know this. One thousand US dollars each. I know

Chapter 8

you two are wanting trekking and meditation, but the deal is too good. The price must be more."

Bradley and I look at each other, wondering where this is going.

Ganesh eases between us onto the couch, pulls out his phone, and starts showing us group photos of backpackers posed in snow-laden mountains.

"Other customers pay much more! This family paid ten thousand US for ten days trekking! Ten thousand for ten days! Much more expensive! Here, a family of eight—six thousand for five days trekking! This, a family of five…"

"Look, Ganesh," Bradley says. "Give it to us straight. Are we wasting our time here?"

Ganesh blinks and sits up straight.

"No time is wasted," Ganesh says. "Never is any time wasted. Time is same and precious for everyone. So no, not wasted. Just one small change."

Ganesh paces the rug from chair to window. "I know we have already shaken, but the price must be higher. Before was not enough and now that I'm thinking… One-thousand and one hundred for each. You see—"

Bradley and I smile and wave him off.

"No worries, Ganesh," Bradley says. "That's fine."

It's a miniscule price increase and the trek is still one hell of a deal.

"Okay, good. Then you pay now?" Ganesh's direct tactics start to remind me of Bradley.

The most I can pluck from my fanny pack is a total of two thousand rupees, enough to cover the cost of a *dal bhat* dinner. An image of my backpack stashed behind the Hostel Yog front desk shimmers before my eyes. Is it still there? And what about my cash envelope tucked away at the bottom? Bradley's in very much the same situation.

True Nature

"As you can imagine," Bradley explains, "this is a much more costly trek than we expected. We need to swing by an ATM and our hostel."

"Understood," Ganesh says. "Ishur will go with you."

Ishur lifts his head from a stack of papers and smiles, ecstatic to be leaving the office.

"One last thing," Ganesh says, shaking his silver wristwatch. "I need your passports. You can leave them here with me. These are required to submit for government application."

My eyebrow raises.

Bradley exhales deeply through his nostrils. "I don't know about that, Ganesh. Can't you just photocopy them?"

Ganesh shakes his head, distinctly left then right. "The government will need to see real passports for permits. There is nothing to worry. They will be safe with me. Everything will be fine."

I swallow down the lump rising in the back of my throat. A lost passport is risky business. I imagine the look on my mother's face knowing I've given my passport to someone I just met. But what can I say? The more I've seen of Ganesh, of his employment at the Tourist Center, his photos, certifications, connections, and Ishur's presence—everything seems legitimate. If anyone's crazy enough to get the job done, it's Ganesh.

I look at Bradley and nod.

"Alright," Bradley says. "Make sure you don't lose 'em."

"Nothing to worry. Nothing to worry."

We surrender our passports, Ganesh delivers some orders to Ishur, then he looks back to us.

"We will meet here in three days for a very important meeting. I will return passports, and you will meet Lama. It is very important you meet Lama before trekking to feel each other's vibration. Until then, you go and pay. Ishur will take you where you need to go. Be safe. We will talk again soon. Take these."

Chapter 8

Ganesh hands us each his business card, which I stuff inside my fanny pack.

"Three days," Ganesh echoes. "Very important meeting. *Namaste*."

We thank Ganesh with one last handshake then follow Ishur through the dark hall, the beaded portal, down the stairway into the foyer, and out the front door. I shade my eyes from the hazy sun and walk alongside Ishur down the city side streets back in the direction of the hustle and bustle.

"You two must be very lucky," Ishur says.

"Why's that?" I ask.

"My father knows many guides. For him to offer his best guide to someone he just met is special. I've always wanted to trek with the lama myself, but I'm not old enough. You will be in good hands. He may not speak much English, but he knows the villages and he knows the mountains. And maybe there is something you can learn about your nature."

I look up at Ishur as we walk. "Thanks, Ishur."

After stopping by an ATM, we catch a taxi back to Hostel Yog. Our usual front desk staff is nowhere to be seen, but thankfully our backpacks are right where we left them. We sneak Ishur up the stairs and inside *Wisdom*. Nina and Daniel's stuff is still piled up on the floor, but they must be out on the town.

We lock the door behind us, draw our cash envelopes from the bottoms of our backpacks, and spread the money across the floor. It must look like a drug deal in progress as we try to add everything up. If anyone other than Nina and Daniel walked into the room right now, we'd have some explaining to do.

It turns out we're only a hundred rupees—about eighty cents short—and we look inquisitively at Ishur.

"Good enough." Ishur smiles, pocketing the cash off the floor. "As my father requested, please return to the office on Sunday. The address is listed on the card. If all goes well, trekking starts as early as Monday. See you soon."

And with that, we embrace Ishur and bid him farewell.

When the door closes, Bradley and I lay onto the floor and burst into joyful laughter. Who would have thought we'd be trekking and meditating in the Himalayas with a Tibetan lama? Best case scenario: enlightenment. Worst case scenario: the whole thing's a sham. We lose our savings, our passports, and it's likely the end of the trip. Other than that, things are looking up.

"We should head to Pokhara tomorrow morning," Bradley says, sitting up.

"If our hike is in three days, shouldn't we just stay here?"

"I don't know how much more time I can spend in this city. It's a lot of back-and-forth travel, but if Ganesh wants us back on Sunday, three days gives us plenty of time to swing by and meet Sajana in Pokhara.

"Plus, I have this feeling we should visit her as soon as possible. That way, she knows we're serious about spending time with her. I'd rather not show up after trekking without knowing what we're getting into. Maybe we can even leave some gear at her place. We've got no other reason to be here, right?"

I think it over. "So to be clear, you want to head to Pokhara tomorrow. We find Sajana's place and get a good idea of what we're walking into. Then we take the bus back to Kathmandu on Sunday to meet the lama, get our passports, and start the hike? Then, after the hike, we stay at Sajana's for the rest of the trip?"

"Exactly."

I guess that makes sense. "Sounds like a plan, brother."

We grab a celebratory dinner at the same place down the street as the night before. After filling our bellies with lemon waters and all-you-can-eat *dal bhat* for ten dollars'-worth of

Chapter 8

rupees each, night falls upon the tourist district, and we call it an early bedtime back at Hostel Yog.

I climb into my bunk and listen to the sound of motorcycle traffic from outside our half-opened hostel window, fulfilling my second one-hour meditation prescription.

For the briefest moment, I consider going out. Isn't that what Daniel and Nina are doing right now? Dancing, kissing, having a good ol' time? Maybe I'll meet someone special.

Instead, I open Hannah's letter one more time. I know we have an early bus ride to Pokhara tomorrow morning, but I want to remember her again, if only for a moment.

CHAPTER 9
THE LETTER

Dear David,

I'm excited for you. I hope you find whatever it is you're looking for in Nepal and that your plane makes it across the ocean. Wouldn't that be awfully terrible if it crashed? Talk about irony. Going down in flames on your way to enlightenment? No one would ever let you live that down.

Of course, it wouldn't affect you personally, seeing as… well, you know, the whole being dead thing. And even if you did make it over the ocean, you could always fall off a cliff, get tied up with the mafia, get kidnapped or robbed…

You know I'm just kidding! I've heard laughter's the best antidote to sadness. I'll miss you, but I know I can't keep you here. I wouldn't want to. Sometimes, people like you need to go and do things like this.

I think everyone needs to pursue their own version of happiness. Otherwise, you take up all sorts of responsibilities, a bunch of business you want nothing to do with later in life, and the pressure starts ramping up like a teakettle. The steam and the whistle builds and builds until… BOOM!

At the very least, you just won't ever feel settled inside your own skin if you keep ignoring it. Things come back to haunt you. And life's too short to settle for anything less.

Chapter 9

I've been having the strangest dreams lately. It's making me think there's not much difference between dreams and real life. We wake up from one and go right into the other. The two worlds blend into each other so deeply that it's hard to really tell what's what. Like two sides of the same coin, or a magician turning over both sides of a playing card. Everyone dreams when they're awake and everyone wakes up from their dreams. I guess it's best not to hold on too tightly to either.

One last thing. Do you think you'll write another book about your travels? I think you're a great writer. I really do. I mean, not the best-of-all-time or anything. You're no Hesse or McCarthy or Murakami—but hey, don't feel bad! If it makes you feel any better, ninety-nine-point-nine percent of the things I read aren't the best. What I'm trying to say is that I like reading what you write. You're different—that's for sure. And you don't have to be the best at something to make a difference or have something to say. Sometimes, you just show up. That's where the magic happens.

Want to know what I think? I bet you'll end up writing one. But it's probably too much pressure to think about something like that right now. There's so much else that lies ahead of you on this trip.

I hope it's an unforgettable experience. Just make sure you write everything down. What you're feeling, descriptions of the people, the colors of the walls in the places you stay. If you don't write that stuff down, you might forget, and when we forget things, it's like they never happened in the first place. That's the importance of memory. It's the knot. Where everything else comes together. Without it, there'd be nothing to tie us to anything else. We'd be like balloons floating toward space.

I'm at my desk writing you this letter, looking out my bedroom window onto a backyard of sunlight and flowers and beautiful black butterflies. The kinds with paper-like wings that open and close like origami, drifting in the wind.

I've spent my whole morning writing, thinking of what I should say to you. I keep second-guessing myself, trying to impress you with my writing, but I decided to write from the heart and say whatever came up. It's not perfect, but that's okay.

I'll try writing to you again in a month or two. Everything will have probably changed by then. Until then, the sun shines, the spring flowers bloom outside my window, and people sip coffee quietly, typing away at their computers. I'm going on a walk through the greenbelt, to be alone with the birds and the butterflies.

- Hannah

CHAPTER 10
PASSAGE

My eyelids peel open to my ribcage vibrating. I must have fallen asleep after reading her letter. I roll over, grab my phone, and stare at the screen with squinted eyes. It's five a.m. and our bus departs to Pokhara at six thirty. Before then, I need to meditate. I lift my face from a drool-soaked pillow and sit.

This early, the hostel is quiet. Pleasantly so. Almost no sounds come from the city. No honking, no jackhammering, no barking, no raindrops pounding against the tin roof. Still, my mind races. I can't stop thinking. Today, we meet the wise woman.

Despite traveling across the world to see her, I know almost nothing about her. Only that she and Bradley have exchanged minimal correspondence. He emailed her, she emailed back. Bradley forwarded me her response right before we came here:

Bradley,

If you wish to know your true nature, you are heartly welcome to come to Nepal and stay with me.

- Sajana

That was it. The entirety of her email.

I understand why such a direct response could cause Bradley to think she's the one. The words "true nature" must ring inside his mind like a delightful chord plucked from a harp.

They resonate with me, too. More than I thought possible. Hiking in nature and experiencing my inner nature through meditation have shaped my life in profound ways. The promise of knowing more is too great an opportunity to resist. Especially with an invitation to stay in a spiritually-rich country like Nepal. A message like that is hook, line, and sinker for any soul-searching hippie.

Beyond this email, only the stories crafted by my imagination give her depth. She lives in my mind like a dream, a silhouette cast against the curtains of my subconscious. I imagine her as a solitary prophet. A recluse meditating in a dark cave or a thatched hut in the heart of the jungle. Sitting there in silence, awaiting our arrival.

I hope she's real. She has to be. After all, we're living with her for seventy days after our trek.

The timer goes off, her apparition disappears, and Bradley and I pack up and hit the road. Before I close the door to *Wisdom*, Nina and Daniel roll over in one of the bunks. Should I say goodbye? No doubt they'll be gone by the time we return, but how deep was our friendship, really? Maybe some people were meant to leave our lives just as quickly as they enter. It's a story that repeats itself when I pass the empty front desk of Hostel Yog.

It's dark and chilly in these early morning hours outside the hostel premises. Bradley and I depart through the gate into the moonlit alleyway and slip away into the dusk. How strange that a place so humid during the day can turn so cold at night.

By the time we reach the main drag, the sunrise and traffic smog warms my hands and ears back up. The brunette at Hostel Yog was right about one thing: unlike the city buses, you can't miss the tourist buses. Six of them line the sidewalk

Chapter 10

like elephants ready for migration. Together, they could shuttle a couple hundred passengers across the country.

Ganesh's voice echoes in my mind: *Hinduism, Buddhism, Tourism.*

Bradley and I stretch our legs in preparation for the eight-hour cross-country bus ride, then we hop aboard.

"Pokhara?" I ask the driver.

He wobbles his head, so I hand him eight dollars'-worth of rupees. This earns us stowage for our backpacks and a pair of worn-down upholstered seats near the front.

The bus smells like the inside of a coffin—cold, dead, and musty. I sit next to Bradley and run my fingers against the headrest in front of me. Clouds of dust soar into the air, and I sneeze. At least the seats recline to a comfortable angle, and a chilly air conditioning flows through the cabin. Before long, the bus fills up with locals, and the wheels start turning.

We plow through traffic then climb a two-lane dirt highway into the hills. The buildings and gray skies fall away in the rearview, and the sun shines down onto the valley.

Looking out the window, I soak up the passing mountainside views around every bend. Jungle foliage shades sections of the highway, tree limbs bounce in the breeze. Terraces ripple down the hills, meeting the rocky banks of a river far below, surging and cutting into the earth like the gash of a knife. It's a relief to escape the city.

No sooner than when I close my eyes does our driver slam on the gas. I launch into the back of my seat as we veer into the oncoming lane of traffic. He must be trying to pass the bus in front of us, but he's insane because it's impossible to see around the bends in the mountainside.

Sure enough, a huge form emerges in the windshield ahead, and I realize we're charging head-first toward another colossal tour bus. My heart pounds against my chest as I grip my seatbelt.

True Nature

This is it. My life ends here. Struck dead on the path towards enlightenment. Hannah was right after all.

Before I can think another thought, we swerve into our original lane, and the oncoming bus whizzes by.

I look at Bradley, alarmed and relieved.

"Round two!" Bradley says smiling.

I clench my teeth as we once again throttle into the oncoming lane, only to avoid another head-on collision at the last second. I look around at the other locals. They're completely unphased. Meanwhile, my fragile existence hangs in the balance of a repeating game of chicken.

To make matters worse, every other bus on the road is playing, too—risking everyone's life to shave mere seconds off an arrival time. Apparently, the life of a passenger is worth no more than the price of admission.

But with every gamble, no one crashes, and my shoulders begin to relax. Novelty and discomfort rusts away with time into adaptation and normalcy. Chaos melts into order. What I once perceived as risk is reframed as skill.

Adjusted to the travails of the road, the ride offers Bradley and me more than enough time to make sense of our lives.

"What do you want in life, David? Let's say you could have anything you want."

I shrug. "No idea."

"Oh, c'mon. There's got to be something. Everyone wants *something*."

I think hard. "Enlightenment would be nice."

"I feel that," Bradley replies. "Hopefully it becomes a reality for both of us soon enough."

Then he chuckles.

"What's funny?" I ask.

Bradley looks off into the jungle then back at me. "I just figured you'd say something else."

I furrow my brow, urging him to continue.

Chapter 10

"A girl, perhaps?" He gives me a few good ribbings with his elbow.

I blush. "Okay, maybe that, too. What about you?"

Bradley cocks his head to the side. "You know, I don't think a woman's in the cards for me in this lifetime. I mean, I guess theoretically, it *could* happen. But practically? I'm not counting on it. Not like I used to."

"Why's that?"

Bradley scratches his chin. "When you're weird like me, your pool of potential applicants grows smaller and smaller as time goes on. At this rate, I wouldn't be surprised if the pool evaporates entirely."

"But what if there's someone out there thinking that exact same thing?"

Bradley yawns. "Like I said, it's possible. I'm just not counting on it."

I nod, also growing tired. With so time spent moving from one place to another, there's hardly been an opportunity to relax. I lean my head against the window, and the carousel of mountainside views begins to disappear.

* * *

Every couple of hours, our bus pulls into a gravel parking lot near the jungle or at the edge of a scenic overlook. At each stop, there's just enough time for everyone to take a leak, stretch, and grab a bite to eat. I buy an apple from a stall, Bradley gets a bunch of local village bananas (essentially, just small bananas), and we take the day's first bites of food before loading back up.

The drive feels endless, our destination far from sight, and yet we progress. I lose track of time as the mountain road twists beside the jungle. I press my cheek against the warm window, watch the sun, and glue my mind to the future.

Stretching during a stop on our passage to Pokhara

Is the wise woman really enlightened? What does it look like when you're enlightened? Does she live in the city or the jungle? Will we be sleeping in some faraway village in some straw hut with mosquitos buzzing around my head? Should I have made a list of important questions to ask her?

For the first time, I feel totally unprepared for our meeting. Hopefully, she offers some guidance for my meditation practice that I can bring to the hike. Guidance that will bring me one step closer to enlightenment.

I peer out the window at the leaves of the jungle trees swaying in the breeze.

The next time I wake, the bus stops.

CHAPTER 11
POKHARA

While everyone grabs their luggage from overhead compartments, dreams still grasp at my consciousness. It's that same familiar daze from when I first landed here. An eight-hour bus ride was only slightly more manageable than the twenty-hour flight.

I step down into the parking lot and glance around. Compared to Kathmandu, Pokhara's skies are still cloudy, but at least I can breathe a good breath and hear myself think.

"Hostel! Hotel! Taxi!"

"We've already got a place to stay," Bradley announces to the swarm of taxi drivers. "We just need a ride into town."

As I grab my pack from storage and swing it over my shoulder, Bradley finds us a ride. We follow a suited man into his taxi. For a long while, the man stares at us through his rearview.

I lean over to Bradley. "Do you have the address…?"

Bradley searches his phone. "That's weird. I'm not seeing one."

I raise my eyebrow. I hadn't wanted to intrude on Bradley's correspondence with the wise woman. Everything seemed so personal and secretive every time I asked. But now, without an address, I wish I had more information.

"Then what are we supposed to do?"

"Chill out, man," Bradley says, noticing my frustration. "There are directions. She says... *Begin at Amar Singh Chowk.*"

"*Amar Singh?*" the driver perks up. "You passed on bus."

"Then we go back," Bradley says confidently.

After a disgruntled head wobble, the driver starts the meter and pulls out of the lot. Is *Amar Singh Chowk* a village off one of those mountainside roads? If so, this could end up being an expensive cab ride.

Even so, we head up the highway. Behind the chain-link fence, I watch a plane take off and sail toward the distant fog. *Pokhara has an airport?* Flying here would have saved us time, but the bus was dirt-cheap anyway. And if the pilots are anything like the drivers, we'd no doubt end up crashing into the mountains. We're here, one step closer, and that's all that matters.

Highway turns to road as we enter a familiar scene: a city center that reminds me of a milder Kathmandu. Pedestrians and motorcycles swarm the lawless streets. Telephone lines droop down like tangled vines between the buildings. Signs and banners cover the bright-painted shop facades of the multi-story buildings. Scaffolding frames the exposed brick and concrete walls.

Nepali covers the shops and billboards. I don't understand the language, but I do speak advertising. A soccer player drinks a yellowish soda from a glass bottle. A mysterious woman wearing trendy shades poses beneath a black umbrella. It's an authentic place far from the guardrails of a city tour.

We take a roundabout and pull into the parking lot of an abandoned gas station.

"*Amar Singh Chowk,*" our diver says.

I look out the window. This isn't the jungle or a cave. With the mountains far off, I guess the wise woman lives in the city after all.

"Thanks," Bradley replies, handing him some rupees.

Chapter 11

I'd expected a much farther ride than what the driver seemed to imply, but I'm not complaining. I'm over sitting in vehicles, and it makes the ride affordable.

We pull our backpacks from the trunk, and our taxi disappears into the throng. I stand there, studying the place. For the first time, it hits me—an utterly vulnerable knowing, deep inside my chest, that I'm far away from home. Of all the places the universe could have pulled me, why here?

I throw my backpack over my shoulder and look at Bradley. "Now what?"

"*Walk north for fifteen minutes,*" Bradley says, reading the directions off his phone.

I chuckle in disbelief. *How specific.* Finding the wise woman seems more and more like a wild goose chase. "Should I set a timer?"

Bradley wobbles his head and rolls his eyes. Luckily, even though the trail was three years ago, measuring walking distance by time is a skill that's never left me. It's ingrained into our legs, so I'm sure we'll figure it out...

We take the road extending away from town, the horizon and sky obscured by a thin fog. As we walk, the weight of my pack presses down on me, and I remember the trail. It feels like home, and I smile.

We pass a muddy soccer field, a basketball court, a children's school hidden behind rows of trees, a produce shop, and a corner store. This part of town looks nothing like Kathmandu's tourist district. Quite the opposite. It's a real local Nepali neighborhood through and through.

With no massage joints or tattoo parlors in sight, we draw the stares of those we pass. A group of children riding tricycles on the sidewalk stops to smile and wave. An old woman sweeping her shop's front steps smiles, too. Even the street dogs raise their heads.

Amar Singh Chowk

While I've traveled abroad before, never have I felt so far removed from the tourist experience. For the first time in my life, I exist as a true foreigner. Someone completely new.

My legs send messages to my brain that fifteen minutes is up, and Bradley checks the directions. *"Take a right at Seva, then turn left behind the hospital."*

I keep my eyes peeled for this word, *"Seva,"* finally spotting a red banner with the word *"Sewa"* hanging above one of the buildings.

"Pretty damn close," Bradley says.

"Yeah, might as well try it."

We hang a right past a corner store, a small produce market, a building with posters of dogs hung in the windows, an open garage with bags of concrete stacked up on the floor, and finally, an empty park with a large banyan tree.

Where's the hospital?

Chapter 11

We ask an old man sitting on a stool in front of the garage, but he simply smiles and shakes his head. "No English."

We thank him with a *dhanyabad* and look around the street.

I point to the building with dog posters. "Maybe they have Wi-Fi?"

"Worth a shot."

We offer prayer hands to the uniformed guard standing in the doorway.

"*Namaste*," Bradley says. "Wi-Fi?"

The guard thinks for a second then nods and turns to push open the door.

"Brilliant word economy," I whisper to Bradley.

"Sometimes, the less words, the better."

The man escorts us inside a drafty hallway, the sound of dogs barking down the hall. He then exchanges a brief conversation in Nepali with the woman behind the front desk. She looks us up and down then scribbles on a piece of paper and slides it beneath the glass.

"*Dhanyabad*," I say.

A momentary smile lifts across her face before she forces it back down and returns to her computer.

Bradley and I throw off our packs, slide down a wall onto the floor, and plug in the Wi-Fi. Four bars of signal pop up on my phone.

"You see this?" I show Bradley my phone.

He laughs. "Go figure."

It turns out this building is the hospital we've been looking for. *Sewa Veterinary Hospital*.

Knowing our destination is only a couple of blocks away, a rising anticipation fills my chest.

A cool air blows over me as we push open the doors to the outside world. Gray clouds cover the skies, and the city seems a few shades darker than last we'd seen.

"Better get moving," I say.

We wrap around back of the hospital, pass beneath the park's towering Banyan tree, and find an alleyway into a tucked-away neighborhood. Bradley and I glance at each other with wide eyes and wider grins. The gated homes lining the block are larger than any we've seen in Nepal so far.

Is this really where the wise woman lives?

The thought of meditating inside an actual home and not some mosquito-infested village eases my mind. Still, something about this block feels strange. Sheltered away from the noises of city traffic, the place feels like a ghost town. So many homes seem vacant and half-built with piles of bricks, wooden boards, tools, and bags of concrete scattered around the yards.

Where is everyone?

"It's the last house on the right side of the block," Bradley says.

The house with the golden gate

Chapter 11

We stop there in the middle of the street, facing the white-brick house with the golden gate. It's one of the few in the neighborhood that seems fully constructed.

"Want to do the honors?" Bradley asks.

I step to the gate, press the intercom, and wait. Thunder rumbles in the east. I press my ear against the speaker, but nothing reaches me from the other side. No beeps, rings, or voices.

I try the button again just to be sure, but still, nothing. Just the empty sounds of anticipation.

I stand back and study the house. Apart from the potted trees in the driveway sticking up over the gate, the place shows almost no signs of life. It's dark inside, the blinds drawn from every visible window. For all I know, it's a façade, an empty shell.

I'd heard such places existed in China. Entire ghost cities erected to inflate employment and GDP. Cities where only the workers live, falling empty the day they're finished, decaying like towns in the 1800s where the gold ran dry. Surely this home wasn't anything like that. I hadn't flown across the world to an empty house with empty answers. No, surely the wise woman lives here, just as her directions say.

An eerie chill runs across my shoulder. I turn around and freeze. A dozen people next door lock eyes with us. I stare at them, and they stare at me. They look like regular people with regular jeans, t-shirts, and shoes, but their gloves make them out to be construction workers.

Bradley and I offer prayer hands but receive only blank stares in return. An imperceptible language barrier thicker than Nepali traffic stands between us. I must look like I feel: totally out of place. They must be wondering what the hell these Hostel Yog-hippies are doing in a place like this.

Their suspecting stares pierce through me. My chest tightens. *Do we look threatening? Have they called the police? Would the cops want to see my passport?*

True Nature

I fish into my fanny pack for the smooth plastic cover, but it dawns on me. I've given it away to a man I don't really know in hopes of hiking a trail I've never hiked before.

Right as I'm really starting to freak out, something wet lands atop my nose, and I look up. An endless sea of dark clouds stretches across the sky. Raindrops pelt the pavement around me. Then, they erupt into a downpour.

"Interesting," Bradley says, matter of fact.

With no nearby trees or canopies, a torrential rain pounds the pavement, pelts my backpack, and runs down the back of my neck. I fling off my backpack, yank my rain jacket from the mesh pocket, and slide it over my T-shirt. A temporary solution at best until we figure out what to do next.

"Ehhhhh?" From behind us, a piercing yell reaches my ears. We turn around and glance upward.

Across the street from the house with the golden gate, a middle-aged woman with long black hair leans over the railing of her second story veranda.

"What you want?!" she yells. I can hardly hear her voice through the pouring rain.

Bradley cups his hands around his mouth and yells back, "Sajana?"

"Ehhhhhh?"

He turns and points to the house with the golden gate. "Miss Sajana?"

The middle-aged woman stares as if pondering something important. Then she turns around and disappears inside the shadows of her home.

Beads of rain drip down Bradley's black hair and run across his face. I step out of the puddle forming in the pothole beneath my feet. My socks and trail runners have already completely soaked through. *I should have worn my Jesus sandals like Bradley.*

"What now?" I ask.

"Beats me."

Chapter 11

No directions, no guidance. As the rain pounds down in sheets, I ponder what my life has come to. This trip isn't at all what I thought it would be.

Desperate for shelter, I consider pitching my tent in the middle of the street. A sense of helplessness and the urge to cry floods my body.

CHAPTER 12
THE HOUSE

As I hold back my tears and search for my tent, a new sound reaches me from above.

"Ehhhhhh! Come!" she yells, beckoning us with a wave of her hand.

It's the woman with long black hair returned to her balcony. She's not the woman we expected to meet. It's not the house we expected to enter. But getting out from under the rain and the gaze of the entire neighborhood sounds a whole lot better than standing here and doing nothing.

We bolt to the front gate and beneath her front porch awning as she ushers forward. We follow her up the marble staircase to the balcony, exchanging grateful *namastes*. In the corner of the balcony, an elderly woman with long silver hair hunches over a loom. I watch her delicate hands pluck the woolen strands taut across the loom, the beginnings of a blanket in the making.

"Mother," the middle-aged woman says, pointing to the weaving woman.

"That's a beautiful blanket," Bradley offers.

The wrinkles in the elderly woman's face bend upward as she glances up from her work. She nods gently and grins, revealing her crooked teeth. "*Dhanyabad.*"

"*Swagatam,*" Bradley replies. *You're welcome.*

Chapter 12

The two of them burst into cackling laughter. His Nepali must appease them.

"I'm glad they liked that one," Bradley says. "That's pretty much the last of what I've got."

Suddenly, the middle-aged woman's eyes widen. She leaps up and disappears through the doorway, soon returning with two plastic lawn chairs. She arranges them side by side on the balcony and slaps the seats with her palms. We oblige, throwing off our backpacks, and plopping down with a sigh of relief.

A gust of wind rushes over the balcony, and I gaze out into a curtain of rain. From here, the house with the golden gate is in plain sight.

Rain hammers the cozy front-yard garden and muddies the soil. The potted trees framing the driveway thrash about in the wind. The T-shirts and socks pinned to the rooftop clotheslines flail about in the storm, hanging on by a thread. There are signs of life in that house after all. People live there, not ghosts.

The middle-aged woman turns away from the balcony and asks me something in Nepali. Thanks to Bradley's few words of Nepali, it's clear she has overestimated my abilities. Seeing my empty stare, she raises her hand to her ear with thumb and pinky finger extended.

"Ohh!" Bradley says. "No phone number. But I have her email. Wi-Fi?"

The woman then shouts some words of Nepali into the open doorway.

Has our quest for enlightenment become us chasing Wi-Fi connections?

Moments later, a little girl with pigtails pokes her head through the doorway.

"*Ba?*" the young girl asks, which I assume means: *yeah, what do you want*?

The middle-aged woman points at Bradley's phone and says some more Nepali. The little girl ever so shyly slides out from behind the doorframe and offers her hand to Bradley. He sets his phone into her palm, and she settles onto the steps beside us. After she hands it back to him, she scampers inside the house.

"We're in business," Bradley says, showing me the successful connection. "I'll shoot an email to Sajana, let her know we think we're across the street."

As Bradley directs his attention toward his phone, I ease back into my plastic chair. The rain doesn't seem to be letting up anytime soon, and what's there to do in the rain? It's another lazy moment where everything comes to a halt and there's zero progress forward.

It makes me wonder how much of my life I have control over. Sometimes, life seems like an endless series of deterministic events. What choice do I have in storms, traffic, and soulmates? Where's the *me* in that? With everything that's happened—could I have ended up anywhere else than here?

There on the balcony, for a passing moment, the thoughts stop. Life feels simple. *Is this what enlightenment feels like? Some everlasting state of contentment dragged out for all eternity?* Whatever it is, for the first time since laying my sweaty back against Hostel Yog's cold brick rooftop, I get the sense that this is where I belong.

The four of us—me, Bradley, the silver-haired weaver, the kind mother in her rocking chair—watch the storm and wait. Bradley sets his phone down and attempts conversation despite the language barrier. This requires the middle-aged woman to summon the little girl into the doorway to translate single words, but it isn't long before we reach a dead end and settle again into silence.

It must be an hour later before the rain slows to a steady drizzle, then lets up completely. The dark clouds disperse, revealing a familiar overcast sky and a few remaining hours of daylight.

Chapter 12

Then a sputtering engine growls through the neighborhood streets. A black figure riding a motorcycle turns onto the block. I lean forward as the bike glides across a pool of water and stops before the house with the golden gate.

The rider dismounts and shuts off the engine, allowing a quiet to descend upon the neighborhood once again. As he unlocks the golden gate, our middle-aged host stands from her rocking chair.

"Ehhh!" she yells, followed by some Nepali.

The driver turns around, removes his helmet, and tucks it under his arm. A young man with a bright smile waves at us. "Hey, guys! Come on down."

"Who's that?" I ask Bradley.

Bradley shrugs. "We're about to find out."

A newfound excitement cascades into my life. Once again, there's forward direction. Somewhere to be, something to do.

Bradley and I take up our backpacks and bow to the two women and the little girl in the doorway. Then we trudge downstairs to meet the young man in the street. He runs a hand through his matted helmet hair then spreads his arms wide.

"Great to meet you," he says, embracing each of us tightly. "My name's Sarod. You must be here to see my sister, Sajana."

"That's us," Bradley says.

"Sorry no one was home when you arrived. It's no fun waiting around for others. When it rains here, everything slows to a crawl. It's not safe to drive motorcycles in the rain or do much of anything for that matter.

Sarod laughs. "People still do it, but I tend to be a bit more cautious. You never know what might happen if you're not careful enough. Anyways, everyone must still be caught up at the temple. I'm sure they'll be home soon. Please, come inside. I'm sure you're both exhausted from your travels."

I'm pleasantly surprised by Sarod's English. He seems like a genuine, kind, and well-educated young man. But who's "everyone?" Who else lives with the wise woman?

Sarod pushes the full force of his weight into the gate, allowing it to slide sideways along its rail and reveal the house in its entirety. He walks his bike into the driveway and drops the kickstand.

"Sahor!" Sarod says sweetly.

An old golden retriever picks himself up from beneath the balcony and lumbers toward us. His long hair drags across the driveway like a broom. He must have been hiding to keep dry.

Sarod scratches the dog's head. "This is Sahor. He's old, but gentle and so kind. You can pet him. He won't bite."

Sahor lying on the front porch

Sahor delicately licks the back of my hand before looking off into the distance, aloof, as if he's already forgotten about me entirely. I scratch the top of his golden-white head as drool falls from his open mouth.

"This way," Sarod says, heading up the driveway.

Chapter 12

We follow Sarod behind the house through a narrow alleyway. There's no backyard—only a few shed-like structures pushed up against the sidewalk and a water basin by the back door.

Sarod turns the faucet to a trickle. Sahor tilts his head sideways, laps up the water, shakes, and shuffles back to the driveway.

"I hope our names aren't too confusing," Sarod says, shutting off the faucet and approaching the back door. "Sahor... Sarod... they sound similar, but I'm sure you'll get used to them." Sarod reaches above his head to the highest shelf of a bookcase and pulls a small key from inside a tennis shoe. "If you ever get locked out, this is how you get back in."

"You must really trust us, Sarod!" Bradley laughs.

Sarod shrugs as he pushes open the door. "I can trust anyone who's come this far."

Bradley and I follow Sarod inside, and a smile spreads across my face. This place is nothing like the empty shell I had imagined.

Flights of marble steps wrap upward into the house. Beneath it, a dozen pairs of sneakers, flip flops, and sandals fill a small alcove by the doorway. A simple but modern-looking kitchen and dining room lie beyond the granite hallway. It's a far cry from a jungle hut or a mountain cave.

"If you don't mind leaving your shoes here, that would be a big help. Things very easily get dirty with all the guests and the rain. Not to mention, it's custom here in Nepal. Your room is right this way."

I slip off my sopping-wet shoes and socks, set them beneath the alcove, and follow Sarod into a door at the end of the hall. Inside are two twin beds, an end table, and a wardrobe. Nothing fancy, but, admittedly, it beats living in the jungle.

"I hope this is okay," Sarod says. "The sheets and pillows are clean, and the bathroom is right down the hall. If you ever need anything else, please don't hesitate to ask."

"Thanks, Sarod," Bradley says. "This means a lot to us."

"Of course. I heard you two are staying for some months, is that right?"

"Well," Bradley begins. "We leave to trek the Himalayas in a couple of days, but we'll be back shortly after."

"Wonderful," Sarod replies. "Now's the perfect time to go into the mountains. As you can tell, the rain is already starting to pick up into monsoon season. It's unpredictable to know when the rains come, but when they do, they hit hard. Anyways, is there anything else you need?"

I shake my head. "Nope, this is great. Thanks, Sarod."

"Sajana and the others should return home soon. Until then, please, take rest."

At that, Sarod waves goodbye. The back door shuts, and a motorcycle sputters off through the neighborhood.

I glance at Bradley. "Got a preference?"

"Nah."

Our shared room in Pokhara

Chapter 12

Too exhausted to change out of our wet clothing, Bradley and I throw off our backpacks and fall onto our beds with a hard thud. The mattress is like a stone slab, and both of us burst out laughing.

"Not too shabby," I say.

"Elegant," Bradley replies with a loud yawn.

With my wet hair dampening my pillow, I give the room a once over. A framed painting of a mountain landscape hangs on one of the empty walls. *Soon I'll be hiking mountains just like the ones in that painting.*

My eyelids close, my body shuts down, and my consciousness slips away.

I soon wake to the sound of the back door slamming shut, then laughter and chatter coming from the kitchen. *Could that be her?*

CHAPTER 13
THE WISE WOMAN

I peek through the door to see two young Western gentlemen fluttering around the kitchen. *Have I woken up in the wrong house? Who are these guys, and what have they done with the wise woman?*

They spot me the moment the door opens.

"You made it!" says the shorter white guy with a clean-shaven head and glasses. He has a strong German accent. He sets down his chef's knife and bows. "My name's Tim. Great to meet you."

"I'm Christian," says the tall one with his matching German accent. He flips back his long flowing hair and offers me *namaste* prayer hands.

They act as if they've been expecting me, so I inch into the kitchen and introduce myself.

"Welcome to Nepal, David. Sajana and everyone else should be home soon. Are you hungry?"

I'm in the right place after all—but what are these guys doing here? Are they the cooks?

"I could eat." It's the truth. The last thing I ate was an apple from our ride into Pokhara.

"Dinner should be ready soon," Christian says, returning to chopping a head of lettuce. "Did I hear you came here with a friend?"

Chapter 13

"Bradley here," says Bradley, stepping out from behind the bedroom door. "What's going on, boys?"

The two Germans laugh and exchange bows.

"How can we help?" Bradley asks.

"Don't be silly," Tim says. "Just relax and make yourself at home. I'm sure travel was brutal. That airport and the roads! Don't get me started. Anyway, dinner's leftovers and a simple salad. Takes no time at all."

"If you insist," Bradley says.

"Do you like yak cheese?" Tim asks.

I stare at Tim for a long moment, caught off guard by the question. *I don't know,* I wonder. *Do I?* I haven't tried it before—yak, he said? *Yak.* A word that I haven't heard in years. The syllable sounds strange leaving his tongue.

"Yak cheese?" I ask, making sure I heard him correctly.

Tim nods. "The lasagna's made with yak cheese. It's yak-everything here in Nepal. Yak cheese, yak milk, yak butter. Really good stuff."

It doesn't sound that great to me. After three years of veganism, I had only recently begun eating animal food products again. A choice that had nothing to do with environmental activism and everything to do with my meditation practice.

My tradition taught me that to make myself pure enough to attain enlightenment, I should avoid ingesting animals. The suffering an animal experienced during its life and death would enter my body and contribute to my suffering. Keeping this diet was a requirement for attending retreats. Only recently did new questions arise. *Was I doing this out of dogma and blind belief? Did refraining from eating animals actually help me?* The answer was still fuzzy, but if I'm eating this meal for free, then I'm like a monk going door-to-door for alms and accepting what is given. If the people here are eating yak cheese, maybe I can loosen my restrictions.

"I—I guess I'll try it."

"You might be pleasantly surprised," Tim says.

I hope so. For enlightenment's sake.

"So how long have you two been here?" Bradley cuts right to the chase, as always.

"Two weeks," Christian says.

"Ten days," Tim replies.

"Not too long, then," Bradley says.

"You could say that," Tim says. "But time is a funny thing, isn't it? In a way, those few days have felt like a lifetime. Maybe my experience is strange, though. Have you ever had that feeling before?"

"Sure have," Bradley says.

I nod but find his response unsettling. If ten days in this house feels like a lifetime, what does that mean for our sixty-five day stay after our trek?

"Wait," Bradley says, putting two and two together, "you guys didn't come here together?"

"Nope," Tim laughs. "We met here. The fact that we're both German is just pure coincidence. Karma, you could say."

Bradley smiles. "Karmic forces at work, indeed."

Tim brandishes the salad with lemon dressing and tosses it in a large wooden bowl. "And how do you two know each other?"

Bradley and I relate snippets of our saga—from fraternity brothers to corporate dropouts to nomadic hikers to meditators. The spiel feels so rehearsed and distant by this point. When something gets repeated often enough, it stretches out and grows thin with time. It becomes perfunctory. It loses its original substance, and it's difficult to relate to the thing it once was. I'm ready to move on from that story and begin something new.

By the time we cover the basics, Bradley leans forward onto the kitchen island. "So how did you two hear about Sajana? That's why you're here, isn't it? To meet her?"

Chapter 13

"That's right," Christian says, leaning back onto the counter. "You know, we first heard about her from a man named Yorn."

"No kidding!" Bradley says. He claps his palms down onto the countertop. "Yorn? The guy who leads Vipassana pilgrimages through India?"

Christian beams. "That's him!"

"Karmic forces indeed," Christian says with a wink. "Tim and I met Yorn on separate pilgrimages through India. I tend to be introverted, but Yorn and I clicked from day one. I told him about my problems and roadblocks with my meditation practice and my desire to meet with a spiritual teacher. After an evening sitting beneath the bodhi tree, he pulled me aside and told me about Sajana. He said I could meet her if I wanted to; I only had to travel a bit farther. And, well, here I am. How did you meet Yorn?"

"He sat a meditation course back in the States where I managed a vipassana center," Bradley says. "I didn't think much of our meeting at the time. We exchanged emails and kept in touch over the years about our practice. Then, years later, when David and I got to talking about meeting a wise teacher, I remembered Yorn had mentioned something about a wise woman. Now we're here, halfway across the world."

All these details were new to me. *Why hadn't Bradley disclosed any of this information to me before? Why hadn't I asked?*

"Life has a way of working out," Christian continues. "So many different paths pulling us in the same direction. And how are you feeling about it now?"

Bradley ponders the question then looks up. "I'm nervous to meet her. I really don't know what to expect."

"What about you, David?" Tim asks.

After everything we've been through, I feel impatient. Like I've wasted my time by coming here. *Where is she? Does she even exist?* I'm not nervous. I just want answers.

I shrug. "I'm still trying to figure that out."

Tim and Christian exchange smiles.

"Perfect," Tim says.

"Sounds about right," Christian says, setting placemats on the dining table. "We felt the very same feelings at first. Questioning, doubting, unsure of our preparation and purpose. Don't worry. Everything will become clearer in time. You give anything enough time, and it's bound to change."

"And surrender your expectations," Tim says, placing water glasses onto the table. "Especially when it comes to Sajana. She's really unlike anything you're imagining."

My eyebrow raises. *What's that supposed to mean? Is she enlightened or not?* Whatever she is, my curiosity and impatience for meeting her grows in each passing moment.

"Make sure to ask her questions," Tim continues, setting out the salad and lasagna onto the table. "If you don't ask, she'll go about her day like all the others. Right after our nightly meditations, she tends to stick around in the temple for a while. If you're lucky, she might say a few words every now and again out of the blue. But Christian's right. Expectations and worry won't do you any good here."

As the two of them finish preparing dinner, I stand around and ponder the implications of our discussion. Why do *I* have to ask *her* questions? Won't she just intuitively know what I need to progress towards enlightenment? Asking questions won't be a problem for Bradley, but I can't imagine myself asking others for help. I don't even know what to ask about.

Tim finishes setting the table then looks up the stairwell. "Dinner's ready!"

"Sit anywhere you like," Christian says while gesturing to the table. "Except here, of course."

Before I can ask about the forbidden silver dish at the head of the table, heavy footsteps come marching down the stairs. A man, short yet strong in stature, steps into the kitchen.

Chapter 13

"Dinner is ready! Dinner is ready!" the man shouts, letting out an infectious laugh. "Very good, very good!" He reaches out to shake my hand, a much gentler handshake compared to Ganesh's. "Shiva. Sajana is my wife. Good to meet you. Please, sit, sit, sit."

As Shiva plops down before the silver dish, Sarod arrives at the backdoor with a handful of groceries.

"*Babu*!" Shiva shouts. The two exchange a brief conversation in Nepali, of which I understand nothing.

Sarod sets the groceries onto the counter and smiles.

Bradley tilts his head at Sarod. "I thought your name was Sarod. Who's *Babu*?"

Sarod blushes. "This word '*babu*' is just an endearing word for, how do you say... loved little one. Something the older generation says to the younger boys in the family."

"I see," Bradley laughs. "How old are you, Sarod?"

"Twenty-eight."

Bradley smiles. "Looks like you're *Babu* to me, too."

Sarod blushes and smiles. "I'm used to it by now."

"Is Nanu joining us?" Tim asks the table.

Shiva laughs heartily. "Who knows? Door is closed. No answer. So secretive! Never answers for me!"

Tim walks over to the stairway. "Nanuuuu?"

"I am coming!" She emphasizes every syllable of her response.

Tim chuckles. "I'll set her a plate."

A thirteen-year-old girl with long black hair scampers down the stairs and prances into the kitchen. She wears a school uniform: a white button-up shirt, long white socks, oxford shoes, and a long plaid skirt.

"I *said* I was coming," Nanu says sarcastically, baring her teeth at Tim. She wraps her slender arms around Tim's neck, pretending she's trying to squeeze him to death. Her long black hair droops over his shoulder as she leans into his ear.

"Not at first."

Nanu rolls her eyes, releases Tim's throat, and plops down onto her seat. "Whatever. Please do not say we're eating the same thing as last night."

"We won't say it, then," Christian says, unveiling and serving the leftover lasagna and side salad.

Nanu buries her head into her hands in the most dramatic fashion then reaches for her fork with a smile. "Well, at least this is food I can actually eat. So much of your other dishes are just… yuck! I mean, not that they are actually bad. Only that I would prefer other foods."

Surprisingly mature language rephrasing for her age, I think to myself.

"We can't eat pizza for dinner every night, Nanu," Christian says. "Our cooking requires what us adults call a refined palate."

Nanu tilts her head to the side, flashes a clever, sarcastic smile, then moves her salad around with a fork.

"Daughter," Shiva says, "where is your mother?"

"I don't know," Nanu mumbles. "I have not spoken with her."

Just as the words leave her lips, the back door opens, and a woman steps into the house. She slips off her tennis shoes beneath the alcove and elegantly removes her full-length poncho. She hangs it onto the back door, revealing a purple V-neck sweater and bright white pants. She looks to be in her forties, her black hair tied up in a ponytail. She tucks a few loose strands behind her ear and places her purse on the kitchen counter.

I watch her every move as she floats toward us with a soft, confident smile, radiating warmth and mystery. Bradley and I stand as she approaches the dining room.

"Mm, yes, so good to see you both," says the woman, giggling. "My name is Sajana. You must be Bradley and David, yes?"

Chapter 13

We nod, and she lets out another endearing giggle.

"Thank you for allowing us to stay with you," Bradley says.

"Yes, this is your home now. Be at your home and enjoy. Is everyone hungry? Oh! You are waiting on me?! No, no, please eat!"

She sits across from me and bows her head. Everyone follows her lead and closes their eyes, so I do the same.

"Thank you for each and everything," Sajana says. "Okay, enjoy."

I bite into the yak-cheese lasagna but hardly taste the food. Instead, I wonder about the woman across from me.

It takes me a while to really notice what I'm shoving into my mouth—the yak cheese tastes like a medium cheddar. After a long rainy day of travel, the warm home-cooked lasagna hits the spot. Also, it turns out that people in Nepal do use forks for some dishes.

Sajana sips her water then tucks the dangling strands of hair behind her ear. "Bradley and David, how were your travels?"

"It's been quite the journey getting here," Bradley says. "But it's wonderful to finally arrive."

"Mm, yes," she replies. "Bradley, you are a meditator and server, yes? We have spoken a bit about this."

"That's correct," he says.

"And David, you are a writer?"

Bradley must have mentioned something about me in their correspondence.

"I try," I say. "It's been a while since I've written anything."

"David wrote a book about our hike," Bradley says casually, trying to spark further conversation. "I'm the antagonist."

Everyone laughs, and we field questions about the trail. It allows us to relive those long-ago moments one more time.

"That's another reason why we came here," Bradley says. "To see you, of course. But we've also made trekking plans very soon, maybe even in the next few days. We're excited to experience the natural beauty of this country."

"Amazing mountains," Shiva says. "You will love!"

Sajana briefly looks up at us, then she refocuses on her food without saying a word, falling eerily quiet.

As we eat, languages of all kinds fly across the room. Tim and Christian recount the day's events in English with spurts of German. Sarod, Shiva, Nanu, and Sajana speak English with interjections of Nepali between the family.

I take bites of my salad and try to decipher the languages, as if concentrating is the only barrier keeping me from understanding, but nothing sticks.

Raindrops pelt the outside world, and a gust of wind rushes through the bows of the trees and presses against the windows. Shiva boils ramen noodles over the stove then carries the pot to the front door a few minutes later.

"Where is my dog?" Shiva shouts with excitement. "Oh, my dog, my dog, my dog."

I watch through the kitchen window as Shiva walks out the front door and slides the noodles into the dog dish. Sahor labors over and slurps up his meal. The sun sets behind the city and night begins to fall.

"Lazy dog!" Shiva laughs. "So lazy! But what to say? He is my dog. Right, Nanu?"

Nanu looks away and Shiva laughs even harder, a laugh so infectious that everyone else bursts out laughing, even Nanu. As everyone finishes eating, Bradley and I start to gather up the dirty dishes.

"No worries!" Shiva insists with a huge smile, stealing the plates from our grasp. "I do this. You sit. I love dishwashing. Good for the mind."

He's right. I've washed many dishes throughout my life, mostly at the meditation center and in my service jobs. There's a certain flow that arises from such a simple task. The mind quiets down, the ego gets humbled, and the heart warms up while serving others.

Chapter 13

We insist on helping, but Shiva doesn't budge. As he takes up dish duty, Sarod says goodbye, Nanu skips upstairs, and Bradley and I chat with Tim and Christian around the table. I hardly notice Sajana's purple raincoat missing from the back door.

"It's about that time," Christian says, standing up and heading toward the back door.

"For meditation?" I ask.

"That's right," Tim says.

"How long do you guys typically sit for?" Bradley asks.

Tim shrugs. "No set time, really. Usually, an hour or so."

Finally, the opportunity to sit with the wise woman. This is what I've been training for.

I reach for my soaking-wet socks and shoes beneath the alcove, but Tim says I won't need them. The temple's right behind the house. I should be fine.

The four of us run barefoot through the rain past the pooled-up water basin, raindrops pelting our shoulders. Tim stops in front of a small shed, turns around, places his finger on his lips, then slowly pushes open the door.

We pile inside a dark and dimly lit space. I close the door behind me, shuffle to an empty cushion, and glance around.

Shadows flicker across Sajana's face. She sits cross-legged atop a throned dais with closed eyes, deep in meditation. Candles, rocks, framed pictures of buddhas, and statues showered with garlands made of marigold flowers sit atop a decorative altar. A gate separates the room in two, protecting another shrine room filled with all kinds of altars.

My heart throbs in rising anticipation as I prepare to jump. I patiently await her instruction for getting started, but no one says a word. She offers nothing to this intimate classroom of students. No instructions, no guidance… nothing. She only sits in silence, meditating.

Did she already forget about us? Is there nothing she wants to share? No wisdom, no pointing out instruction, no guided meditation?

I might as well go for it, then.

The moment I shut my eyes, the strangest thing happens. I feel myself slipping away. My body dissipating and dissolving. The temple walls expand, and I expand along with them.

What's happening? In my three years of practicing meditation, I've only felt this sensation a handful of times before, but never to this depth, and never so suddenly. A psychedelic state like this usually takes me at least an hour to access. To witness the world behind my eyelids changing so fast sends my heartbeat into a quickened frenzy.

My reality fades away fast in each passing moment. *I can't stand it. I'm not yet ready to leave my body. I don't want to die.*

I flutter my eyes open and breathe deep to ground myself in the world before going back in. *Why do I keep stopping myself from leaning into death? Did I just prevent myself from achieving enlightenment?* Maybe *that* was my moment, my missed opportunity, the death of my ego. I'd ruined everything by opening my eyes.

Nonetheless, I continue. While unable to reach that same depth, time feels unfamiliar, even nonexistent. I flow in and out of some of the most deeply powerful and calming states of my life.

What's up with this place? Maybe there's something special here after all.

With the five of us packed into such a small area, the room acts as a pressure cooker. The room seems to be sealed from all sides. No sound seems to enter the space, and no sound leaves it. Without air conditioning, my body heats up, requiring precise attention to keep my breath stable and my heart steady.

Chapter 13

Just when I think I might exist in this state of mind forever, she speaks.

"Tim," Sajana says, finally.

I squint in the dark, just enough to peek at what's happening. Tim rises and sits on a small cushion before her dais. Then she lays her hands upon his shoulders and begins to chant. I have no idea what she's saying, but it sounds quite beautiful. The chant repeats for a couple minutes, then she stops.

"Christian," she says.

Tim and Christian swap places, and the same process unfolds.

Once her chanting concludes, she says, "Good. Now, take rest. Take rest."

As the two Germans stand and exit the temple, Bradley and I remain seated. Silence permeates the room.

"Thank you, Bradley. Thank you, David," she says dismissively. "You may take rest now."

Bradley rises and takes a seat on the cushion at Sajana's feet. "Before we sleep, can we speak about something important?"

"Yes, of course," she says, giggling. "You may ask whatever it is you want."

Bradley swallows and clears his throat. "There's so many things I want to talk to you about," he says, his voice slightly quivering. "But it's important that we disclose our intentions for coming here. We came to Pokhara to prove our commitment to staying with you, but for now, we can't stay long. Starting as soon as Monday, we'll be trekking for three weeks. We plan on returning to Pokhara after the trek, if you are still willing to have us."

Sajana peers down at Bradley from atop her dais and a gentle smile slowly spreads across her face. She takes a deep breath, then exhales.

"Yes, I know this," she says firmly. "I heard you speaking of this at the table. I thought it best not to say in front of everyone, but it must be told now. I'm sorry to tell you this, but the trekking plan won't work. Yes, it's best that you call and cancel the trekking."

I glance up. *Cancel the trek?* My stomach drops, and a hollow emptiness fills my body.

She nods compassionately. "Yes, you see, I leave in one month to tour Europe for the summer. If you trek now, when you return, you will have only ten days to spend with me. I'm afraid this is not enough for the two of you. Better you spend more time with me now, one full month, while you are here. Since you are here for ninety days in Nepal, you can trek another time after I leave. Trekking will be waiting for you, but now is not the time.

"After your trekking, you are welcome to stay here as long as you wish. I will not be here, but as I have said, this is your home now. And if you have come all this way, stay and be where you are now. You have come here to find your true nature, have you not? Yes, and if this is why you have come, I feel this is what is best for both of you."

I sit stunned and silent, thoughts slamming into my mind like motorcycles piling up in the street. *Cancel the trek? I can't afford throwing away such a sizable chunk of change. We've already scheduled our meeting with the lama. Ganesh has our passports. And didn't Sarod mention something about Nepal's monsoon season approaching?* Hiking the Pacific Crest Trail in the pouring rain was miserable. The thought of giving up such a perfect opportunity flips my world upside-down.

Bradley looks just as shaken as me, sitting up straight, frozen in time. I can tell his mind is elsewhere, churning through the information, trying its hardest to put things back together. Finally, after some deep thought, he snaps out of it.

"In that case," Bradley says, "I'll need to inform our trekking company of our cancellation as soon as possible."

I glance at Bradley. *What the hell? You're really wanting to cancel?*

Chapter 13

Dizziness spreads over me as my vision of hiking the Himalayas with our unlikely guide slowly fades into the night.

"Yes, good," Sajana replies. "Please keep me updated with your plans."

"One last thing," Bradley says while rising to his feet. "The trekking company in Kathmandu still has our passports. Is there any way we can have them delivered here?"

Sajana presses a finger to her bottom lip. "Mm, yes, there is a way these arrangements can be made. But do not worry about any problems. What is important is staying here. If you need to make a call, you can do this now. It is the only way this will work."

At that, Bradley bows and walks out the temple door, his shadow receding into the rain.

I sit there, momentarily stunned, my once expanding world now crumbling down around me. Not knowing what else to do, I stand up and run after Bradley, following him into the downpour. Sajana's request seeps into my mind like a poison, slowly taking me over, shaking me to my core. We can't give up on trekking. Not like this. Not yet.

I run into the house, slam shut the bedroom door, and glance at Bradley sitting on his bed, phone in hand.

I snap, "What do you think you're doing?"

CHAPTER 14
STONE & BALANCE

Bradley sighs and leans forward. "Cancelling."

"Can we talk about this first?"

Bradley tosses his phone onto his bed. "There's not much to discuss. I don't like it either, but she's right. I came here to find my true nature, and for that, we need to stay with her for as long as possible while we've got her—longer than just a week. So if she says to cancel the trek, then that's what we do."

I plop down onto my bed. "I don't understand. Why do you think we'll find our true nature here and not on the trek? Don't you remember how special the trail was?"

"The trail's done, David. Just let it go."

"Weren't you the one who said our trek was 'divine timing'—an *omen*, even? We were given an opportunity, twenty-one days of hiking the Himalayas with a Tibetan lama… and now you're just going to give that up?"

"Yep."

I throw my head back and exhale. After so many dreams of hiking the Himalayas, how it all ties in with my plans for enlightenment, I can't let that go. Is Bradley overestimating the wise woman's insight, meanwhile throwing away the ideal opportunity?

We've heard so little from her, and I'm doubtful that she holds more promise than a Tibetan lama in the Himalayas.

Chapter 14

But I must admit, I'm intrigued by her presence, generosity, word choice, and the depth of our most recent meditation session. At the very least, I agree that spending one week with her isn't sufficient training.

So maybe we stick around here for a while, but is there a way we can still trek?

My mind shifts again. Why does Bradley think *he's* solely in charge of this decision? Does he not care about my preferences? Doesn't he know how much this hike means to me?

Maybe, if trekking is so important to me, I'll hike the trek by myself, without Bradley. The thought crosses my mind then immediately recedes. No, it wouldn't feel right. Bradley's my best friend. We're on this journey together, through thick and thin. Then again, maybe our paths to enlightenment are more separate than I originally thought.

How does he expect his plan of staying with the wise woman to play out? I decide to test the waters.

"If you're set on cancelling, how do you plan on getting your money back?"

Bradley picks up his phone. "I'll ask."

As he emails Ganesh, I lean back on my bed and glance at the painting of the mountains in the corner of the room. The ridgeline and peaks seem to have faded ever so slightly. The colors appear faint, some strokes of paint lifted from the canvas, evaporated into thin air.

I must be tired, loopy from all this conversation. I'm seeing things that aren't there. I blink and look over at Bradley, sitting there in silence, thinking.

His face lights up. "Here's an idea."

"Yeah?"

"There's a chance we don't have to cancel."

A glimmer of hope returns to my stomach. "Right, but what do you mean?"

"I mean, maybe Ganesh lets us delay the hike. Once Sajana leaves, we can go off and trek, same as before, just a few weeks later."

I scratch my head. It's too late to ask Sajana to reschedule her Europe tour, but rescheduling our hike isn't out of the question. "Ganesh would have to reschedule our permit dates and coordinate with the lama. If we let him know now, maybe he can make it happen. The only remaining concern is: what about monsoon season?"

"Beats me," Bradley replies. "I guess we can ask Ganesh."

I sigh, still resigned to our hiking plan, wanting to hold onto what had been laid out so perfectly for me mere moments ago.

"I've got a feeling there's something special about Sajana," Bradley says. "You just have to give her a chance."

I exhale a long, deep breath. Of course he thinks she's special. Meeting her is one of the primary reasons we flew around the world. I just hope he's right. "Alright. Let's see what Ganesh says about all this."

Bradley pulls Ganesh's business card from his fanny pack and dials him up. The line rings on the other end and the voicemail picks up. It seems unlike Ganesh and Ishur to miss a business call, but it's understandably late.

Bradley explains the situation over voicemail. "Something important has come up, Ganesh. We need to move the dates of our trekking permits back to June. We still want the lama as our guide and will arrange for someone to pick up our passports. We look forward to hearing from you as soon as possible to confirm this change."

Bradley hangs up, sets his phone on the end table, and lies down.

I fall back onto my bed, buzzing with adrenaline. There's no way I'm going to be able to sleep without an answer, so I stare at the painting.

Then, the end table vibrates.

Bradley hands me his phone. "Check it out."

Chapter 14

It's a text message:

Yes, Sir. That is fine. We will do this. Thank you. -Ganesh

A grin spreads across Bradley's face. "How about that?"

"That's it?" I ask. It seems too good to be true. "What about the Lama? And monsoon season?"

"It's a bit unclear, isn't it? I'll reach out again tomorrow. But it sounds like good news for now. I think we can trust Ganesh on this one. The hike is still on, and we can stay here with Sajana. I think we should let her know."

I can't sleep at this point anyway. "Might as well."

Bradley and I charge through the rain and slip into the temple. Sajana's still meditating in the dark amid flickering candlelight. I get a strange feeling she's been expecting us.

The two of us sit down on cushions and Bradley delivers her the news.

Sajana adjusts her bracelet. "Yes, this is good," she says with closed eyes. "As I've said, staying here is what is best for both of you. At times, the mind can feel so rushed to go from one place to another. We forget what it means to be in one place for some time.

"Now there is something we must discuss. I know it is late, but now that the trekking is delayed, there is space to understand. I'm afraid something is still not good."

Still not good? After all of that, what else could possibly still not be good? I lean forward and await the latest breaking news.

"In the first moment of meeting you," Sajana says, finally. "I can feel what is happening with each of you, and I noticed something important. You have likely already noticed this, what is happening between you, but it is best to make this clear."

Still with closed eyes, Sajana rubs the palms of her hands against her knees before allowing them to settle. Then she speaks clearly, without hesitation, as if reading words written on the backs of her eyelids. Words that flow effortlessly from her lips.

"There is a special bond between you. This much is obvious, I am sure. Why else would you travel here together? But what you may not know is that this bond is shared only between spiritual partners."

"Spiritual partners?" Bradley asks.

I recoil a bit, too, at her reading.

"Yes, spiritual partners. When I say this word, *spiritual partners*, understand what I am saying. I do not mean a soul partner or someone who is romantic with you, as two souls joined together in this lifetime.

"No, a spiritual partner is different. This bond is for those who walk the same spiritual path, perhaps the strongest of all bonds, interconnected through each and everything. One may leave for some time, and the paths seem to split, but at some point, like the threads of a blanket, they reunite. Such is the blessing and the curse of spiritual partners."

I look over at Bradley. *Spiritual partners, huh? I guess it makes sense.*

Similar thoughts have crossed my mind before. Through so many phases of life, I find myself inexplicably tied to Bradley again and again.

While hearing this doesn't totally surprise me, the plain and matter-of-fact delivery of this message, especially from someone who has only just met me for the first time, fascinates me. If she already understands the subtle dynamics of our relationship, what else might she know about me? I find myself curious, sliding to the edge of my cushion.

"At first glance, some might think you are very similar people. But you are very different people with two very different minds, each here for different reasons. You see, each and every being has their own questions, conditioning, and expectations. And this is where there is a split."

"A split?" I ask.

Chapter 14

"Yes, a split. Something has happened to the bond. It is difficult to explain, not easily put into words, but what I can say is this: Fixing this bond is one of the reasons you have come here to Nepal. Whether it can be mended, this will be up to you. It will take hard work. The problems that caused the bond to break reside within each one of you. Like two halves of a whole, two wings of a bird. Without one wing, a bird cannot fly."

I look at Bradley, then back at Sajana.

She sighs. "Of course, what I am talking about goes much deeper than birds and wings and things like this. This is only the surface. There are many levels to understanding. As you can imagine, such things deep below the surface are very complicated and difficult to explain. Impossible, really. The only way is to say that, in the end, this split is a problem of flow."

"Flow?" Bradley asks.

"Yes, flow. The flow is gone. Only when this returns will the bond heal and the split mend at the deepest level. You will come to understand further soon enough. For now, do not worry yourselves. Please, stay with me as I speak. I don't mean to confuse you. I hope you can understand what I'm saying to you.

"When we use the mind, we are limited by language, and everything can so easily be confused. But it is the best we have. I'm sure this is a lot to hear at once, but what's important is something totally different yet very much the same thing.

"Because all of life, our problems and desires, are interconnected. There is no separation between them. Only connection. Since your time here with me is short, we must take important steps now. First, is this. Bradley, will you come and sit here again?"

Bradley sits before her, and she lays hands on his shoulders with outstretched arms. Their bodies remain still for some time. Rain falls outside the temple, time stands still.

True Nature

"Yes," she says, resting her hands atop her lap. "I'm afraid it's true. You are like stone."

"Like stone?" Bradley asks. His lip trembles with fear and confusion as he speaks.

It makes sense to me, but it's still surprising to hear. In my eyes, Bradley commits steadfastly to his decisions. *Is that what she means when she says he's like "stone?"*

"Yes, stone. Your body and mind are like stone."

"You can feel that… from touching my shoulders?"

"Yes, your shoulders are very tense and hard like rocks. This feeling has spread to your whole body and mind. You have come here with so many of questions. And you wish to discover what is your true nature?"

Bradley nods. "Yes, I do."

"In that case, you must listen. The reason you are very tense and like stone is because you are closed. This closing is what is keeping you from understanding your true nature."

"What can I do about it? This feeling that I'm like stone?"

"It will take time and practice, but here is what you will do. Because your body is very weak and your energy is very low, you will eat and drink water. You will spend time resting. And most of all, you will practice opening."

"Opening?" Bradley asks. "How exactly do I practice opening?"

"I will explain more in a moment. But first, I must ask, do you know why this has happened to you, Bradley?"

Bradley thinks for a while and sighs. "Yeah, I think so…"

"Yes." Sajana shuffles up straighter and looks Bradley directly in the eye. "I will be very clear, because it is important for you both to hear this. You see, I have seen cases like this time and time again. The problem is always the same. It was not good for you to do course after course, month after month of meditation. Too much of anything leads to imbalance.

Chapter 14

"In your quest to untangle yourself, you've only created more and more knots. More tension, more confusion. In this process, you have really become closed, Bradley. To other paths and other ways of thinking. Like a one-track mind, you have only focused in one way for so long and created so many of boundaries around yourself. With such tight boundaries, how can anything get in? Such is the nature of the mind. To this end, the solution is you must open yourself.

"This is your duty while you are here. I will be here with you to help, but this is your path. Only you can face this within yourself. I cannot do any facing for you. So if you wish to know your true nature, this is what you must do."

Her words descend upon the room like storm clouds. Bradley's chin lowers to his chest, and he nods solemnly. A single tear, glittering in the candlelight, falls from the corner of his eye.

I've never seen Bradley so utterly speechless and struck. The sight of it shakes me. Much like her initial email, it seems like she's once again struck a chord with him—this time, a different note.

Sajana turns to me and nods. "David, will you sit here now?"

I swallow hard, take Bradley's spot at the feet of the wise woman, and close my eyes. Her outstretched hands land softly atop my shoulders, and warm sensations vibrate through my body. I take a deep breath, trying to cleanse my mind for a proper reading. Then Sajana returns her hands back into her lap and smiles.

"You are very open, David."

I look up, somewhat surprised. "Really?"

"Yes, opening is not a problem for you, this much I can say. It is also the case that you don't have nearly the same questions for me as Bradley does. In fact, at the deepest level of your mind, you may not know why you have come here in the first place and what it is you want to ask me. These questions remain inside you, questions with answers very important for you. So instead of opening, you must take a different approach. You must balance."

"Balance?" I ask, tilting my head.

"Yes, balance. This is very important for you. You see, there is a fine line between opening and closing yourself. So long as you are open, you will always grow. But the mind is like a delicate seed.

"Too much water and sunlight can so easily kill a seedling if it tries to grow too quickly. Too little water and sunlight, and the result is the same. It is a question we must all ask of ourselves whether to open or balance. This is the importance of balance."

I nod, though I still have no idea what all this means for me or what role balancing plays in my quest for enlightenment.

"This is the work of both of you. Until this is settled, your true nature will evade you. One will remain closed, the other imbalanced. Things will be stuck, unable to move. The spiritual partnership will never be mended.

"I tell you this not to discourage, but because once there is flow, many things will become clear to you. I know this may be difficult for you, but you are strong and will find your way. This is what we will do while you are here.

"You can understand now why it is I have asked you to stay," she concludes. "OK, it is already very late, and the days ahead of you are long days. Now, please, take rest. Take rest."

After speaking these final words, Sajana stands and proceeds out the temple door. I sit beside Bradley in the darkness, my mind in a daze, the candles still flicking on the altar before me. I have a thousand questions but don't know what to say.

What just happened? My mind shuffles through the details. She seems to be right about Bradley, but what about me? Opening and balance weren't taught in our vipassana meditation training—so how does this fit in?

Chapter 14

As Bradley departs behind Sajana, it takes me some time to find the strength to stand and exit the temple. Beneath the night sky, the rain drenches me as I walk the short distance back the house, but I couldn't care less.

The world grows fuzzy as I step into the house. Even the narrow hallway seems as if it's collapsing in on me, and I escape its fate by shutting the bedroom door behind me. Bradley's already in bed with the lights off. I climb into bed and pull the quilt over me.

That night, Sajana's words linger, lodged deep in my mind like shrapnel. Single words pierce the insides of my brain, stick in the grooves, repeating.

Opening... Closed... Stone...

Balance... Water... Light...

A bird with broken wings...

Flow... The flow that isn't flowing...

"Everything's flipped upside-down," Bradley says.

"What?" I ask, despite knowing. "Upside-down? Oh, yeah."

I close my eyes as the news presses me against the bed. *What is this house? Who is this wise woman? What about our trek? What was with that sit in the temple?*

There's something strange about this place, about us being here. Nothing is as I had imagined it. I sink into sleep as raindrops pelt the window and a loud gust of wind rushes through the streets.

CHAPTER 15
THE ROOFTOP

"Psst!"

I peel open my eyes from the middle of a dream. A shadowy figure stands in the bedroom doorway.

"So sorry to wake you both," Tim says. "But Sajana's ready for our morning meditation on the rooftop."

"Thanks, Tim," Bradley says, rolling out of bed.

I blink hard and check my phone: Four a.m. *Is my phone not yet adjusted to the time zone?* I stare longingly at the screen waiting for the numbers to change, but nothing changes. Four. Zero. Zero. The dark bedroom window only confirms my dreaded suspicions.

Before I know it, the door shuts, and I'm alone. I lay unmoving between my slab and quilt, rethinking why I came here. I'm used to waking up this early at meditation retreats, but I didn't expect that routine here.

Knowing everyone must be expecting me, I groan, wipe the sleep from my eyes, and drag my feet over the edge of the bed. My joints snap into place as I lift my legs into hiking pants, slip on a baggy T-shirt, then drag myself through the open doorway.

Something's not right. Something's wrong with the flow.

Chapter 15

The hallway is as dark as the bedroom, offering me hardly any visibility. *Where do I go again?* The answer stiches itself together like the strands of an unraveled blanket.

Meditate... Sajana... Rooftop.

The roof.

I run my fingertips along the painted stubbles of the wall and find the handrail. The smooth marble steps curl endlessly up the spine of the house. Had the house grown taller as I slept?

My eyes adjust to the darkness by the time I reach the second story. I make out the distinct shapes of a sofa, an armchair, a flat-screen television, an ornate rug, and closed doors (maybe bedrooms for the family?). One thing's for sure: this isn't the rooftop.

I continue higher, finally reaching the third floor. A faint light shines from behind a cracked door at the end of the hallway. A light to the outside world.

As I step onto a balcony, a freezing gust of wind slams into me. Besides the wind, it's quiet here. Off in the distance, the faint outline of a city shrouded in darkness glows beneath dusty clouds and a pale moon. Beside me, a spiral staircase twists into the sky.

I take the steps, slippery and cold to the touch, still wet from last night's storm.

Balance.

I grasp the railing and ascend as if climbing the final precarious peak of a mountain. The wind tosses my hair across my face. The fog residing inside my head still lingers.

There on the rooftop, Bradley, Tim, Christian, and Sajana sit in meditation like stone statues wrapped in shawls and facing the empty skies. I plop down onto an empty cushion, wrap the shawl around my shoulders, fold my hands atop my knees, and close my eyes. Biting winds slip through the openings of my shawl, and as everyone else in this city sleeps, I shiver.

I feel mixed-up, unsure of what's going on. My old tradition only practiced meditation indoors. They said the elements —sunrays, insects, wind—distracted the mind unnecessarily. Undoubtedly, meditating on a freezing cold rooftop is a challenge, but Sajana must be testing our abilities. If that's what it takes…

Before I do that, I peek at Bradley's statue-esque posture. *Stonewall Bradley,* a friend back home once called him.

"It won't stick," he'd replied.

He sure does sit with perfect posture, though. After his three years of living at a meditation center, abiding by a strict and defined indoor practice, what does he think about all this? About sitting outside? About his closed body and mind? I can only imagine how much a shock it must be to leave behind those old beliefs and ways of living.

Time stretches onward, then it fades away. Cold winds rush between the houses, tear through the alleyways, and blow over me in waves. The only warmth I can conjure is the slightly warmer air exhaled through my nostrils. The cold keeps me awake, the air slaps me right when I'm on the verge of nodding off. I focus my attention to keep from shivering. The last time I was this cold and sleep-deprived was on the trail. There, I had the option of walking to warm and wake up. Here, there's no escape.

Just when I think things couldn't get any worse, a man shouts in the distance. I open my eyes and glance around. *What the heck was that?*

The yell comes again. A peculiar yell that begins soft, continues for fifteen seconds, then crescendos into a powerful shout at the top of his lungs. No one in danger yells like that, that's for sure. Which can only mean one thing: he's shouting on purpose.

But why? Who in their right mind practices yelling, and before sunrise, no less? I listen in utter disbelief as the guy practices primal screaming. A one-man crowd cheering on a breakaway leading to a goal. A man turning Super Saiyan.

Chapter 15

Whatever it sounds like, he's got some nerve yelling at five o'clock in the morning.

His screams offer me no answers, dragging out my perception of time into infinity. Surely the whole neighborhood hears him, but no one yells back except a chorus of neighborhood dogs.

Then he stops, and the suspense thickens in the silence. *Maybe that was the last one.* No one can possibly keep going on like this forever. Even the human vocal cords have their limits.

Another long yell erupts through the gaps in my anticipation.

Thirty more days of this? I'll never find enlightenment at this rate and in these conditions! I must be losing it, going insane, in disbelief that we postponed the trek for this. *Come to think of it, has Ganesh given Bradley any updates yet?*

When yells finally stop, I only remember how cold and miserable I am. I shiver, my nervous system wrecked. *How long did he yell for? How much longer until this meditation is over?* For all I know, I'll live out the rest of my life sitting atop this roof.

Then, finally done fighting these thoughts, my mind quiets, and a dull sense of surrender flows through me. New sounds emerge—an early morning symphony of roosters cuckooing. Neighborhood construction workers hammering away. Engines revving.

Morning looms near, but I don't want to be the first to move. I remain still until there's shuffling, footsteps, and a warm sunlight touching my face.

My eyelids flutter open, and my lips separate. A crimson sun floats in the eastern sky, shrouding the sprawling city of Pokhara in a dim glow. Buildings fan out in the distance like steps leading to grassy hills. Beyond the hills, snow-covered mountain peaks tower above the city. Mountains that rise into the skies and pierce the clouds.

As everyone departs downstairs, the sight of the distant mountains draws me nearer to the rooftop's edge. After three hours of brutal meditation, I'm vulnerable and easily swayed by nature's intoxicating beauty. I gaze outward, soaking up the panorama, breathing in the cool, crisp air. My eyes water, and I wipe away a tear. It seems the more time I spend truly looking inward, the more beautiful life appears when I glance outward.

The pleasant feelings fade faster than they arrived. It only takes me a moment to realize I'm wiped.

Rooftop view from the house in Pokhara

I head downstairs to our bedroom, ready to turn in for a quick nap.

"Hey!" Christian says from the kitchen. "Are you hungry?"

I lift my hand off the doorknob and turn to see everyone bustling about the kitchen.

"Oh, yeah. Sure." I'd much prefer sleep, but food isn't a terrible alternative.

Chapter 15

I decide to make myself useful, cutting up bananas, apples, grapes and throwing them into a bowl with pomegranate seeds and a splash of lime. A proper fruit salad for the table. Even though I'm exhausted, it feels good to work with my hands and to give back to those around me.

Meanwhile, Tim stuffs toast into a breadbasket and says something to me, but the words don't register. I stare blankly back at him and blink hard.

"How embarrassing," Tim laughs heartily. "I'm terribly sorry. Speaking German is such an easy habit for me to slip into, especially with Christian around. Anyways, I was asking how your morning meditation went?"

"Not bad," I say, holding back a yawn and mixing the fruit salad. It's a flat out lie, but after this morning, I'm not quite in the mood to get into conversational details.

"Glad to hear it," Tim replies, grabbing silverware from the cabinetry. "Those long sits in the early morning can be extreme for some people. But you've attended those vipassana retreats. You and Bradley must be well-equipped."

It's true we're accustomed to meditating for ten hours a day for ten days straight (and in Bradley's case, a thirty-day retreat), but a three-hour meditation in the freezing cold while listening to some guy yell his lungs raw is a different story.

Come to think of it, how did Bradley handle that meditation?

I turn to see him sitting at the dining room table, slumped over, head down in contemplation. He looks like a shell of his former self, as if his soul has crawled out of his body. He's not the same Bradley I've known from before. The Bradley from the trail. The Bradley who boarded a plane with me to travel across the world. Last night's diagnosis must still be haunting him.

"*Your body is like stone,*" she had said. "*You really have become closed.*"

Words like that could do a number on anyone. Especially to a man who considers himself an experienced and advanced practitioner.

While it's disheartening to witness Bradley's state, my dark side derives pleasure from his misfortune, and a sense of superiority arises in me. Maybe I'm ahead of him on this path after all. Maybe I was right by not committing full-time to a meditation center.

But are these thoughts crossing my mind because of our competitive relationship or because of my awful morning meditation? Either way, I feel pretty damn good about myself right now.

Christian lays napkins on the table and Tim announces breakfast up the stairwell. Shiva barrels down the stairs as his usual bright and energetic self, Nanu slumps into the kitchen too sleepy to care, and Sajana floats to her seat with her usual processional flow. There's only one person missing.

"Should we set a plate for Sarod?" I ask Tim.

Tim shakes his head. "Sarod lives downtown with Goma, Sajana's mother. Maybe we'll visit her later."

A trip downtown to meet Sajana's mother? I'm too tired to get excited about that journey, but I am a bit intrigued.

Everyone gathers around the table and bows their heads. I do the same.

"Thank you for each and everything," Sajana says. "Okay, please eat. Especially you, Bradley."

Bradley nods solemnly and returns to eating.

Talk about kicking a man while he's down. I can't help but smirk, joyfully basking in his suffering. On that note, is my enjoyment in the suffering of others rooted in my own suffering? It's too much to think about right now. An extravagant breakfast buffet sits before me, and it's time to feast.

After devouring my peanut-butter toast and fruit salad, Bradley and I manage to convince Shiva to let us wash the dishes. It's an arduous task cleaning up everyone's dishes,

Chapter 15

but we split the duties. Bradley soaps, and I rinse, toweling them off and placing them in the drying rack. *Good for the mind.*

Meanwhile, Shiva leaves to drive Nanu to school and go to work. Sajana and Tim drink tea in the living room. When I place the last dish onto the rack, Christian appears at the bottom of the stairs wearing his backpack.

"You're leaving?" Bradley asks. It's the first sign of life I've seen from him all morning.

"Onto the next journey," Christian says.

I didn't realize our arrival would coincide with his departure. We exchange hugs, and I wish him well on his next voyage, which he says is drinking ayahuasca in South America.

One thing after the next, I guess. I've taken psychedelic mushrooms a few times before. As eye-opening as those trips were, I've found meditation to be a more profound, insightful, and potent practice. While mind-altering medicines can unlock states of consciousness, they're not for me right now. The answers I'm looking for won't be found in substance.

As Christian steps into a taxi parked in the street, I wonder again why some people leave our lives just as quickly as they enter.

It's not even nine o'clock yet and the day already feels full by my standards. Desperate for sleep, I sneak into the bedroom, flick off the lights, and hop into bed. Just a quick nap, I tell myself. My body relaxes and my mind drifts into dreams.

"David," she says.

I lift my head from the pillow. Her shadowy figure leans through the doorway.

"It's not good to nap before noon," Sajana says gently. "You really should stay awake during these hours. Awake and alert. Then, if you must, a short nap around two or three in the evening. But no earlier, and no longer than thirty minutes. Yes, this is best for you."

True Nature

I sit up while hiding my disappointment.

She smiles. "Today is a big day for you and Bradley. I'm going to teach at the school now, but I have asked Tim to show you and Bradley around the city. There is much to see. It will be good for you to walk. Please be mindful and remember what I have told you. Okay, I will see you this afternoon."

The door shuts and the room goes dark once again. I sigh. The last thing I want to do is stay awake on only five hours of sleep, but maybe she's right. If I'm here until our trek starts and returning afterward, I should familiarize myself with the city. A walk doesn't sound too terrible, either.

I haul myself out of bed and find Bradley alone on the living room couch staring at a cup of hot tea steaming in his hands. Quiet, reserved, introspective. He's missing his shell.

I sit on the couch across from him and exhale through my nostrils. "Where's Tim?"

Bradley brings the tea to his mouth. He takes a long sip and sets it back down. "Upstairs, I guess."

"Oh, right." I pause to look him over. It was fun enjoying his suffering at first, but now I'm genuinely worried for him. "You okay, man?"

He shrugs. "I'm fine." His eyes close. "Just a bit tired, that's all."

"Yeah, same."

"Hey, guys," Tim says, appearing in the living room doorway. "How about a walk around town?"

Both of us nod, but neither of us moves.

Tim smiles. "When I first got here, I felt so disheartened. Walking around the city really helped lift my spirits. It's a nice day outside, and we can visit Sajana's mother, Goma. What do you say?"

Do I really have a choice?

"Sure," I reply, mostly curious about what Goma's like.

Chapter 15

Bradley takes another sip, sets down his cup, pushes it across the table, and nods.

"No rush," Tim says. "Whenever you're ready. I'll wait by the front gate. Oh, make sure you bring a rain jacket. You never know when the weather might turn."

I glance out the window. It's sunny, and there's not a cloud in the sky. *Is the weather that unpredictable here?*

CHAPTER 16
GOMA

I snag my rain jacket, stuff it into my daypack, and follow Tim out into the world. It's a bright and sunny morning as Tim, Bradley, and I stroll the neighborhood side streets chatting idly, hopping puddles, and kicking rocks. Beyond the homes and buildings, snow-covered mountains poke above the horizon.

Tim was right. The sunlight lifts my mood and there's much to see.

We cross a stone bridge and follow a milky-white stream into the city. The water smells like sewage thanks to heaps of trash that fill the mesh wiring installed above the stream.

None of this bothers the three elderly women washing their clothes in the milky water. I can't imagine the water makes the clothes any cleaner, but the women must know better than me—they live here, not me.

The sidewalk bends alongside a butchery, a motorbike repair shop, and a golden shrine in the middle of the road. We pass a group of elderly men sitting quietly in a park beneath the shade of a large Banyan tree. The road bows beside a temple atop a hill skirted by jungle. A family of monkeys holler in the dense brush.

I try to orient myself to the city, but the longer the road stretches, the more disoriented I become. My mind still

Chapter 16

seems shut off since freezing during this morning's meditation.

Nevertheless, Tim shuffles ahead calmly and confidently, one step at a time with a downward gaze and arms clasped behind his back. It's the stride of a man who knows his way around. Someone with all the time in the world and nowhere to be.

Me, on the other hand—I'm still ready to get caught up on sleep.

We soon come to a wide, trafficked bridge and peer over the side into a deep chasm. Empty soda cans, plastic chip bags, and cigarette cartons litter the riverbank below.

I sigh. *Wasn't this supposed to be a place where people honor nature? How am I supposed to find my true nature when no one else around me respects theirs?*

"There's not much of a garbage collection system here," Tim says as we lean over the rail and stare into the chasm. "The infrastructure just doesn't exist yet."

It's something I hadn't considered. Maybe this country hasn't yet benefitted from a "green" movement. Maybe different cultures have different values. Maybe these people have more pressing concerns beyond chip bags and soda cans. They have families to feed. Early morning primal screams to endure. Clothes to wash in milky-white streams which get hung up to dry in the rain.

Over the bridge, the city appears in an instant. Buildings shoot up, powerlines crisscross the streets, motorcycles honk, and the crowd thickens.

Bradley, Tim, and I swim upstream against a mass of uniforms, suits, and brightly colored saris. Old ladies sell fruit from crates on the sidewalk as grandchildren tug at their blouses. Young men in white T-shirts and blue jeans display tennis shoes spread out across blankets. A homeless man offers his outstretched palms. Our footsteps push us forward into the thick of it.

I glance up at the billboards plastered above the city. There's a handsome, well-groomed man drinking beer from a glass bottle. Next, a beautiful, smiling woman in cap and gown framed by the words "Study Abroad in Australia."

I thought a nice stroll around town would help ease my mind. Yet somewhere between the trash and the advertisements, I find myself even more disillusioned than before.

And then it hits me: I miss the trail. Life was simple there. I knew my purpose—a gift from the trail itself. All I had to do was wake up and walk. I knew what the trail required of me amid rain, sleet, and snow. Progress was clear and defined in miles. I felt supported and confident because so many others walked with us and shared the same goal. All that ended after six months, where the trail met the highway.

It's no wonder I so often find myself traveling with Bradley. No one else lives this way. No job, no partner, wandering around, searching for enlightenment. Two lost souls seeking a better way to live, anticipating that moment when everything clicks and falls perfectly into place.

I swear, even the hippies at Hostel Yog have real responsibilities and jobs. At least for now, we have Tim, too. A fellow journeyman on the path.

"Here we are," Tim says, leading us into a nearby plaza. "If you ever need to buy anything at all, this is the place."

"Bhat-Bhateni Superstore Shopping Mall" reads the banner, then, under it, "Welcome to a Great Shopping Experience."

Great.

The doors peel open automatically, and the chaos of the city evaporates as we're sucked into a spacious mart. I grab a rickety pushcart and follow Tim and Bradley down the aisles of packaged foods. Trailing us, a peaceful chant pipes through the overhead speakers.

Om Mani Padme Hum... Om Mani Padme Hum...

Chapter 16

Tim guiding us through Pokhara

Tim tosses a bag of muesli, a box of green tea, and packages of noodles for Sahor into our cart.

Om Mani Padme Hum... Om Mani Padme Hum...

This haunting song swirls inside my head all the way through the produce section, mixing with memories of the yelling man. My world starts spinning.

"You alright?" Tim asks.

"Yeah, I'm fine," I reply.

Balance, David.

I breathe deep, lean against the cart, and march to the check-out. We split the bill, load everything into our day-packs, and return to the chaotic city streets once again.

The rest of the morning blurs by. We walk every which way, entering and exiting through different doors and alleyways. I get the sense that Tim's walking around solely for pleasure, but I'm along for the ride at this point—

no questions asked. Half there, half gone. Bradley drags along, too. No one says much.

We buy bread from a German bread store, fruit from an organic produce shop, then we wander through a maze of clothes racks and movie-rental shelves. It's been years since I've stepped foot in a movie rental store. They're not a thing in the US anymore, like the small towns where the gold ran dry.

I scan the spines of the old movie boxes and feel myself transported to my childhood. To sunny afternoons spent playing tag with friends, running around aimlessly on the playground, seeking nothing. For a moment, nostalgia floods my brain and pulls me deeper down the aisles.

The heavy groceries in my daypack bring me back to the present, and I realize I have no clue where I exist in relation to the house with the golden gate.

"You ready to head out?" Tim asks.

Wandering the streets of Pokhara

Chapter 16

I startle and snap to attention. "Yeah. Are we heading back soon?"

"One last stop," Tim says happily, pointing to the alleyway ahead. "Goma's house is just around the corner. Sajana's mother is getting old and hurting these days, but she's so very sweet. It would mean a lot to her if we stopped by."

I sigh and stick behind Tim and Bradley through a congested side street, hugging the brick wall to avoid the motorcycles. Past a discount clothing store, Tim pushes open an iron gate into a much narrower alleyway. We take it to the back and around the corner where the three of us enter the back door of a turquoise-painted building about three or four stories tall.

I drag the bottoms of my sandals across the straw doormat, slip them off beside the shoe pile, and head upstairs behind the others. On the way up, framed black-and-white photos cover the stairwell. I recognize some of the faces—Sarod, Shiva, Nanu.

One in particular catches my eye: a photo of a young girl standing in an open field, gazing into the camera with a soft imperceptible smile.

"You coming?" Bradley asks.

I blink hard, shake my head, and continue upstairs through the doorway.

There, an old woman with a round face and long black hair lays on the couch beneath the light of the living room windows. She gently pushes herself upright at our arrival, the wrinkles in her face curling upward.

"*Namaste, namaste,*" she says, waving to us.

"How are you feeling today, Goma?" Tim asks.

Goma points to her legs. "Ah, paining, paining... milk tea?"

"Don't worry. You keep resting. We'll just—"

Before the words leave his lips, Goma rises to her feet, shuffles to the kitchen, and sets a kettle on the stove.

"Should we... help her?" I whisper to Tim.

Tim shakes his head. "She likes to do things herself. Best we just enjoy ourselves for now."

I plop down on the white, sunlit couch across from Tim and Bradley and gaze out the window. With the clouds gone from sight, the mountains appear just as amazing midday as they did at dawn. *My trekking poles dig into the earth, the sun shines down on me, a cold mountain air whisks across my face.*

The kettle's sharp whistle pierces the silence and returns me to the room. Goma presents a tray of mugs. I take one of the warm cups between my hands and take a sizable sip of milk tea. Like lava, the scalding hot liquid burns my entire mouth, rushes over my tongue, and scrapes my taste buds clean-off. I nearly spit the whole thing out but somehow manage to hold it down as I carefully return the cup to the table.

Meanwhile, Bradley tilts his cup back and starts chugging the drink with huge gulps. I imagine him mouthing to me the words: *mind over matter*. Even though it's an imagined scenario, I find myself already getting annoyed at him.

Between losing myself in imagined moments, staring out the window, and sipping tea, I pick up parts of Tim and Goma's conversation here and there. Sarod is teaching at the school, Goma says. Maybe he will get married soon.

Another man finding his soulmate. Another reminder to feel alone.

After the conversation ends, Tim places his cup on the table. "Would anyone like to join me for a quick haircut across the street?"

"Not a bad idea," Bradley says, rising off the couch and running his hand through his medium-length hair. He glances my way and grins, the first I've seen from him all day, as if to ask: *you coming?*

Chapter 16

I grip my hair and clench my teeth. I haven't cut my hair since I started the trail four years ago. *Why get rid of it now?*

"Y'all go ahead," I reply.

"You sure?" Bradley asks.

I nod.

"Suit yourself," he says with a shrug, and the two of them disappear down the stairwell.

The room falls quiet with just Goma and me. Even though we're located smack-dab in the city center, the room is sheltered and peaceful, a haven from the hustle and bustle.

With Goma's legs propped up on pillows and her head resting on the couch pillows, I stare out the window and get back to drinking my milk tea. I don't want to seem rude by not finishing. Even with melted taste buds, the drink tastes incredibly sweet and delicious. I down it quickly, wondering how something could taste so good.

As the last bit of liquid slides down my throat, a surge of energy courses through my veins and light up my head. *Wait… is this milk tea caffeinated?*

I've avoided coffee for years and I'm incredibly sensitive to caffeine. The smallest dose keeps me up all night. But it's too late. It's already spread throughout my entire system. The milk tea courses behind my eyes, accelerates my heartbeat, and throttles me awake from the inside out. This jolt of energy lifts me from my introspection.

"Thanks for having us here, Goma."

"Mm, yes. Good."

"It really does feel nice to be here. I'm still getting used to everything—the city, the schedule, the traveling. I think it just takes time. Anyways, it means a lot that you would open your home to us. This milk tea is really tasty, too."

"Good," she says with a smile. "Good, good."

Her smile shines so bright and genuine, and her expressions feel so heart-warming. Despite her pain, I can tell strength surges through her body.

"Your daughter, Sajana," I say. "She's special, isn't she?"

Goma smiles, takes a deep breath, and places her feet on the ground.

"Oh, no, that's okay. You can sit—"

Before I can dissuade her, Goma lifts herself up and beckons me into the stairwell. I oblige. One by one, Goma leads me down the steps, pointing at the photos hung on the wall and telling me names.

I was right about some of the faces. Others live in faraway places: USA, New Zealand, Australia, she says. A family spread across the world. Pulled away by the city's billboards.

Then Goma points to the photo of the young girl standing in the field with a soft imperceptible smile.

"Sajana," she says with great delight. "Very young. Thirteen."

I study the photo again. "Did something special happen to her that year?"

"Yes, special. Very sick. Hospital. Lots of paining, paining."

I scratch the back of my neck. "Oh, I'm sorry."

"Mm, yes. Better now. Much better."

As if that concludes our tour, Goma walks back up the stairs and passes through the doorway. I stand there a moment, me and the photo.

"Did you miss us?" Tim asks, appearing in the doorway, his head freshly shaven. "Sorry it took so long."

My jaw drops. While Tim looks very much the same, Bradley is almost unrecognizable. His short hair and wispy beard have been wiped clean from his head, replaced by a tight buzz cut and clean-shaven cheeks. I struggle to reprogram this new image of nearly bald Bradley into my mind. Who the hell is *this* guy? I hold back my wince and flash a smile at his arrival.

"You missed out, brother," Bradley says, grinning. "The guy at the shop gave us the royal treatment. Back massage,

Chapter 16

scalp massage. The works. He even cracked my neck back and forth a few times too, practically free. I felt so bad at what he was charging. My tip was more than the cut! If you ever change your mind, I wouldn't mind paying him another visit."

"Yeah, sure..." I nod, still nearly speechless over Bradley's sudden changes. I also can't help but notice how much better his mood seems compared to this morning. As if he's coming to grips with something, slowly starting to fill himself back up.

"It's probably time we head back to Sajana's for dinner," Tim whispers to me and Bradley. "Let's say goodnight to Goma and head out."

We do just that, thanking Goma for her company and milk tea. Her eyes shimmer as she embraces me warmly.

"We'll be back soon!" Tim says as we head through the doorway. With her house so close to the city center, I have no doubt he's right.

I walk down the steps, passing the framed photos one last time, the image of the young girl with a soft imperceptible smile now etched into my mind. Something special happened to Sajana that year. If I could find out what, maybe I could recreate that awakening for myself, too.

CHAPTER 17
SELF-DESTRUCTION

On the way home, the skies glow orange and the shadows of buildings cast themselves into the alleyway. Tim leads us past vaguely familiar landmarks: the bridge and the trash-laden chasm, the golden stupa, the large Banyan tree in the now empty park, the temple atop the hill, the repair shop, the butchery, the milky river.

We follow everything to its end, into quiet and familiar neighborhood streets, and to the house with the golden gate.

"It's been a long day," Tim says, leading Sahor to drink from the basin. "What do you say we keep dinner simple tonight?"

We split the duties of preparing spaghetti, garlic bread, and a side salad for the whole family. The only things keeping me awake are the milk tea and the task at hand. I must admit, it feels good to serve. Since we're staying here for free, it's the very least we can do.

By the time dinner is ready, everyone seems to arrive home all at once. First Nanu and Shiva, then Sajana, all strolling across the kitchen floor into the dining room. Even Sarod joins us for dinner, saying that Goma has already gone to bed.

"May each and every beings be happy," Sajana says, and we begin eating.

Chapter 17

I twist spaghetti onto my fork as Sajana looks around the table.

"Tim. Did you go into town today with Bradley and David?"

Tim finishes slurping his bite of noodles and nods. "We went shopping and visited Goma."

"And we got haircuts," Bradley says.

Sajana giggles. "Yes, I see."

Nanu reaches over and rubs the top of Tim's head, reading it like a crystal ball. "It feels... *weird*."

"It does, doesn't it?" Tim says. "I'm still getting used to it myself."

"David," Sajana says.

I look up.

"You did not cut your hair with your friends?"

I shake my head. "Nah, not today."

She nods. "Yes, maybe next time you will feel ready."

I take another bite of salad, wondering what kind of teachings these are. Opening and balancing, walking around the city, getting haircuts. How is any of this bringing me any closer to enlightenment?

"Sajana?" Bradley asks. "Back at Goma's house, there were family photos hung in the stairwell. Does the rest of the family live in Nepal?"

"We are fortunate to have a large family," Sajana says. "Sisters, brothers, cousins, and children. But many have left the country. Maybe they will visit home every few years, but now, their lives are in new places."

Her words echo the "Study Abroad in Australia" billboards spread throughout Pokhara.

"It's common these days," Sarod says. "A lot of my friends moved away for schooling and jobs. Only the private schools teach English, which as you know is necessary in today's world. There's not much opportunity here. Unless you want to work in tourism.

True Nature

"Personally, I consider myself lucky to be a teacher. Many of my friends are ashamed to work in the fields or get a job that's perceived to be only for the poor. There's a caste system here, and the government is corrupt. Only the few at the very top benefit."

"It's true!" Shiva says, shrugging and laughing. "Very corrupt!"

"Women are also treated unequal to men," Sajana says. "Many women need the husband's approval for dress and leaving the house. In this way, our family is different. Each and every one is raised with equal treatment, fully supported in their life choices. We encourage all to do what they believe is best for themselves."

"True, Nanu?" Shiva asks his daughter with a smile.

"I *guess* so," Nanu says, staring at her spaghetti.

Sajana giggles. "Yes, in society there is progress. Slowly, slowly everything is changing. But for things to be equal for women in Nepal, it may take tens of years, one hundred years or more. Who knows for sure? For example, we still have arranged marriages. The man chooses the woman. If the families agree, the two are married. In countries like US, it works differently, yes? There, you have love marriages. Here, that is far less common."

I wipe my mouth and nod. *Love marriages, huh?* I hadn't thought about it like that before. I guess I've taken the whole institution for granted. Never in my life would I have to decide between the two processes. But it still makes me wonder what an arranged marriage would be like. Would my life be easier if I didn't have to find my soulmate? If she was just handed to me?

I take another bite of spaghetti and shake my head. *Am I crazy?* I'm so far from marriage, I shouldn't even be thinking about it right now. And yet the thoughts continue like a milky-white stream full of garbage.

It seems like an arranged marriage takes away from the romance. Where's the mystique of finding a soulmate?

Chapter 17

It makes me question the success rate of arranged marriages. Then again, as I look around at this wholesome family surrounding the kitchen table, it seems to be working for Sajana and Shiva.

After a second plate of spaghetti, I set down my fork and lean back in my chair, my stomach expanding to the limits of its capacity. I reach for empty plates, but Shiva insists on doing dishes and doesn't budge.

"Good for the mind," he says.

As Shiva finishes up the dishes, Bradley, Tim, and I chat until we notice Sajana's purple raincoat missing from the back door.

"About that time?" Bradley asks.

Tim nods and rises from his chair. The three of us gather by the alcove and head outside. It's nearly nightfall. The water basin is full of yesterday's rain, and the walkway has the slightest touch of wetness embedded into the concrete. We walk barefoot toward the temple door and slip inside.

It's a familiar scene from the night before—a dark room lit only by the warm, quivering glow of candlelight. Sajana sits upon her chair, her face shrouded in shadow. After settling onto our cushions, I shuffle into a comfortable position and arrive at complete stillness.

I don't know how long the mediation lasts. I estimate just over an hour, but it's hard to tell. Time tends to fall away during meditation, and it seems especially warped in this space.

After enduring the pressure cooker, Sajana breaks the silence by calling us up one at a time. She lays her hands upon our shoulders then tells us to take rest.

"Sajana," Bradley says before any of us can leave. "Could you explain more about opening up?"

After a long day of keeping to himself, I can tell Bradley's got a lot on his mind.

"Yes, of course," she says, sitting still and comfortably. "I have explained this to Tim, but this is very important for both of you. You must understand what is opening and how you can open yourself. Here is how you can open."

She closes her eyes, and with a deep inhale, she stretches her arms out wide and tilts her head back to the ceiling. She holds the position for ten seconds, breathing. Then she slowly exhales, returning her head upright and her hands in prayer position against her chest.

"This is what I mean by opening. Now you try."

I close my eyes and reach my arms out wide. *How ridiculous.* Is she implying that opening up is a matter of physically stretching out your arms? I'd done plenty of this stuff in yoga classes before: backbends, bridges, wheels—heart-openers, they call them. I never believed extending my chest could cultivate open-mindedness.

Perhaps I'm having such trouble accepting this opening practice because I'm already open. After all, Sajana had said that I was very open, so this must not be for me. I'd better keep my focus on balancing and leave the opening to Bradley.

"Good," Sajana says to us after some time. "There is something important to remember about opening. If we open ourselves too much, we can become so lost that we destroy ourselves. There can arise too much of energies that may harm you. Before this happens, this is the time for balance. Here is how you can balance."

This time, she wraps her arms around herself and squeezes tightly, her chin falling to her chest. The three of us practice this same maneuver. Arms out wide, then hugging ourselves. *So, this is what she means by balancing?* If I wasn't a hippie before this, there's no doubt I've fully breached the territory.

"Now go outside and feel the nature," Sajana says. "By being with the outer nature and observing your inner nature, you will learn about loving, caring, and sharing. Go, and then return here when you have finished."

Chapter 17

It's cold and dark out. I follow Tim and Bradley outside and pace the driveway beneath the night sky, the half-waking moon and the stars shining faint like crystals.

What am I supposed to do again—feel the nature? I glance over at Tim as he squats down and wraps his arms around a potted tree. I bite my lip to keep myself from bursting out laughing. The sight of a grown man delicately hugging a thin little sapling looks like pure comedy. I didn't realize feeling the nature meant *feeling* the nature.

Meanwhile, Bradley back-bends in the middle of the garden. He lifts his chin towards the moon and flings his arms out wide as if trying to rip open his chest.

I heave a heavy sigh.

Balance...

I stand in the driveway and wrap my arms around myself, breathing as the wind blows over me. I squeeze tighter. A slight warmth rises in my chest, but even that fades away in the cold.

I stare at the tree in the corner of the driveway, walk over to it, and exhale through my nostrils. Worried the tree might snap between my arms, I end up hugging the space around the tree, the leaves brushing up against my chest.

Nothing grandiose happens. No epiphanies, no breakthroughs, and no enlightenment. After a long day, I'm no more balanced and starting to get frustrated.

As Tim and Bradley return to the temple, I patrol the driveway, making sure to give appearances that I've spent a long time balancing and done a good job on my assignment. Only then do I rejoin the others on cushions in the temple and wait for further instruction.

"Good," Sajana says. "Now take rest. But before you sleep, it's important for you to do more balancing, David. Bradley, keep opening yourself."

I bow my head, say goodnight, and pace the driveway a few more times before calling it quits and shuffling to bed.

True Nature

I close the door and relinquish my body onto my stone slab of a mattress. Then, I roll over.

"Have you heard anything else from Ganesh?" I ask.

"Not yet," Bradley says. "I'll touch base with him tomorrow and keep you updated."

I exhale and close my eyes.

"She's right, you know," Bradley says out of the blue.

I lift my head then drop it again. "About what?"

"About us. The flow being blocked. Opening and balancing. Everything. It's crazy how I'm only just now seeing this."

I sigh, just wanting to go to sleep. "What do you mean?"

He shrugs. "Maybe I stayed too long and grew too dependent at the meditation center. Maybe my beliefs became dogma. Maybe I put too much stake in one technique and one way of meditating. Maybe I destroyed myself.

"Don't get me wrong, I wouldn't trade my time there for anything else in the world. It's just that, at a place like that, it's difficult to create a life of your own. It's hard to really know yourself and lose your individuality to the collective. It muddies the waters when trying to distinguish programming from intuition.

"I really thought I had it all figured out at the center. Now look at me. Everything's breaking down. For the first time in my life, I'm not sure who I am anymore. Or if I ever knew at all." Bradley sighs. "I probably sound insane telling you this."

I shake my head. "That makes two of us. I'm still not sure about this whole balancing thing. It's not the teaching I expected to hear."

"I guess we have a lot more work ahead of us."

I guess so. And deep down, I'm afraid this work won't produce the answers I'm looking for.

I must have fallen into sleep at some point because I wake in the dead of night to the room spinning at an uncontrollable speed.

CHAPTER 18
UNPLEASANT SENSATIONS

Knots twist inside my stomach. The room is burning hot, and I sweat under the sheets.

Was I dreaming before this?

I throw off the covers, but everything keeps falling apart. I try meditating while lying in bed, but everything keeps twisting, spinning, heating up, dragging me in, pulling me under. I'm swept away by a force outside my control, pulled by a rushing river, skydiving without a parachute.

I can't take it any longer. I leap out of bed, dart into the bathroom, and purge. The seconds pass like minutes, the minutes like hours, and right when everything's settled, the tide rolls in and pulls me under again.

By the end, there's nothing left inside me. I slump onto the bathroom floor and bury my head into my clammy, lifeless hands. It's been forever since I was this sick. I've forgotten what it feels like to be siphoned of energy, on the edge of death.

What caused this? The food, the city water, or something more subtle—a mound of anxieties, a bundle of worries—buried deep inside me? Stuff like that can't stay in there forever. It has to leave somehow, by whatever means necessary.

Of what use is my meditation practice in times like these? Where's the equanimity and insight I've acquired?

I take pride in imagining myself as someone who's practiced, but this sickness surpasses my capabilities. Could the enlightened avoid illness or bear its suffering to such a tolerable degree that they remained unaffected? Does wanting to feel better make me addicted to pleasurable sensations? There's got to be something I can do to pull myself out of this.

Come to think of it, I've been in a funk ever since arriving in Nepal. Poor sleep, sitting for long periods of time, extensive fasting followed by gorging on *dal bhat* and spaghetti, the unexpected side-effects of milk tea. To start, I could do a better job balancing my sleep and nutrition.

With what remains of my energy, I shuffle down the hall and crawl into bed. The side of my head throbs against my pillow.

From behind my closed eyes, I sense a light fall across the room and a shadow drift through the doorway. She rests at the foot of my bed and her warm hand lands on my forehead.

"It is as I thought," she says gently yet firmly, setting a cup on the end table. "You must not let this happen again. It is best that you drink and rest. Stay in bed and meditate here."

Then she disappears out the door with Bradley in tow, and I'm left alone in the darkness.

I prop myself up against the wall and take deep breaths with the warm mug clasped between my fingers. How did she know I was sick? Maybe my vomiting woke up everyone in the house.

I try sipping the hot liquid, but it only sends my belly into a panicked frenzy. I can't stomach anything. Whatever's inside of me wants nothing to do with anything on the outside. I set down the cup, bury my head into the pillow, and moan. For hours, my insides twist a terrible dance to the beat of my throbbing head.

It isn't until nine o'clock, when the sunbeams slip through the blinds onto my bed, that some semblance of my former self returns to me. Dishes clatter in the kitchen. Doors open

Chapter 18

and slam shut. A long silence settles upon the house. Best I try to get on with my day, too.

I stagger back into the bathroom, my camp towel and toiletry bag in hand. Opening the door is like returning to a nightmare. Horrible things happened here. I brush away the foul taste lingering in my mouth and glance at my face in the mirror. *Jesus Christ.* It's even worse than I had suspected. My sunken-in face looks like I've been run over by a fleet of motorbikes. I rub my eyes, but the same sickly face stares back at me.

I strip and turn on the shower, but no matter which way I turn the valve, the water remains freezing. After showering in the cold water, my handkerchief-sized camp towel immediately soaks through from toweling my hair, so I push the remaining water off my body with my hands and squeegee the puddles into the drain. I'm not a hundred percent myself, but I'm well enough to get dressed and step out into the world.

Tim, Bradley, and Sajana drink tea on the living room couches, each with stories written across their faces. Tim's bright and joyful expression, Sajana's restful smile, and Bradley's concentrated gaze. To them, I must look like a ghost rising from the dead.

I take a seat on the couch and watch Sajana's lips move. It takes my mind a moment to refocus. I tune my mind to her voice like a radio dial trying to clear away the static.

"As I was saying," Sajana continues, "there is no separation between us and nature, only interconnection. One cannot live without the other. You can imagine this, yes? And if you do not wish to imagine, you can experience.

"One example. When a baby is born, it is born into nature. The air the child breathes is from the trees, and the space it occupies is the space of the earth. We cannot live without these elements. They are part of us. We are nature itself.

Therefore, we can learn from this, to be in ourselves, to connect to nature. This is why it is our duty to love, care, and share with each and every beings."

Her eyes open and close like shutters. Her words, while not the most grammatically correct, spill from her lips like a stream of compassion and clarity, arriving without thought. Never have I sat with someone who so clearly embodies the present moment. I'm dragged along with her into the here-and-now by no choice of my own. A simple reaction of my body aligning to meet her presence. This is why I'm here. I lean forward, and the world sharpens into focus.

"Another example," she continues. "I'm sure you must be wondering why, in the early mornings, we sit outside on the rooftop. You see, if the weather is pleasant, we go to feel the nature. Sometimes, the nature invites us. Other times, it closes. It is very important to know the difference. Soon we will go deeper into the nature so you can learn this from your own experience."

Experience nature for myself? Wasn't that the purpose of our trek? The trek we delayed to stay here?

Sajana glances at her phone and giggles heartily. "I must leave to teach for the college now. Please continue listening to yourself and spend the morning as you wish. Bradley, I can feel from you that you are still very much like stone. Keep opening yourself. And David, you are feeling better, but you still need much of balancing. I will see you when I return."

At this, she stands from the couch, grabs her rain jacket, and departs out the back door. Like that, we're left alone once again.

As Bradley and Tim go off to meditate on the rooftop, I find my eyelids growing heavy. I know she said to keep balancing, but how does she expect me to do so on such poor sleep?

I sneak into the bedroom and close my eyes. A part of me feels guilty for sleeping when I shouldn't, but I'll make sure

Chapter 18

to balance as soon as I wake up. I'll finish my meditation and… I'll write. It's been months, but maybe it's finally time to get back into it.

With this new plan, I lay down to sleep. Then everything goes dark.

CHAPTER 19
INTO THE NATURE

"David," she says. "It's time that we go now."

I lift my head from my pillow and rub the sleep from my eyes. "Go where?"

"Into the nature," Sajana says, smiling. "You are having a hard time, and nature is inviting us out, so we will go. It is a very important trip. There are things we must do while we are there. It is only for one night, so you do not need to bring much. Be ready to leave soon."

As the door shuts and Bradley follows her out carrying his daypack, I realize it's eleven o'clock in the morning. I'd slept for two hours, ruining my writing plans. With all this change, balance seems impossible. At the very least, I do feel better.

I roll out of bed, stuff a change of clothes and toiletries into my daypack and walk into the hall. Sajana's standing in the kitchen.

"David, will you come sit here?"

I reluctantly sit down at the dining room table and await her judgment.

"Eat this." She places a small bowl of rice and yogurt in front of me. "It will help your stomach. Then meet us outside."

After retching my guts clean last night, I'd considered fasting today, but jumpstarting my gut bacteria makes sense,

Chapter 19

too. I force-feed myself the dish. It's mild and easy on my stomach. Then I go outside to meet the others, still no idea what it means to "go into the nature."

To my surprise, Tim's in the middle of the street shoving his backpack into the trunk of a taxi and saying his goodbyes to Bradley and Sajana. He's leaving already? I feel like I was just starting to get to know and like the guy. I wait my turn then offer him one last embrace.

"Short and sweet," I say.

"Life's like that sometimes, isn't it?" Tim says. "The days are long, but when it's all over, your time spent here will feel as if it's been ripped away from you in the blink of an eye. Enjoy the rest of your time here, David. Whatever you're looking for, I hope you find it."

"Thanks, Tim. You, too."

As Tim's taxi disappears around the corner, I stand and think. He was right about time—it feels irrelevant here.

Sajana turns to Bradley and me and gestures to the motorcycle helmets sitting on the windowsill. "We are taking the scooters. Who knows how to drive one like this?"

I glance at the scooter and begin to sweat. I don't—that's for sure. I've never driven anything like that in my life. I wipe my forehead while imaging trying to pilot through Nepal's chaotic streets.

Likely disappointed by my lack of willingness to volunteer, Bradley sighs and snags the keys. "I'll drive."

"Good," Sajana says. "Once Amit arrives, we will leave to the village."

On cue, a motorcycle pulls up and stops before the golden gate. A young man wearing a black helmet, matching leather jacket, blue jeans, and black tennis shoes swings his leg over the seat and dismounts.

He removes his helmet and rests his shiny pair of aviator sunglasses atop his head. He's a Nepali guy who looks about our age. The young man pushes a few strands of his slicked-back hair behind his ears and smiles.

"My name's Amit. It's an honor to meet you." His voice emanates a friendly, gentle, and serene presence.

Bradley and I shake his hand.

"You know how to ride one like this?" he asks Bradley.

I was just about to ask him the same question.

Bradley studies the control panel for a second then nods. "I can figure it out."

"Wonderful," Amit says. "We'll go now and catch up later. I think you will enjoy where we are going."

Amit mounts his motorcycle, throws on his helmet, and revs the engine.

"Please be safe," Sajana yells to us while hopping on the back of Amit's bike. With her round sunglasses still resting atop her nose, she grabs the young man's shoulder. "It will be a long ride. Stay close. Do not get lost."

Bradley rolls the scooter down the driveway, hops on, and starts the ignition. He slides the visor of his helmet down and nods. I push the house gate closed, strap on my helmet, and kick my leg over the back seat.

"You're gonna want to hold on tighter than that," Bradley says. "You don't want to fall off, do you?"

I scoot closer and squeeze Bradley's ribcage tighter. Then, we take off. I curl my toes as we glide up the neighborhood street behind Amit and Sajana, the air rushing across my helmet.

We pass the park with the Banyan tree, the veterinary clinic, the corner store, and stop at a busy intersection. Sajana turns around with a smile, and the two of them peel out and disappear up the road.

"Shit," Bradley announces.

Chapter 19

Amit introducing himself before our departure

He must have thought we couldn't make the turn, because his last-second hesitation allows a new fleet of motorbikes to clog up the road. I squirm and furrow my brow, waiting for the traffic to clear up. Since neither of us any idea where we're going, we really can't afford to lose them. Bradley looks both ways, grasps the handlebars, then leans forward.

"Hang on."

Maybe that travel health insurance was a good idea after all.

Our scooter bolts forward into a flurry of beeps and honks. I clench my teeth, prepared to black out and wake up in a full body cast, but my impact against the concrete never arrives. The oncoming horns and engines swerve around us. We're alive.

I glimpse ahead through a forest of motorcycles and spot Amit and Sajana's bike through the gaps in traffic. Our poor little scooter doesn't have much horsepower, but Bradley races to catch them. We weave between traffic, leaning side to side ever so slightly, before finally pulling up behind them and sticking close to their tail.

Following Amit and Sajana up the streets beyond Pokhara proper

The four of us zoom forward past shops, markets, and stupas on either side of the city blocks, the heat of the day beating down on us. Riding on a bike offers a much different perspective compared to riding inside a taxi. Suddenly, the rules of the street make sense. There's a method to the madness. Honking isn't mindless. It signals your bike's existence in space for safety reasons, especially when changing lanes, passing, or turning. As the ride goes on, I feel more and more like a fish swimming through the ocean current.

Just when I start to feel my confidence rising, a flock of old women pass by. They ride handsfree and without helmets on the back of their husbands' motorbikes, their legs dangling off the side and their sari dresses flapping in the wind. I must be the only passenger in the entire city wearing a helmet and holding so tightly onto the driver.

Chapter 19

When I try relaxing my embrace on Bradley's ribcage, a pothole nearly throws me from the scooter.

"You got this?" I ask.

"Just chill, bro. Hang on."

I do exactly that, grabbing on even tighter than before.

Before long, the city and its traffic slips away as we climb the highway into the foothills. The view atop the rolling hills is incredible. Green grass terraces contoured to the mountainside descend into the valley. I sit up straight and let go of my grip on the backseat of the scooter. The breeze whips my shirt, and I smile.

The sound of the wind rushing by makes conversation impossible. I point to a herd of mountain goats, but Bradley doesn't say much. He's focused on the road ahead.

The drive stretches on and on. An hour later, Amit and Sajana's motorbike slows down and turns onto a gravel road. My entire body vibrates as we rumble over the rocks, shaking me up. I'm thrown into the air and back down onto my tailbone with hard thuds.

The fatigue of holding onto Bradley sets in. Riding outside the confines of a car cabin is exhilarating but taxing on the body. I can only imagine the concentration required on Bradley's behalf.

I peer down into the valley. Any mistake would send us toppling over the embankment into certain death. I cling tightly to the vehicle, ride the rocks, and await our arrival.

Eventually, the road's switchbacks grow too steep to carry our combined weight, so I jettison the vehicle and hike uphill.

"Hop back on," Bradley tells me at the top. "I figured it out."

He's right. This time, Bradley's wide snake-like turns offer us enough traction to inch up the switchbacks.

The road levels off to a more gradual climb, and a banner stretches overhead: "Ulleri Village: Welcome to You."

True Nature

Village homes made of rock and clay and straw line the road. I hold my breath as we pass a poultry farm. Crop fields reach up past my shoulders. A yak pulls a plow through a dirt field. A herd of bison carry supplies beside us. Villagers of all generations stare at us with big, curious eyes. I wave, and they wave back.

We park next to Amit and Sajana's motorbike at the top of a hill and turn off the scooter. A serene quiet descends upon the village. There's no barking, no honking, no yelling man. Only a light breeze and the sound of crickets chirping in the grass.

Bradley and I step to the edge of the hill and overlook the valley. I glance at the dreamland laid out before me, a sprawling village nested in the clouds. Distant mountains, taller than the hills beneath our feet, line the horizon. The sky and the sun are so close I could touch them.

The enormity allows me to space out and peer over the valley. So many of my worries fade away. *If I didn't have goals in mind, this would be a nice place to settle down and enjoy a simple existence.*

"It really is a beautiful village," says a man's voice.

I turn around to find Amit approaching.

"Thanks for leading the way," I tell him.

"No problem," he says.

"What a drive," Bradley remarks while reaching down to touch his toes.

"Ulleri is a longer drive than most," Amit says. "But whenever Sajana goes into the nature, I make sure to join. These are very special trips. They don't happen every day."

I can see why he thinks these trips are special. This place is beautiful and quiet and peaceful…

"Baloo!" Sajana exclaims.

I jump as a bushy-tailed village dog darts between my legs. He runs circles around our group while barking loudly. I guess some things you can't escape, even in the village.

Chapter 19

Baloo settles at Sajana's feet, and she kneels to scratch his head. He's dirty, likely hasn't been washed in months, and his fur is patchy in spots, but he's adorable. As he scampers over to me, I pet him, too. Then he turns and disappears up the stepping-stone path.

"Come," Sajana says. "We will follow Baloo."

CHAPTER 20
ULLERI VILLAGE

I throw on my daypack and trail the others, passing beside hip-height stone walls, wheat fields, and village homes.

Bradley makes conversation as we walk. "How long have you known Sajana, Amit?"

"Ever since I was a child," Amit says. "I've always felt close with her. She's changed my life, so I try to find different ways to serve her and the family."

"That's great. It's a wonderful family and a wonderful house."

Amit nods, putting one foot in front of the other, trailing just behind Sajana. "The house in Pokhara has especially good vibrations. Of course, like anywhere else, you must be in the right mindset to find yourself there."

"What do you mean by that, Amit?" I ask.

"The house is no different than any other phenomena. It only amplifies what's inside you. Whether it's Sajana, the house, other people, or the nature around us, they merely serve as our reflection."

I think on Amit's words. It's true. I can't escape myself—no matter where I go. The world serves as my reflection. After all, the inputs must ultimately pass through me. What my mind interprets informs me about myself. So far on this trip, it's been a lot of unpleasant reminders, especially

Chapter 20

getting sick. Hopefully, whatever was wrong with me in that house is gone now. I don't need to worry. I need to focus on being here, in nature.

The next time I look up from our hike, Baloo sits in the middle of the path patiently awaiting our arrival. Upon seeing us, he leaps over a stone wall into the front yard of a village home and disappears through the doorway.

I study the two-story house. It's made of brick, patched together with clay, and set upon a stone foundation. The porch's wood-paneled shingles appear warped in parts, matching the roof. The authenticity of the place cannot be understated.

As we open the gate, a large woman emerges from the door. She sets her straw broom against the façade of the porch and charges down the steps with cackling laughter. Her arms fling out wide to hug Sajana. One by one, the hefty woman makes her rounds, hugging everyone with fierce embraces. When it's my turn, she pulls me close, enveloping me in her ample bosom. For a moment, it's impossible to breathe. When she finally lets me go, she looks into my eyes with a joyful smile and says something in Nepali.

"Her name is Seti Chama," Sajana says to us. "Her English is not good, but it is no problem for us. This village home is where we will stay. It is also the home where she grew up as a child. She is fortunate to own a home in the city as well, but she visits here when the nature opens itself to us. It has that purpose for us as well. Come, there are things to be done."

Following Sajana and Seti Chama's lead, we haul sticks from a pile in the front yard and carry them into the house. I slide off my sandals and pass through the doorway into a dark and cluttered room. I pace the linen potato sacks and rugs lining the clay floor and set the sticks beside the stove. As Seti Chama gets to working on the stove fire, I sit down and study the place.

Our Ulleri village home

Two cot beds and a metal wardrobe press up against the wall. Jackets and sweatshirts hang from the walls, canteens from the support beams. Towels dangle from a rope near the kitchen window. A wooden table overflows with chalices and cookware. Stashed beneath it are pots, pans, kettles, and a huge rice cooker.

It's only one room, but with the clay stove in the corner, it's everything one needs to survive. It's cool and dusty, and after a long day's scooter ride, I can't help but smile. Shelter is shelter. A roof over my head is good enough.

Seti Chama kneels, snaps the twigs, and pushes them into the low clay platform. She sets a match to the sticks, blows into the side-hole to fan the flames, and sets a large wok upon the hole directly above the fire.

With no AC, the only ventilation is the open door and the high-up window. The rich smell of campfire smoke fills the room and heats the space. I get the sense I'm just as much outside as I am inside.

Chapter 20

While Amit and Sajana begin cutting potatoes, Bradley fixes his eyes on the hundreds of small, dirty brass chalices. They're exactly like the ones in Sajana's temple, but still dirty from last use. When he squats down and begins to wipe them clean, I wince. Bradley helping means I'm helping, too.

I push a straw mat under my heels, squat down, and begin to polish the chalices with a thin white cloth. As I wipe away the black, waxy residue, I wonder why we're spending so much time on such an unimportant project. There's no enlightenment in chores. Then again, the time spent doing dishes and sitting for long hours brought rewards and taught me patience. Is that part of what Sajana is trying to teach us?

Finally, we root the clean chalices with fresh wicks, fill them with hot ghee poured from a kettle, then set them aside to cool. Meanwhile, the spicy aroma of cooked potatoes fills the air, and Seti Chama serves us each a large plate of potatoes as we work. Still wary from my morning sickness, I munch on a single soft and spicy potato—more out of politeness than hunger.

Sajana lights one of the chalices and holds it out in her palm. "Do you know what these are for?"

"Not really," I say.

Sajana smiles. "We light lights to send well-wishes to friends, family, and all beings. You never know the benefit your well-wishes will bring to another being. Not to mention the benefit it brings to yourself."

I stare intensely at the flickering flame, losing myself in the light.

"Come," she says, returning the chalice to its place on the altar. "Now we can go further into the nature."

Finally—a real adventure.

I gather my daypack, fill my water bottle from a hose in the front yard, and follow Sajana, Amit, Baloo, and Bradley up the path toward the northern hills.

"We are going near the top," Sajana says. "There is something special there to show you."

Sajana and Baloo leading the way

Bradley and I look up at the peak, and our eyes widen. Finally, a chance to channel our old hiking life and put our latent abilities to the test.

"Let's get it," Bradley says to me, marching to the front of the group.

I follow him up the narrow path, climbing hard and sweating beneath the hot sun. The path leads us beyond the village, higher through lush green grass plateaus. It doesn't matter when the trail disappears beneath our feet. In our excitement, we make our own way. We trek through the downtrodden grass fields, weaving between the blooming acacia trees and boulders.

Then Bradley and I stop. We've forged too far ahead of Amit, Sajana, and Baloo. Sure enough, we backtrack to find

Chapter 20

them waiting by a large boulder in an open field. When we approach, Sajana wraps her arms around the giant rock.

"It is important to feel and love the nature," Sajana says. "When we love the nature, the nature loves us, too. By feeling, we see how we are a part of everything."

As Bradley and Amit embrace the boulder, I sigh. *Not only are we tree-huggers in-training, but now we're rock-huggers, too?*

Nonetheless, I place my cheek and hands against the stone. I must admit, with the hot sun beating down on us, the cold rock surface cools my face and a sense of gratitude arises in me. This somehow feels slightly less ridiculous than tree-hugging.

"Before we go on," Sajana says. "We must first prepare ourselves."

Prepare for what, though?

Sajana sits beneath the shade of a large acacia tree, and the four of us circle up beside her. Even Baloo sprawls out in the grass between us. As I prepare myself for what might be an hour of meditation, Sajana starts chanting.

"*Om Mani Padme Hum... Om Mani Padme Hum.*"

I recognize it immediately. It's that same chant from Pokhara's Bhat-Bhatani supermarket. Another sound following me from the city.

To make matters worse, Amit and then Bradley join in.

I don't even know what those words mean! I clench my jaw. From my past experiences with yoga, I've always thought chanting was silly. Plus, the vipassana lineage says chanting creates artificial bodily sensations. These sensations distract the mind from the body's natural sensations, which are the root of suffering.

But I don't want to be the only one not chanting. I might as well give it a try. What's the worst that could happen?

I quietly join in on the chant but notice Bradley's chant growing louder. *Is he challenging me?* I furrow my brow and keep my *om* tuned to a low volume, waiting for the chant to end.

Finally, Sajana culminates with one last *om*, and we settle into silence. My face relaxes. A long, drawn-out wind blows across the grass and through the bows of the trees.

"David," she says.

I open my eyes.

"What did you feel during our meditation?"

"Uh, it felt good. Very pleasurable."

She shakes her head. "No, we are not just doing this for good feeling—to be swept away in pleasure and bliss. There is more beyond this. In everything we do, there is meaning. Do you know what is the meaning?"

Her question catches me off-guard. *What's the meaning of feelings?*

Well, my habit-pattern is to pursue pleasurable feelings, avoid unpleasant ones, and label them each as either good or bad. But maybe pleasant feelings aren't *good*. And maybe unpleasant feelings aren't *bad*. If I only seek what's pleasant, I might quit when times get tough and never reach the fruits of my labor. Similarly, if I always avoid what's unpleasant, I could be ignoring key indicators for growth and change. Yes, she's right—feelings do serve a greater purpose. These bodily sensations convey useful information. If anything, they're neutral signals which inform and can be used to improve my experience.

In turn, feelings aren't meant to be judged—they're meant to be understood, embraced, and balanced. If I focus on deepening my awareness of ascribing meaning to all things, maybe I'll see something I've missed all along.

"I think I'm starting to understand," I reply.

"It is something to consider more." Sajana nods. "And Bradley, why do you think we stopped here?"

Bradley shifts around in the grass. "So we could learn how to chant?"

Chapter 20

Sajana shakes her head.

"So we could feel the nature?"

Another head shake.

He scratches the back of his neck and thinks for a second. "So I'd let go of wanting to reach the top?"

Amit and I snicker.

"Mmhm," Sajana says.

Perhaps I, too, had been narrow-mindedly focused on getting to wherever it is we're going. Maybe this sort of ambition is what led me to lose track of the present and become unbalanced. I shouldn't get too far ahead of myself. One step at a time.

Finally, Sajana stands from the grassy plain, and Baloo hops to his feet. "And now, we are ready."

CHAPTER 21
THE FALLS

We stand from the grassy field and enter the tree line at the far edge of the plateau. Beams of light shine through the cracks of the thick jungle canopy overhead as my footsteps dig into rich, wet earth.

I once spent many months in a place like this and so little time since then. For the last three years, I'd isolated myself inside dimly lit coffee shops trying to write a book about the trail. The project consumed my life. When I finally completed it, I collapsed on my bedroom floor and wept tears of joy. It felt as if I had removed a huge weight from my shoulders. Unfortunately, in the days following, I would notice a new burden: *now what?*

After plumbing the depths of my trail story, I didn't want to write anymore. The very thought of starting over made me dizzy. I even wondered if writing was a viable tool to help me transcend suffering.

I gave up writing and kept meditating. My isolation was no longer spent in coffee shops but in meditation retreats. After three years of such behavior, it's no wonder I'm burnt out. *How often had I stepped outside? How could I have forgotten the centering effect that nature has on me? Why haven't I made more time for it?*

Where's the balance?

Chapter 21

As questions circle my mind, I keep trudging through the jungle behind the others. I push foliage away from my face and swat at the high-pitched whining of a mosquito invading my inner ear.

I notice Amit pluck leaves from a plant and shove them into his pocket. It seems strange to take from nature, but I don't say anything. There's no point in causing unnecessary conflict.

Soon we meet a bubbling creek, and I notice an ominous roar thundering in the distance like the sound of a powerful rain shaking up the earth. Sajana and Amit wave for us to follow them and the sound upstream through jungle. We do so, fighting through vines and branches with the shallow water swishing over our feet. The higher we trek, the deeper the creek, and the steeper the climb. Soon the rocks grow to the size of boulders, requiring us to crawl and leap from boulder to boulder.

I slip knee-deep into the creek and gasp. *Why did I wear these stupid sandals? They don't offer me any traction!* Then I glance ahead to see Sajana and Amit hopping from boulder to boulder in their sandals. I sigh and continue the climb.

The roaring sound of heavy rain reaches its climax as I press myself up and over a boulder. There, I find myself standing in a wide-open glade, gazing up at a towering waterfall.

What a wonderful dream-like oasis! Shimmering falls span the glade like a tattered curtain draped across the mountain. A river of water spills from the cliff, crashing down into a large murky pool.

The pounding force of the falls against the pool reverberates through the glade and shakes up my insides. The water splashes down hard, and gentle mist reaches me from the edge of the jungle and kisses my face. I understand now why we've traveled here, so far from the city.

Amit unravels a foam pad strapped to his pack and lays it on the ground at the edge of the mist. It makes for a great spot to throw our stuff onto while staring at the scene.

True Nature

Sajana leans in close, having to speak loudly over the sounds of the falls. "Now go and be in yourselves in these moments. You will need this for your journey."

The afternoon is hot and humid, and I'm sweating from the climb. A dip in the water does sound rather pleasant.

As Bradley and Amit kick off their sandals and make their way into the pool, I remain stunned by beauty. I've seen plenty of waterfalls before, but none like this. Hidden deep in the high jungle, untouched by humanity. If such a place existed in the US, there'd be lines of people waiting to pay an entry fee.

"David," Sajana says. "What do you see?"

"A waterfall," I explain.

She laughs. "Yes, this is true. What else?"

I shrug. "A pool?"

"Do you observe all the elements present here at this waterfall?"

"The… elements?"

"Yes, the elements," she says matter-of-factly. "Wind, earth, water, and fire. They are all present, and there is something you can learn from each of them. You see, David, there is so much we can learn from nature and the elements. You've experienced this before, but it is so easy to forget. This is why we return, again and again, to remember what we already know. The outer nature can always teach us something of our own inner nature."

Sajana reaches out her hands as if to catch a few droplets of mist.

"Take, for example, the wind. It comes and goes. Arises and passes away. When it is gone, never does nature cry or feel sorry. When the wind returns, neither is nature happy. Nature does not judge. It only carries on with the flow of life. This is because nature understands a deeper truth—that much like the wind, everything is always coming and going. Nothing disappears.

Chapter 21

"More examples," she continues. "When the leaves of a tree fall from the branch, a tree does not panic or celebrate. Whether or not there are clouds in the sky, nature knows this is the way things must be. Everything is part of this process; everything is always perfect.

"The rain and fog dance with each other just like the sun and the moon. This is nature's way of balancing. There cannot always be one side showing itself. Sunshine every day creates a desert. Rain, an ocean. You see the importance of balance?"

I nod, still processing the information.

"Perhaps this will help you, David. You see, each of us has our own special element. An element that resonates with us more than all the other elements. Do you know what is your element?"

"I'd have to think about it," I say.

"Too much thinking," she says gently. "Look at your friends. Amit's element is earth. Have you noticed how much of groundedness he has? And Bradley. His element is water. Do you see how much of happy he is like a child standing under the waterfall?"

Sure enough, I turn to see Bradley standing beneath the most pulverizing spot of the falls. His arms stretch out wide, trying to peel his chest in half. He's filling himself up more and more, inviting something new inside his once empty shell.

Sajana looks up into the sky, then back at me. "I feel your element is *espaysh*."

Espaysh? It takes me a moment to grasp her pronunciation. "Oh, *space*?"

She nods.

"Space—you mean like outer space?"

Sajana giggles. "No, what I mean is the *espaysh* around you. The open air and open nature. Open *espaysh* where you can look up and see the stars and the skies."

I lift my head up to the blue skies above the jungle canopy. Now that she mentions it, I do like space. Like the wide-open views from atop Hostel Yog and Pokhara's rooftops. The miles of lush desert in southern California. The expansive mountaintop vistas and ridgelines in Washington. Gazing up at the Oregon night sky, the moon and stars hung about in space.

"I guess I do like space."

Sajana nods. "This is just the beginning for you."

If this is the beginning, we've got a long way to go. I'd better start making up for lost time.

"Sajana," I ask. "What were we chanting by the boulder? *Om Mani Padme Hum*? What does that mean?"

"Yes, this is just a mantra. Sounds that repeat. You see, all of us have thoughts repeating inside our minds. What repeats becomes our reality. Whichever you choose is up to you, but this one can be very helpful.

"Each word has its meaning. *Om* is the qualities of the Buddha; it is in everything. Mani is the intention for enlightenment, the jewel. Padme is the lotus flower which grows from the mud; it is wisdom. *Hum* is no separation, connection between all things. Having explained, what is important is not the words but that you feel the words is helping you."

I nod. "But what if I can't *focus* during these mantras? Let's say, because other people might be annoying me?"

Sajana giggles as if knowing exactly what I'm talking about. "Do not worry about anything related to others. What they are doing, how they sound. You cannot control any of it. Just be in yourself. Listen to your own heart, your own potential. This is what's important."

"Okay. Thanks, Sajana." Easier said than done, but I'll try my best.

"Now go and join your friends. Learn from the water element with Bradley and Amit."

Chapter 21

I slip off my Jesus sandals and wade into the murky pool. It's freezing to the touch, but I mush forward until the water rises to my waist. The force of the falls slapping against the water grows intense as I approach.

I lean my head in, and the cold water slams against my shoulders. I gasp, and the sheer force nearly collapses me, but I stand in just the right spot to keep from falling over. I breathe for some time, smiling.

Everything is good and well until I head back to shore. Sharp, painful, and prickling sensations engulf my legs like a thousand needles stabbing into me. I lift my leg above the surface and gasp. There are a dozen leeches latched onto my skin.

Imagining the leeches burrowing into the first few layers of my skin, I race toward the shore.

"David!" Amit yells.

I turn around as he rushes towards me.

"Use these," he says. He offers me a few leaves from his pocket. "And don't worry about the bites. If anything, they purify the blood."

I'm unsure about the whole blood purification thing but this is a moment of crisis. I grab hold of a leech with the leaf and rip it clean-off. One by one, I repeat the process, ripping leeches from my legs and tossing them back into the water. By the end of it, trails of blood run down my legs, making me look like a wounded soldier. Thankfully, it looks worse than it feels, and I'm grateful for Amit and his remedy.

I kick-back to sun dry and watch the falls with Amit. "It's a beautiful view."

Amit nods. "It's special. No one knew about this place before Sajana came, not even the village people."

"She discovered this herself?"

"That's right. Occasionally, she gets feelings and chooses to follow them to places she's never been before. As for this place, I remember I received a call from her early one morning.

True Nature

She said she wanted to take a ride into some faraway village. I hadn't heard of it before—I don't think she had either—but I'd gotten calls like this from her before, and I knew what to do. I didn't question the idea. There was no point anymore. I just hopped on my motorcycle, picked her up, and followed her instructions.

"When we finally arrived at the village, we took this same route into the hills—through the jungle and up the creek—and there it was. Before we left, we told everyone in the village the way to the falls. It's why she's so loved by the people here and why it is such a special place."

"I don't get it. How does anyone know to go to a place they've never been before?"

Amit shrugs. "That's usually how it happens, doesn't it? I mean, how did you know to come here?"

I wipe the last of the blood from my legs and nod. Sometimes, following your intuition pays off in strange ways.

"David," Sajana calls out to me.

I look up to see Sajana standing by the edge of the pool, holding a pair of scissors and beckoning me with a smile. I shake my head and laugh as I walk toward her.

"Your hair holds habit-patterns," she says, patting the top of a rock. "It's time to let them go."

Maybe she's right. I love my long hair, but I've held onto this identity for long enough. A little change could do me some good—no harm in that. It's a small loss, but I know it'll grow back. Plus, it's common for monks to shave their heads. I don't want to go full-on monk-mode like Bradley, but there's something to be said about the middle path, about balance.

I sit down and brace myself.

Snip.

A noticeable weight lifts from my head. I wait in place, anticipating more snips, but she's gone easy on me. Sajana places a matted clump of hair into my palm and points to

Chapter 21

the creek. Her message is clear and direct, delivered without words.

I kneel before the creek, set down the clump into the water, and watch as the strands separate then disappear downstream. I didn't expect haircuts and waterfalls to bring me closer to enlightenment, but the smallest things, even those symbolic, serve their purposes.

Sajana delivering me some wise words

We sun-dry in the glade until the sun sinks below the mountains. It's getting near dark, so Sajana lifts herself up and says it's time we return.

Together, we gather our belongings and navigate down the creek, through the jungle, and across the wide-open grasslands. The rock trail on the outskirts of the village leads us closer to home as the sun descends further into the horizon.

As we walk, I notice Bradley making conversation with Amit. It's obvious Bradley's changed. Something has shifted inside him. He's more joyful and playful. He's opening up quicker than I thought he would.

As we arrive at the village edge, an old man, barely skin-and-bones, greets us on the path and bows to Sajana. Excluding Seti Chama, I've never met a happier human. His toothless smile beams with joy. He shakes our hands, says something in Nepali, then takes off in a different direction.

"He wants to give us gifts," Sajana says. "We will wait for him."

When I look over the man's shoulder to see where he's gone off to, I notice his home is nothing but three stone walls and a concrete slab—no roof, no windows, no doors.

The old man soon returns and graciously hands us two huge bags of *saag*, which are edible jungle leaves. *How could anyone with so little so be generous?*

I don't know if I would act the same way if I had nothing. No matter what I achieve or earn, it's never enough to be satisfied. I'm always chasing more and better. And yet this man feels rich enough to offer us everything he owns with a smile on his face.

As night descends across the foothills, my eyelids droop and my feet grow weary down the cobble-stone path. All this sickness, sleep deprivation, travel, and hiking has taken a toll on my body. A quiet night's sleep inside Seti Chama's village home would do just the trick to get me back on track.

As I imagine myself resting beside a warm, flicking fireplace and wrapped in woolen blankets, the distant sounds of pounding drums, clashing symbols, and whistling flutes rattle my eardrums. It's closer to noise than music—the kind of nonsense that makes me wish I didn't have ears.

"What are those noises?" I ask the group.

Sajana turns to us and giggles. "I had almost forgotten. The villagers have new instruments and want to play for us tonight at the house."

I glance at Bradley sidelong. *Village music at this hour?*

It's the worst possible news, but what choice do I have? If I need to stay up and endure a few songs, then that's what I'll do.

Sure enough, Seti Chama's front yard is filled with villagers, including the featured band—a group of young men

Chapter 21

playing their newly acquired drums, cymbals, and flutes on the porch. The band stops playing when we reach the house and shouts something at us.

Amit laughs. "They're asking for the tourists to dance."

"Dance?" I ask. *I thought we were here to listen.*

A brigade of children suddenly push Bradley and me into the middle of the yard. The crowd cheers.

I look at Bradley and sigh. "We doin' this?"

Bradley wobbles his head. "Let's show 'em what we've got."

With everyone circled around us, we might as well play along. If it's a show they want, it's a show they'll get.

The music is fine at first. Bradley and I sway to the strange, slow, and methodical music beneath the moonlight. But soon the tempo increases so that the only way to dance to the rhythm is to fling and flail my limbs wildly about. Faster and faster, Bradley and I twist and turn, a cold wind whipping across our bodies.

Our ridiculous movements send the crowd into a laughing frenzy, clapping as the song goes on. The rhythm pulses through my body, my joints open and loosen. I haven't moved my body like this in ages. Not since Hostel Yog's rooftop. When the song finally ends, I'm dripping sweat and sucking air.

"Again, again!" a group of kids shout, pushing us back into the middle.

Bradley stares intensely at the children, who laugh and stare back at him. All the kids flock together, circle around us, and begin mimicking our moves. Bradley and I take turns leading our own little dance troop by pounding our chests, roaring, crawling, donkey-kicking.

The children link hands, and we run in circles. The kids laugh, and the villagers clap to the noise.

Bradley leading the troop

How many songs have passed? Five or six, is it? It's impossible to tell.

When the music finally stops, the band packs up and exchange prayer hands with us. Bradley and I chug water on the porch steps, drenched in sweat.

"The tourists can dance!" one of the little boys says in English.

As the remaining villagers depart for the night, Seti Chama serves us each a plate of potatoes and *saag*, the jungle greens given to us by the old man at the edge of town. I stare at the dish, still concerned about getting sick again, but I haven't eaten much today. I should eat this—I just have to be careful with quantity.

Bradley and I handfeed ourselves the savory and spicy leaves and potatoes. Then we lay down on the clay floor, set straw mats behind our heads, and close our eyes.

Seti Chama stands over us and cackles.

Chapter 21

Amit laughs, too. "Seti Chama says we are sleeping in the attic."

I glance longingly at the empty beds, but there's no point in asking. I'm done trying to figure out this place. *I want sleep, so just tell me where to go, and I'll go.*

Exhausted, I follow everyone up the ladder into a dark loft.

"What's with all the potatoes?" Bradley asks.

"They're everywhere!" Amit laughs.

Hundreds of potatoes are spread across the floor, making the attic more suitable for storage than sleeping. So we begin the arduous task of pushing piles and piles of spuds into the far corners of the attic to clear space for sleeping spots.

Amit can't stop laughing the entire time. "Work in the village doesn't stop!"

Bradley lays down onto some blankets and kicks his feet up onto a huge pile of potatoes. "They do make for a fine footrest."

Sajana and Seti Chama join in on the laughter.

I clear enough space for my legs, throw down a blanket onto the hardwood, and sigh. It's such an absurd situation, I have to ask, "Amit, what's wrong with the beds downstairs?"

"Nothing," he says. "We have to sleep closer to the potatoes!"

It's nonsensical rationale, but sometimes jokes like that land the hardest. The laughter is infectious, and I find myself laughing, too.

The giggling dies down as we wrap ourselves in blankets and pack together like sardines. Sajana and Seti Chama sleep in the far corner of the attic, and the three of us guys cram side by side closest to the stairs.

As my head hits the pillow, I glance out the small window framing a dusty moon. I've been pulled in a thousand different directions these past few days. Hopefully, I can find a manageable routine to make slow and steady progress toward my goals. Maybe that's what I need for balance.

And with that, I turn off my headlamp and close my eyes.

* * *

I wake in the middle of the night to Amit and Bradley snoring and wheezing like trains whistling down the tracks. As hard as I try to fall back asleep, it's impossible, so I tiptoe down the ladder and walk outside for a breath of fresh air.

I sit at the edge of the front porch in the quiet, staring out at the starry night sky. I wonder how Hannah is doing.

"David?" a voice asks.

I turn around to see Sajana standing in the doorway.

"You cannot sleep?"

I shake my head. "I guess there's a lot on my mind."

"Mm, yes." She giggles and sits next to me. "This is normal for the mind. The snoring doesn't help much either."

I crack a smile, and we sit in silence for some time.

"I have more questions for you, Sajana."

She laughs. "Yes, go on."

I clear my throat. "I know we haven't talked much. It's just that… there's been so much going on these last few days. I haven't had much time to think."

She smiles, waiting for me to continue.

"I wasn't sure why I came here at first, but the questions are starting to come to me… I guess I just want to know what's possible.

"Every now and again, interesting moments pop up in my meditation—glimpses of wholeness or oneness, you could say. They're life-changing moments where everything comes into perspective. But none of them last. They come and go, and I'm back to being regular old me again, with the same old desires and stories as before.

"I've thought that maybe there was something outside of meditation that would fill in the gaps. I've tried reading the right books. I've tried studying theories, models, and concepts,

Chapter 21

but filling my head with ideas doesn't help much either. In some ways, it turned me into a parrot.

"But when you speak, it's... different. I can tell that the things you're saying you didn't just learn from a book. They come from a place of wisdom. It's something you've experienced..."

"Yes," she says, picking up before I'm able to form a coherent question. "It has always been like this. If you wish to hear my story, I will explain. It is a long story, but it is important that we share our stories. You never know what you might learn and feel from another person."

Could this be her enlightenment story?

I prop myself up into a comfortable seat against one of the wooden beams and nod. "Yes, of course."

As if passing through a doorway that exists only behind her eyelids, Sajana closes her eyes and speaks.

CHAPTER 22
SAJANA'S STORY

"You see, David, ever since I was a child, I was loved by others," Sajana begins. "My name itself bears the meaning, 'one who is loved by everyone.' It is in my nature. Saying this sounds like so much of ego, but I cannot change the way things happen. Just like I have my own nature, you have yours. There are things that come easy to you and things that will go against who you are.

"My whole life I was so quiet, always listening to others. Only when it was necessary did I speak my voice. Which brings me to this story…

"One day, when I was a young girl, a boy came to visit our village. I do not remember the exact reason for his visit. Maybe he was sent to buy food for his family, but he was alone—and he was a strange boy. Very quiet and did not say much. Because he was so strange, many kids in the village began to make fun of him, throwing rocks, things like this.

"So I shouted and told them to stop. And I explained to them: Can't you see this boy is from another village, raised in different nature? What choice does he have in his nature? We should not treat him poorly simply because of this.

"The village kids were stunned. Everyone turned around to stare. Like I said, this was so unexpected of me. To be yelled at by this little girl, my words must have reached their hearts.

Chapter 22

They set down their stones and walked away. Afterwards, when everyone had left the village square, the boy walked up to me and handed me this."

With her eyes still closed, Sajana shows me her hand and a beaded bracelet gripping her wrist. It's a beautiful bracelet made of what looks like giant seeds. The smooth seeds glisten beneath the starlight.

"I cannot say what would have happened to him had I not spoken," Sajana continues, "but that day, we became friends. I remember I was so much of happy of how the universe rewarded me for using my voice. You never know the difference even the smallest gestures can make."

I smile. She's really made a difference in people's lives since the beginning. And not just instructing people to hug trees and rocks, but life-saving stuff. Much like the boy, she might be different from me, but there's a noticeable generosity that accompanies her presence.

Sajana opens her eyes and smiles as a gust of wind blows across the porch. "I tell you this only to describe the beginning of my own nature. Even as a child, I could feel myself becoming more in touch with the nature.

"Often, I would go into the jungle and not return for many days, only returning when I felt the time was right, when I was open and balanced. I felt so safe during these days, not a care in the world, but my family was so much of worried! You can imagine Goma's face when I finally arrived home! After so many days!

"More time passed, and I continued to change. When I had grown even more into a young woman, I remember a painful sensation began in the bottom of my foot. I could not explain the reason for this pain, but this feeling grew like a fire burning inside my bones and spreading into my legs. It was so much of pain that I was put inside a hospital."

"I spent so many of days lying in the hospital bed. I could not do anything at all, getting up only to eat and drink and stare out the window. I felt so useless between those walls, away from the outside nature, and I became very sad and depressed. I even thought that maybe, just maybe, my body might be taken from me."

I can feel myself sitting up straighter as I listen.

"Since there was nothing else to do, I started meditating very seriously. Eventually I realized something new. Even though pain remained in my body, I began to change. There was so much of pain, but no added suffering on top.

"While this was happening, friends and family would come to visit me to see how I was doing and leave in such a good mood. They were surprised by what I had to say, but it was only what I had learned from the nature and through self-observation. Friends would come and go and tell more friends. So many people wished to hear these teachings. Perhaps this is how you have heard about me."

I nod. "Yes."

"Eventually, the lines of people coming to see me became so huge that I could not speak to everyone in one day. I gave so much of myself, speaking to as many as I could before resting, and I became more and more sick. My condition worsened, the fire in my bones spread higher into my chest."

Sajana looks down at her sternum and presses it with her fingers. She takes a deep breath as though she can feel it again, just for a moment.

"The medical doctors and spiritual healers visited me, but none knew what to do. No one could help me. One doctor accused me of faking my sickness, saying I was using my pain for attention."

Sajana laughs.

"I asked him, 'why would I choose this bed? Do you not think I would stand up and leave now to return home if I had the choice? I do not wish things to be this way, but this is the way things are.'"

Then she sighs. "Months passed. Many hard days. Eventually, the time had finally come when the doctor says my body

Chapter 22

will soon go, that my life will end. Everyone came to visit that day—my family and even those in faraway villages."

A sudden swell of emotions stirs in me, but I try to remain calm.

"They took me from the hospital and brought me outside on a stretcher into the open air for my body to feel the nature one last time before its passing. There was so much of sweating and hard to breathe. I couldn't move. But I was fully conscious and confused in these moments.

"As they were carrying me outside, I thought, *Why do they think my body is passing? It is in poor condition, yes, but now is not my time. I know what is my karma in this life.* In that moment, I knew my purpose was to spread love to all beings. It was so clear to me. Clearer than anything. And that is when it happened."

I scoot to the edge of my seat and sit even taller.

"All at once, I woke up. My arms flew wide open like this. All I could see was light everywhere, no darkness, and Buddha in everything. I could feel myself swimming in the flow of nature, connected to all energies, everywhere. And my pain was gone.

"When I climbed down from the procession and walked, everyone was in so much of shock and disbelief. But there was no denying it… ever since that day, I have known my path. Yes, still my body feels pain, the sickness returns every so often, and one day my body will leave. But so long as I'm alive, with whatever energy I have left, I will spread love to each and every beings. That is my true nature."

I try to keep the rising emotions held inside me, but I notice my fingers pressing into my eyes to wipe away a tear. We sit together in the silence of the night. She waits patiently, discerning that I'm trying to take it all in.

Finally, after I'm able to hold back another tear, I look into her eyes. "Thank you, Sajana."

She nods. "Yes, but the story does not end here. It keeps going. Do you think I was swimming with Buddha and light

True Nature

in every moment of my life from that day on? You see, there are many awakenings, but none of them last forever. It is our nature to return to as we were before, and at the same time, things are never the same. So we must continue to face darkness and pain, because that is where our own awakening and potential awaits."

Sajana stands from the porch and steps into the doorway.

"It's time we get back to sleep. I have said a lot. You already understand this, but you will understand more clearly soon enough. This work continues when we return home to Pokhara in the morning. Until then, it's time to rest with the potatoes."

We both laugh. Then she smiles and disappears into the house.

I stare out into the valley, darkness blanketing everything. I try to consider all she just told me. If her enlightenment came by way of a near-death experience, from seeing light in the darkest moment of life, what does that mean for me?

It's too much to take in, and my mind begins to shut down. Maybe the answers will come to me in time, in the days ahead, when the *real* work begins, just like she said.

I tiptoe into the attic and find my place on the floor between Bradley, Amit, and the potatoes. Everything is changing. Slowly.

I wake up hours later in a coughing fit. My throat and lungs burn from the inside out, and heat tinges my nostrils.

I realize then that I'm engulfed in a thick cloud of smoke.

CHAPTER 23
SWEPT AWAY

Amit and Bradley shoot up next to me, also coughing their lungs out.

"Fire!" Amit yells. "Run!"

My heart races, and Bradley, Amit, and I immediately scramble to our feet. We clamber down the steps through the smoke and dart outside into the open air.

As my watery eyes clear up, Seti Chama and Sajana emerge from behind the outhouse carrying piles of wood. Then Amit, Sajana, and Seti Chama burst into laughter.

"I couldn't help myself," Amit says, scratching the back of his neck. "This happens every morning. The smoke from the fireplace goes up into the attic. All part of living in the village."

Good one, Amit. At least the house isn't burning down.

As Seti Chama cooks us breakfast, I dry my eyes in the sunlight then stare at the mountains across the valley. The five of us eat a meal of potatoes and jungle greens on the porch and watch a red and orange sunrise paint the sky. The view and the fresh air are nice, but I'm ready to head home.

Finally, Sajana stands and says it's time we go back. Our departure happens quickly. We exchange one last embrace with Seti Chama, follow Baloo down the path to our bikes, and Bradley and I load up onto our scooter. Bradley revs the engine, everyone waves goodbye to Seti Chama, and we follow Amit and Sajana's motorcycle down the rocky road away from the village.

"Thanks for Visit," reads the banner overhead.

Ulleri departure

My body shakes as we rumble down the mountain. When we turn onto the highway, the wind blasts across my helmet, and we speed through the hills toward the city. I don't say much to Bradley, and he doesn't say much to me. I'm exhausted and looking forward to catching up on sleep.

The ride home seems much faster than the ride to the village. It's still morning when we arrive at the golden gates of Sajana's house in Pokhara. Amit drops off Sajana and waves goodbye.

"I'll see you soon," Amit says. Then he zooms down the block and around the corner.

Sajana turns up the driveway and leads us into the house. She stops us as we're heading down the hallway toward our room. "Bradley, David. Now that Tim and Christian are gone,

Chapter 23

a new space is best for you. Pack your things and follow me."

Bradley and I gather our backpacks from our bedroom and follow Sajana up the stairs. Second floor, third floor…

Just as I'm wondering if she wants us to live on the rooftop, Sajana turns away from the balcony door and places her hand on a knob. I hadn't this door noticed before. I must have been half-asleep when passing it on the way to our early morning rooftop meditations, thinking it nothing more than a broom closet.

Sajana pushes the door inward and says, "David, you will sleep here."

I step inside and glance around a small bedroom with a low bed, an empty bookcase, and a bathroom door. The room is clean, quaint, and simple, offering no distractions. It's much more cell-like than our previous living quarters.

"And Bradley," Sajana says, "you will stay over here on this side. Come this way, both of you."

I set my backpack at the foot of the bed and follow Sajana and Bradley through the open doorway. My jaw drops. The conjoined room is expansive, larger than any room in the house. Floor-to-ceiling windows line the walls. Sunlight glints off the polished marble flooring. Two stone goddess statues sit ominously with prayer hands in the corners, keeping watch over piles of yoga mats and meditation cushions. A Japanese futon topped with silken white sheets lays spread out across the floor.

"This space may feel like a big change for you," Sajana says. "But these rooms will help you be in yourselves. It is good to change your environment. A change of place can make what once was old new again. Please, make best use of what is here. When you are settled, come downstairs."

As Sajana vanishes out the door, I stand in the doorway and consider her words. Leaving the US for Nepal has been quite the change of scenery, but I wonder if it's only brought more questions than answers. I have to make use of my remaining time here. Maybe these new rooms will help.

"Not too shabby," I say.

"Impressive," Bradley replies, dragging the futon to the corner nearest the bookcase. "Hey. I'll see you downstairs. I'm going to get settled in."

I nod. Much like on the trail, we've already spent so much time together. It's reasonable that he wants some space to himself.

I unpack my stuff and check out my new digs. All in all, it's an upgrade from the downstairs situation. It's not complete privacy—there's a shared bathroom and an open doorway separating our rooms—but at least we have our own sleeping spaces.

My new cell

I open the window above my bed and lay down, allowing a gentle breeze to fan across the back of my head. The sound of children dribbling basketballs and laughing at a nearby school pipes inside my room and bounces off the yellow-painted walls.

Chapter 23

I consider passing out but then remember Sajana wanting us to come downstairs. When Bradley slips by, it's just another reason to get up and on with the day.

By the time I arrive downstairs, Sajana's already halfway out the back door, fitting her arms into the sleeves of her purple raincoat.

"You do what you like while you're here," she says. "I don't tell anyone what it is they should do here. It is always up to them. Be in yourself and ask yourself this question. Remember to balance and open. If you wish to go into the city, keys to the scooter are on the counter. Okay, I will see you this afternoon when I return."

And with that, the door closes behind her, the golden gate rattles, an engine sputters off, and an eerie silence settles into the home. For the first time in what feels like an eternity, I have no assigned activities. Nothing to do and nowhere to be. Just me and Bradley, alone.

"I'll be upstairs meditating," Bradley says, trotting back up the stairs.

Make that just me, alone.

I walk into the living room and sit on the couch. *Which meditation technique should I practice?* I could practice breath-centric meditations to harness concentration, body-scanning meditations to cultivate awareness, equanimity, and insight, or loving-kindness meditations to help me be more loving... But where do I start? There's only so much time in a day.

Overwhelmed, I stand and stare out the window. Dark clouds fill the skies, and rain begins to fall onto the garden. Heavy winds rip through the neighborhood streets, pushing the rain diagonal. Clothes hung on rooftop clotheslines flap and crack in the wind. Beads of rain crash into the window like pebbles. Gutters overflow and dump water onto the sidewalks. Grassy soccer fields flood and turn to mud. Rain slams the treetops and rustles the canopies. Limbs break and crash to the ground.

I imagine the dogs, curled up and huddled together on the front steps of the gated shops. Empty glass bottles, aluminum coke cans, and cigarette butts washed away into the rivers, swept into the sea. A hermit crab searches the ocean floor for a new shell and finds an aluminum coke can.

It's only been a few days, but I miss my old life. My friends and family back home. Biking the city, swimming in the springs, frisbee in the park. I miss physical touch, lying beside someone special. I miss *her*.

So why did I come here? What good is enlightenment if it takes me away from the people I love?

As I peer through the window, I'm reminded of my dependence, for living off the kindness and generosity of others. If I were a successful writer, I'd have the money to support myself in my search for enlightenment. I wouldn't be here, relying on others.

Then again, I've had plenty of money before, and I recall being just as miserable as ever.

I sit back on the couch, pick up my phone, and capture what comes to mind: stories about the trip thus far, descriptions of Ganesh, Sajana, Bradley. None of it feels insightful, but it's my first time writing since the last book. Words begin spilling out of me onto the screen. The act of capturing events and emotions into the written word excites me, and I write in disbelief of the sudden outpour of creativity.

Then I stop and massage my temples. *Isn't writing how I got here in the first place? Getting lost in words, trapping myself inside coffee shops all day long, finding purpose in achievement?*

At an even deeper level, doesn't involving myself in narratives deepen my attachments to thought and the material world? Isn't meditation the true practice for unravelling that attachment?

Between writing, enlightenment, and soulmates, it's frustrating carrying so many desires. Each manifests as a voice inside my head, pulling me in what feel like different directions.

Chapter 23

I notice how my mind has separated spiritual and material desires as two independent pursuits, but could the two be more interconnected than I had imagined?

Perhaps living with the wise woman was a good decision after all. Now that I'm no longer pulled in a thousand directions, I can make some choices of my own. Apart from the ongoing construction next door, it's quiet and clean. Well-suited for meditation and introspection. It's no doubt a unique situation. Sajana and her family are completely different from anyone I've met, here or elsewhere. Who in their right mind opens their home rent-free to spiritual seekers from all over the world?

Writing in my phone on the living room couch

Maybe I'm here to find balance in everything. To question and allow. To observe and listen. To learn about these desires and let them go. To understand who I am and who I wish to be. To follow everything down to the bottom.

And maybe meditation isn't the only way to get there. Maybe I have time for all of it.

So I pick up my phone and continue writing.

* * *

That night, after our evening meditation in the temple, Bradley heads to bed.

I sit down on the cushion in front of Sajana and take a deep breath. "Sajana, there's a question that's been on my mind."

"Mm, yes." She giggles.

I clear my throat to make room for the incoming words. "What should I be working on while I'm here?"

Sajana leans back in her chair, and a candle flame glitters in her eye. "Mm, this is an important step for you, David. I have been waiting for you to ask what is on your mind. Everyone has their own process. You have been balancing, so good.

"As you know, there are many techniques for meditation. Many are good options, I am sure. At the same time, each and every one of us is different. It is important to listen to yourself. For you, I see something different… for you, I see…"

I scoot to the edge of my cushion.

"For you, it is your writing. Focus on your writing."

The words catch me off-guard. "My writing?"

"Yes, your speech and your words. This is your karma. To you, it might seem like just words, but it is much more than that. At the essence, it is love. It is reaching other's hearts, seen and unseen."

"But what do I write about?"

"I cannot give you a topic. Only you can do this for yourself. But I have a feeling I know what you'll write about. The spiritual journey, yes? Mm, this is what I think you might do."

Chapter 23

I laugh and nod. Makes sense. It's exactly what I've been doing.

"Please understand," Sajana continues. "While writing is important to you, everyone's karma in this world is different. Do you know what I mean by this? Karma is very simply what you are meant to do in life. It is your purpose. How you fulfill your spiritual path. It is the meaning in everything.

"For some, their purpose is to be a good friend, mother or father, brother or sister. For others, it is service to others. And for all of us, it is presence in each moment. This is why each person must know themselves and follow their heart in every moment. Do you understand?"

I nod, mostly convinced of my limited understanding. "One more question…?"

She smiles. "Yes, of course you may ask."

"What do you think about love? You and Shiva had an arranged marriage, right?"

"You have many questions about love, David." Sajana giggles. "I will try my best to answer. This is true: Shiva and I had an arranged marriage. It is very common in Nepal. At the time, I was only eighteen years old and so very unsure about myself.

"At first, like many people do, I wished change for Shiva. I saw in him only the things I wished he could be. The mind might think change is best for others, but this is not the case. It is common that the change you wish to see in others is simply the change you wish to see in yourself.

"This desire is your own projection. This is your wish, not theirs, so it is yours to manage. In managing, you must be careful. You cannot force others to change, or it will backfire. The more you force change on another person, the more you will become more separate, and boundaries will form between you.

"This is how many relationships end, not because of anything to do with the other person, but because of what is happening inside ourselves. When we are unhappy, we tend to push away the people we love. Instead, if you want to change someone, then first you change yourself."

"How exactly do I do that, though? How do I change the way I love?"

"You love so that you no longer need any changes from that person. Instead of needing change, you offer support. Only then, change may come. You work on yourself so that this person may one day see your contentment and wish to see the same change in themselves.

"When you love another person, this changes the nature and the entire environment around you. This creates the conditions to make others' change possible. When you change yourself, you may notice that you never really cared about the other person's change.

"It is the change in yourself that you wanted all along. It is you who wishes to feel a certain way. Accepting yourself and others fully, no matter where they stand in life, this is what is meant by unconditional love, real love."

I sit there, absorbing her words. So if I want to experience love, I'm the one who needs to change? And I do this not by *trying* to become more loving, but by unconditionally accepting who I am in this moment? It's easy to say, but it seems like I need more practice to truly feel it as my reality.

"Thanks, Sajana. I'll work on it."

"Mhm."

She stays seated, as if knowing I have more questions. I feign a smile and swallow down the lump stuck in my throat.

"You have more questions?"

Finally, I come out with it. "Do you think I'll ever find my soulmate?

Sajana smiles. "Yes. You will. Do not worry yourself."

My heart warms. "Thanks, that's everything for now."

"Good. Take rest, David."

As I return to the house and drop into bed that night, part of me is still beaming inside. Sajana knows so little about me,

Chapter 23

much less anything about my work, and yet somehow my purpose is clear to her. She affirmed my karmic path, *and* she thinks I'll find my soulmate.

How quickly things change. I'd imagined enduring a thirty-day silent meditation retreat at this house, but instead I'm learning how to open, balance, and pursue creativity. My expectations are ground to dust and swept away by the wind. I'm not sure what's left of me.

Where does this path lead, how deep does it go, and to what end?

CHAPTER 24
A FIRE SPREADS

A week passes. I spend time writing, meditating, and walking the streets of Pokhara. While I try to focus on balancing myself, I find my attention taken by Sajana.

She's not what I had expected an enlightened person to be like. She doesn't live as a recluse in the jungle. Nor does she dwell in the mountaintops or some faraway cave, meditating day and night, trying to cleanse herself of impurity. Sure, she meditates, chants, holds ritualistic pujas, and ventures into nature, but her days overflow with worldly responsibilities.

She does laundry and cooks for the family. She works as a professor at the local college, manages a nearby orphanage, and attends to any visitors that walk into the home. She's on social media. She owns a smartphone. I find her using it constantly to serve others via texts and phone calls.

People contact her often. Relatives, friends, and past students. They call wanting to catch up or consult her perspective regarding their sicknesses, sadness, and desires. She makes time for everyone, counseling with fast-talking Nepali and chanting. I can't help but listen to her from the other room, trying to pick up whatever wisdom I can grasp.

All in all, her days are… *mundane*. Boring.

Nothing adds up. I thought enlightened people didn't participate in the material world and society. My mental image

Chapter 24

of what an enlightened person should be crumbles in her presence. Had I misled myself with preconceptions, unreality, and imagination? And if that's the case, what other false notions of reality has my mind consciously or unconsciously created?

After my talks with Sajana, I feel close to her. But for some reason, the closer I feel toward her, the farther Bradley seems. His conversations with her become more and more private. One afternoon, I hear them talking in the living room. He's asking her about past lives, alternate planes of reality, and Buddhist cosmology. It's clear his interests differ from mine.

Our diverging perspectives seem to be driving us apart. I try asking more than once how he's doing, but he'd rather not share. He doesn't seem in the mood. So I stop asking. But that doesn't make me any less curious. The two of us only speak when life necessitates it. Just enough to head into the city, buy groceries from the downtown market, and return home again.

Bradley's change seems dramatic and noticeable compared to mine. After living for three years at a meditation center, the process of opening looks evident and obvious compared to the subtleties of my balancing. Either that, or I'm not doing a good enough job.

I can tell he's opening up to new perspectives, softening his stances, and shedding a past that no longer serves him. It seems that no matter how deep one's conditioning, a supportive environment with proper guidance is sufficient for transformation. I can't help but feel like I'm once again no longer ahead of him. If anything, he's either at the same level or even ahead of me.

True Nature

Bradley meditating atop the roof until sunrise

* * *

The next morning, after our rooftop meditation and breakfast, Sajana's phone rings. This call is different from the others. She runs from the kitchen into the living room. From the speaker phone, I hear a woman on the other end crying out in pain. Her screams send chills down my spine.

Chapter 24

"What's wrong?" Sajana asks. "Breathe. *Bistaré, bistaré.* Slowly, slowly. Do not worry. Quiet your mind and listen."

Sajana holds the phone to her lips and utters a beautiful chant until the screams finally stop.

"Take rest. You will be better soon. There is nothing to worry. I am always with you."

When the phone call ends, Bradley and I step into the living room to see Sajana lying on the couch. Her face looks clammy, her rosy cheeks drained of color, reminiscent of my own sickness when we first arrived. I haven't seen her like this before.

"Is everything okay, Sajana?" I ask.

Sajana's eyes remain closed as she speaks. "It feels like there are pistols firing inside my head. Like fire is spreading across my back and body."

"Is there anything we can do to help?" Bradley asks.

Sajana shakes her head. "You are already helping. I can feel your *metta*, the love you are sending me in these moments. I will be fine. There is so much of pain, yes, but it is only the mere sensations of pain. No added suffering layered on top. Keep being in yourselves, opening and balancing."

As much as she says to be in myself, I can't help but worry for her as she lays there in a sweat. I wonder if the same sickness that led to her awakening has returned—or if it had ever really gone away.

That afternoon, a knock sounds at the front door, and Sajana's father, a quiet, kind, and gentle man named Devendra, steps into the living room. He sends his love from Goma then tells Sajana to lay down on the living room carpet. He takes his time, methodically stretching Sajana's legs, leading her through various exercises and tells her to see a doctor. Then he leaves.

It's a kind gesture, but I have my doubts that it's enough.

I ask, "Sajana, are you afraid you'll die if you don't take care of yourself?"

Sajana smiles. "It may seem for a moment like there is something to lose, something to hold onto, but there is nothing. We never had anything in the first place. One day, when the body passes, we will return to this natural state. So what is there to gain? What to attach to? What to fear?

"This is why we love unconditionally and share with all beings. Only the gods can go on living forever. I am no god. How can I be a god with this human body? And so, if I am human in a human body, there is nothing to hold onto."

* * *

Devendra returns the next day with Sajana's prescribed medicine purchased from the drug store. She's in great pain, but she continues her phone calls and our nightly discourses, chanting while lying down on the couch. She hardly sleeps, wakes up at three in the morning, and begins again.

It's the sort of schedule that would wear anyone down to the bone. I wish she would rest and stop working so much. Her life seems unbalanced, overextended, and on the path to self-destruction.

Could it be that some teachers struggle to follow their own teachings? That our work is the very source of our pain?

And yet she serves as if she's unable to live without it. As if serving itself was the source of her energy.

The days pass, and Sajana's health improves steadily. Bradley and I wake at four in the morning and, on days when the weather is clear, we meditate on the rooftop in darkness and endure the yelling man until the first sunlight warms my skin.

We prepare and eat breakfast with the family, and when it comes time for normal human beings to start their day, everyone leaves for work and school—except Bradley and me.

By this point, it's a familiar routine. We clean the house. We write. We walk or scoot into town. We visit Dharapani

Chapter 24

market, the German bread store, Goma's house, and the local food stores.

I pass the people in the city: the uniforms, suits, dresses, and beggars. And a new perspective arises. I've lived these lives before. Student, worker, vagabond. Maybe I'm not as alone as I thought. Maybe I do belong here. Maybe others feel like I do, lost among the crowd.

To my great relief, Ganesh finally confirms we will indeed be hiking with the Tibetan lama guide. In preparation for the trail, Sajana says we must go into the nature.

In accordance with her suggestion, every few days, Amit pulls up to the house on his motorbike and we fly away from the city on scooters over the hilltops. After exploring far-away temples and villages, we return to the house completely exhausted.

One night, we find ourselves stuck high up in the hilltops, waiting for a raging storm to pass beneath the awning of an abandoned house. When it doesn't let up, we drive down the hills through the storm, returning to the house sopping wet.

Eventually, the rain makes it almost impossible to travel anywhere. We spend our trips to the market hiding under umbrellas and covered in rain jackets. One moment it pours, and the next, the sun shines again.

When the sky darkens, we prepare and eat dinner with the family, meditate and chant in the temple, then sleep.

Every few nights, I dream about Hannah, recalling for a moment what it's like to lay next to a woman. And as my desires for love remain, the day of our trek approaches. Nothing lasts, much like our time in Pokhara.

Thirty days pass, and Sajana tells us that tomorrow, she will leave.

CHAPTER 25
DEPARTURE

The next morning, Sajana gathers Bradley and me and leads us behind the house to an open-air room just beside the temple. The space is nothing but a large clay firepit. We sit around the edge of the pit as Sajana lights a fire and begins chanting.

We *om* as the fire blazes and a thick smoke fills the space. The smoke warms my face to the edge of my pain tolerance and makes my eyes water. Tears fall down cheeks, mostly because of the smoke, but also because it's our last day with Sajana.

Finally, we stop chanting, and the roaring crackle of the fire dies down into silence.

"I am heading on tour today," she says with closed eyes as if suspended in deep meditation. "I will serve in Europe and retreat for some time. How long I will be gone? I don't know. Months, perhaps. By the time you return from your trekking, I will be gone. Before I go, there is one last thing I must tell you.

Sajana opens her eyes and looks at Bradley. "As much as you have opened, Bradley, and as much as you have balanced, David, and the flow is returning slowly—I'm sorry to say this, there are still things you have ignored. You have

Chapter 25

both only been working on the surface. You must go much deeper into the essence of who you are.

"As you go out into nature and do your trekking, you will test what it is you have learned. The journey has only just begun. This trek will not be easy. You will face many challenges in a short time. You have become comfortable here in the city. This is why it is important that you feel the nature. Use what you have learned here and discover your true nature.

"As for your lama guide, I sense something special about him. Your teachings continue with him and of course by listening to your own selves. I don't know when we will see each other again, but don't worry. Know that you are always welcome here and that I am always with you, in each and everything. Hopefully, you will understand why it is you have stayed. Now take these. They will serve as reminders on your journey."

With that, she hands Bradley a beaded bracelet.

"Bradley," she says. "Your bracelet is made of the seeds of a bodhi tree, the tree under which the Buddha was enlightened."

Then Sajana hands me a necklace.

"David, your necklace is made of mala beads, beads used for prayers and counting blessings. May you both find what you are looking for. Thank you for all your help while you were here."

I nod, take it in my hand, and place it around my neck.

For a while, we sit in silence and stare at the fire until the smoke dies down. Even then, we wait as the coals glow a bright red and only a few whisps of smoke rise from the ashes.

Finally, I hear Amit's motorbike sputtering up the road. The engine shuts off, and the golden gates creak open. It's finally time. Bradley and I hop on the scooter and follow behind Amit and Sajana to the airport.

It's a vaguely familiar location. I remember passing this tiny airport on our taxi drive into the city and the wild goose chase we took to find our new home in Pokhara.

The whole family is already waiting in the parking lot by the time we arrive. Together, Goma, Devendra, Shiva, Sarod, Nanu, Amit, Bradley, and me wait on the grassy lawn until Sajana says her plane is finally ready to depart.

"Sajana," I say. "I have one last question for you."

She giggles. "Yes, David?"

"Do you mind if… if I write about you? If I share your story with the world?"

Sajana smiles. "Of course. You can write whatever you like."

I nod, clasp my hands together, and bow. The mala bead necklace dangling from my neck lifts from my chest and hangs in the air. With tight embraces and tears in our eyes, it's clear how much she means to her family. A family that I, too, now feel a part of.

Waiting for Sajana's departure at the Pokhara airport

Chapter 25

And with that, Sajana turns around, waves goodbye, and disappears through the front doors of the Pokhara airport.

* * *

It's quiet back at our home. I walk the stairs to my bedroom and stare out the window. Nothing to do, nowhere to go. Not until our hike, which begins next week. I'm thrilled and nervous for the upcoming adventure. Sure, Bradley and I will return to this house after those twenty-one days, but this trek is most likely my final shot at enlightenment.

For the next seven days until the hike begins, I dream about Hannah. The same dream since the beginning.

CHAPTER 26
THE LAMA

"Now we go," Ganesh says. "If we miss the bus, no trekking!"

Bradley and I scramble out of bed, stuff our backpacks, and rush out the front door of Ganesh's homestay.

The roads are empty at six in morning. Only a cold wind rushes through the Kathmandu alleyways beneath an overcast sky. With the wind blowing at our faces and the weight of our backpacks pressing us downward, I exert more effort than I'd like at this hour to keep up with Ganesh's brisk pace.

While I suck in air, trying to catch my breath, Ganesh fishes into his coat pocket and hands us each a slip of paper: our trekking permits for the next twenty-one days.

"I lose big!" he says, laughing and shaking his head. "Big loss for me. I pay lama, food, guesthouses, but I can't help myself. I see you two, and what can I say? I see a glow in your eyes. Desires of meditation and trekking. I want to help! But I lose big!"

Ganesh sighs and grins. "Still, so many people this will help," he insists. "You will see. And remember, his name Lama Dai. Best guide. Very good. No one better!"

I sure hope so. My expectations for our trek with this Tibetan lama are sky high. *What wisdom could he impart to us? Could he lead us into the perfect conditions for enlightenment, the same conditions that so many monks seek in the Himalayas?*

Chapter 26

Whatever we'll find, I'm itching to get back on the trail after a four-year hiking hiatus. If these less-trekked Himalayan trails require a guide, who better than a Tibetan lama?

Chasing Ganesh through Kathmandu

By daybreak, we reach a crowded street with locals waiting curbside. Unfortunately, none of the parked tourist buses in the area catch Ganesh's interest. Instead, he paces the sidewalk in his polo, khakis, and shiny brown dress shoes. He steps off the curb to study the passing buses, glancing frequently at his silver wristwatch. Beads of sweat drip from his receding hairline, which he wipes away with the back of his hand to avoid reaching the collar of his white polo shirt.

Ganesh turns to me. "Nepali buses. Always late, so slow."

With the idle time, Bradley and I sling off our packs and squat on the sidewalk. I press my knees outward with the help of my elbows to force the opening of my hips, which tend to tighten up in the early mornings.

We must look ridiculous squatting on the sidewalk, especially Bradley. His wool socks rising past his calves accentuate his long legs and extra-short shorts. His recently bought white hemp T-shirt looks to be the freshest part about him. At least he's wearing his trail runners, one of the few times he's done so here in Nepal. What a relief knowing we won't have to deal with either of us hiking barefoot again.

As I stand up to straighten my legs, Ganesh takes off in a full sprint down the street after a tour bus.

"Fast!" he shouts, waving his hands in the air. "Come, fast!"

Bradley and I immediately throw on our packs and make a mad dash towards the bus, my pack smacking my back as we gallop up the street. When Ganesh catches up to the bus, he slaps the steel shell with his palms, and the bus comes to a halt.

We reach the vehicle, and the door slowly draws open. A skinny, old man wearing a red baseball cap, maroon vest, sweatpants, and flip-flops steps down onto the street and bows.

"Lama Dai!" Ganesh says.

The creases in the old man's cheeks and the cracks in his sun-tanned skin slide upward as he smiles. The two men exchange a firm handshake.

Bradley and I introduce ourselves to Lama Dai, but based on his curious, absent-minded gaze, it's unclear whether our names register in his mind.

Ganesh turns to me and Bradley. "Lama can call me if anything is needed. Otherwise, we will talk after your trekking. You are in good hands now."

"We always were, Ganesh," Bradley says, shaking Ganesh's hand. "And don't forget, we'll write about you in our blogs and put in a good word for *Everest Holiday Trekking Expeditions*. Lots of people will read!"

Chapter 26

A huge smile spreads across Ganesh's face. "You share! You share!"

We nod. *Yes, Ganesh. Pending our survival, we'll be sure to tell everyone.*

Bradley steps up onto the bus with a giddy laugh and pats the lama's back. "We're going to have fun together, Lama Dai."

Lama Dai chuckles softly and nods. It makes me think his version of fun is different than Bradley's.

Lama Dai's arrival

The bus, only halfway filled with locals, gives us a choice in seating. I take a seat near the front, Bradley heads all the way to the back, and Lama Dai sits across the aisle from me.

As the bus pulls forward, we wave goodbye to Ganesh from the window. It's going to be a long drive. Nine hours, Ganesh told us. But the distance is worth the wait. A small and necessary price to launch ourselves one step closer to enlightenment.

True Nature

I drift in and out of sleep beneath an orange sunrise as we leave the city behind, rattling up twisting mountain roads. I want to dream and dream deeply, but the bus throttles my brain around like dice.

The sun, pinned against the sky, disappears and reappears around every curve of the mountain as the hours come and go. I gaze at the passing landscape, which flips back and forth between lush jungle and grass terraces rippling down the mountainside into the valley. Every so often, scattered village homes made of brick, mud, rock, and corrugated tin pass us by. Cows and oxen gnaw mouthfuls of grass in the middle of the fields. Villagers crouch and fill woven baskets with crops. Prayer flags strung up between the homes flap in the wind. Views that remind me of Ulleri.

I turn my head around to see Bradley spread across the row of empty seats at the back of the bus, his legs kicked up for some shut eye.

Lama Dai must notice me awake because he moves seats next to me. Although he doesn't say anything, I guess this is my chance to talk with a Tibetan monk. But where to start?

"Lama Dai, how is your meditation going?"

The old man stares back at me quizzically. His wide brown eyes seem to be gazing into the window of an empty house. I curl my legs up onto my seat, place my hands atop my knees, and close my eyes.

"Meditation?" I ask again.

"Oh," he says with a smile. "Yes. Good."

I brace for more information, but he leaves the matter at that. Getting answers from Lama Dai might be harder than I thought, but I try reaching for more.

"You grew up a monk? Is that right, Lama Dai?"

As if a light had just switched on in his mind, Lama Dai's face lights up. He fishes into his pocket, opens his wallet, and hands me an identification card with his picture on it. I'd seen this photo before. It was the photo Ganesh first showed

Chapter 26

us back at his home office. The photo of an old man either too tired to open his eyes or gazing into the sunlight.

"Yes, lama," he says proudly, pointing at the card.

Hiking Guide Certification, it says. It's not exactly what I was asking about, but at least it does seem to confirm he's a legitimate guide and indeed, a Tibetan lama.

I smile, dig out my passport from my fanny pack, and show it to him. "David."

"David," he repeats, nodding.

"Bradley," I say, pointing to the back of the bus.

Lama Dai nods again, returning his card to his pocket and his gaze out the front windshield.

"I'm looking forward to meditating and trekking in the mountains with you, Lama Dai."

Lama Dai smiles and nods. Our conversation ends there.

A wave of disappointment rushes over me. I'd expected insight from this guy. Not only that, but the language barrier seems too thick to penetrate—which is putting it lightly. This guy literally does not speak English. How are we going to get through this hike if we can hardly speak with him? In a way, it feels like we're screwed. At the very least, it's going to be a long and challenging three weeks in the Himalayas.

I look out the window beside me and watch the passing scenery. I guess this is just the way things are. Nothing I can do about it. As I lean my head against the window, my eyes draw to a slow close. I can sense the wheels beneath me crushing gravel, a metal hunk of a machine carrying me up the road.

I jerk forward suddenly and wake to find us parked outside a touristy restaurant at the edge of the jungle.

"*Dal bhat,*" Lama Dai says, pointing out the window.

I shake my head and pat my belly. "Pugio," I say, which means full.

Lama Dai raises his eyebrow. "Sure?"

"Yeah."

Lama Dai smiles and follows the crowd into the roadside restaurant. I squat down in the dirt parking lot and watch Bradley juggle a hacky sack pulled from his fanny pack.

"Not hungry?" I ask him.

"Nah. You?"

"Nope."

I stand to stretch my legs and Bradley passes me the ball. We used to play all the time on the trail, but that was a long time ago. It takes some time for our reflexes and coordination to return, offering us a few good rallys and a few good laughs.

"So how's Lama Dai?" Bradley asks.

I chuckle. "He seems… chill."

"Did y'all talk much?"

"I doubt we'll do much of that on this trek."

"Works for me. So long as he knows the mountains, that's all that matters."

While Bradley rallies to himself for what's admittedly an impressive amount of time, I ruminate on the situation. Unlike Bradley, I was hoping to have some insightful conversations with Lama Dai, and his lack of English-speaking disappoints me, especially after how fluent Sajana was.

After another rally ending with my failure to return, I start to lose interest.

"I'm gonna rest," I say. "Feeling tired."

"Sure thing," he says and continues to juggle by himself.

I sit on the curb and think about our upcoming twenty-one-day trek through the Himalayas. I'm not getting any insights from Lama Dai, but maybe there's something else that awaits me. The trail didn't disappoint, and this trek is the closest possible scenario to simulate a similar but next-level experience. Hopefully, it's enough time to find what I've been seeking.

Chapter 26

Before long, a flow of people returns to the parking lot and reboards their buses. Lama Dai nods at us, and we board ours, too.

We're on the road once again. I lose track of time, nodding in and out of sleep through the twisting mountain roads. With no more planned stops for bathroom breaks or *dal bhat*, our few remaining stops seem oddly dream-like.

An old woman slaps the bus, hobbles down onto the dirt road, and disappears into a thicket of jungle trees. With no buildings or homes around, I have no idea her destination. Nevertheless, she vanishes into the trees, the wheels kick up dust, and we continue up the dirt road.

I also recall a large man in a white tank top hauling a styrofoam cooler into the middle aisle. He pats the top, gives some instructions to the driver, then bows. As we're leaving, a young man rushes for the door last second and crushes the cooler beneath his heel, causing the smell of fish to fill the bus. I slide down my window to keep from vomiting and stick my head out into the warm breeze of the passing world.

What must be hours later, my eyes peel open to someone tapping my shoulder.

"Sati Khola," Lama Dai says.

I look around. The bus is empty save for Lama Dai, Bradley, and me. This must be the end of the road.

I yank my backpack from the overhead storage and step onto the dirt behind the others.

Bradley turns to Lama Dai. "That's your backpack, Lama Dai?"

Lama Dai smiles and nods.

I stare at Lama Dai's pack. *What the hell is that? Does it even weigh five pounds?* It looks like a school kid's backpack—not anything serviceable for a three-week trek through the Himalayas.

I lean forward and tighten my shoulder and hip straps. It hardly alleviates the weight of my forty-five-liter backpack, which is stuffed with a sleeping bag, tent, cookware, and cold weather clothing. Someone's unprepared for this hike. And I have a small, unsettling hunch it's me and Bradley.

We walk the only dirt road in town, which passes between a mountain of jungle and brightly painted village buildings. Beyond the village, the resounding sounds of a river fill the valley. On the other side of the canyon, mountains rise to touch the cloudy skies.

Lama Dai leading us to a guesthouse in Sati Khola

Lama Dai scouts the guesthouse facades. Owners sitting in rocking chairs or sweeping porches exchange words of Nepali with Lama Dai from a distance, but Lama Dai has his sights set elsewhere. Somewhere specific. Like pacing Kathmandu's tourist district for just the right restaurant.

Then Lama Dai stops in the middle of the road and tilts his head sideways at one of the guesthouses as if to inspect its general quality. It's a two-story, pink-painted guesthouse with two tables beneath a corrugated awning. Lama Dai

Chapter 26

gestures for us to wait, walks beneath the awning, up the porch steps, and disappears through the doorway.

Bradley and I stand and wait beneath the partly cloudy skies, sweating in the warm humidity. The sound of the river roars like a lion charging through the canyon.

Before long, Lama Dai remerges with another old man by his side, and waves at us.

"Is this the place?" Bradley asks, stepping up the porch steps.

Lama Dai smiles and turns up the hall.

Bradley smirks at me. "I think that's our answer."

Our first guesthouse at the trailhead

We follow Lama Dai up the narrow, open-air hallway past the guesthouse rooms. Near the middle of the hall, the old man presents to us a small room complete with two twin beds topped with rose-patterned sheets and a window with wooden shutters. Minus the shiny marble floor and regal décor, it reminds me of our downstairs bedroom in Pokhara. A room stripped down to the bare necessities.

Our simple shared bedroom

"Where are you staying, Dai?" Bradley asks while throwing his backpack beside the bed closest to the door.

Lama Dai grins and points down the hallway.

"So we're stuck sharing and you get your own?"

The lama nods.

"Lucky you," Bradley says. "I'm only kidding, Dai. We're used to it."

I must be used to it, too, because wanting my own room hadn't even crossed my mind before Bradley mentioned it. It makes me think that Bradley really might want his own room.

"*Beesonay,*" Lama Dai says, placing his hands together against the side of his head. Then he turns and vanishes down the hall.

Rest.

Chapter 26

With our hike starting tomorrow, I might as well get all the rest I can manage. I sit onto the rose-patterned sheets to find a rock-solid mattress—nothing new thanks to Sajana's house.

As I slip off my shoes and lay down, I consider how hiring a guide has its perks after all, especially if no one here speaks English. This part of town seems like rough territory for me and Bradley to haggle with our barren Nepali vocabulary.

"Any Wi-Fi?" I ask, glancing over at Bradley lying down on his bed.

Bradley tosses his phone next to him. "Nah."

I reach inside my fanny pack to check for myself but my phone's dead. I must have forgot to charge it at Ganesh's homestay last night. So I search the room for outlets but the search turns up empty. In fact, there's no lights in the room at all. *Strange. Is there no electricity here?* All good. I've lived for days without Wi-Fi while hiking the trail and attending meditation retreats. It's a relief to no longer need that in our search for enlightenment.

Nevertheless, a dead phone is of no use. I fish into my pack, connect to my external battery, and begin to doze off.

I re-open my eyes at the flick of a lighter and the smell of smoke. I turn over to see Bradley standing on his bed waving around a sage stick like a wizard casting spells.

"What are you doing?"

"Smudging."

I cough. "Why?"

Bradley lets out a deep groan. "To cleanse the place. Purge out negativity, get rid of evil and unwanted spirits. You never know what unseen things might be lurking here. Where we're going, we could use all the help we can get."

I raise my eyebrow as the ritual runs its course. *What am I supposed to say to that?*

I'm skeptical about such beliefs—maybe he's right, and better safe than sorry, I guess—but I can hardly breathe with all this smoke. The smell, while different from that of hot, rotting fish, is equally as terrible.

"Mind if I open a window?" I suggest.

"Just enjoy it," he says, situating himself onto his bed to meditate. "It'll be gone soon enough. Everything's impermanent."

I scoff under my breath. I know it's true, but does that reasoning justify selfish behavior?

As Bradley settles in meditation, I reach for the wooden shutters, but the moment I lift the window, the roar of the river pours into the room. The sound is so loud that I have to shut it immediately.

I guess I could be a bit more flexible. *You can deal with it for now, David. Balance.*

I'm glad I stayed at Sajana's before this hike. I'll need these tools of opening and balancing these next three weeks. It's hard to say if this is a better or worse situation than Sajana's house, but with Lama Dai hardly speaking a lick of English, I feel like I'm once again my own teacher.

I sigh and lay back down, still frustrated from the residual smoke, but my body grows heavy. I consider fulfilling my second hour of meditation, too, but that grueling nine-hour drive really took it out of me. I sure could use a short nap. Hopefully, by the time I wake up, the smoke will have cleared out and my mind will be fresh.

CHAPTER 27
THE NIGHT BEFORE

It's six o'clock in the afternoon when I wake to the faint smell of smoke now buried into my pillow. I roll over to find Bradley's bed empty. It's not quite time for dinner, so maybe he's out exploring?

I slip on my sandals and pace the hallway. One by one, I peek into the rooms, but other than ours and Lama Dai's, the rest are empty. It's the same on the second floor, too.

I sigh. *Isn't this supposedly the start of the trail?* If so, there should be at least one or two fellow hippies here. I remember Sarod mentioning monsoon season, but I hadn't heard about it since. Could that be why no one's around?

I walk to end of the hall and stand on the balcony overlooking the jungle. The sound of the river stampedes through the dense canopy, and I immediately know where Bradley went.

I walk the road past quiet guesthouses, searching the jungle for a trail down to the river. Ahead, our tour bus sits parked in a stream. Two young men splash water against the vehicle with buckets, polishing the hunk of metal to its original color.

I make my way downhill, following beside the rocky stream, hopping atop boulders down to the river, remembering the rocky path near Ulleri village that led to the waterfall.

Sure enough, Bradley sits at the bank, his feet dangling in the rapids.

We share nods as I approach.

The sound of the river consumes the valley. It's an unbelievably powerful river, its flow never-ending. There must be so much snow up in those mountains, and I wonder what it will be like to reach those heights.

I stare at the rapids white-capping over the boulders stuck in the river's wake. Falling in would mean certain death, so I wedge myself between boulders at the river's edge to soak my feet. The snowmelt numbs my toes, worthwhile preparation for the miles of hiking that lay ahead in the coming weeks.

The silty canyon river

Just then, a sharp whistle pierces through the river's roar and strikes me from behind like a dart. I turn around to see Lama Dai standing by the village, waving his hands back and forth.

"I think he wants us to come back," I yell at Bradley.

Chapter 27

Bradley stares at the rapids, unmoved.

"Did you hear that whistle?"

Bradley rolls his eyes. "Be up soon."

I strap on my sandals and return to the village. Lama Dai sits out front of our guesthouse beneath the corrugated metal awning, a cup of tea set on the table before him. I sit across from him as he quietly sips from his cup, a neutral expression worn on his face.

There we wait until the sun sets behind the mountain walls and darkness shrouds the valley. The guesthouse owner sets a small lantern onto our table, and a chorus of cicadas chirp loudly in the jungle brush. Occasionally, the headlights of a jeep pass by in the darkness.

When Bradley's shadowy figure finally emerges from the darkness, he sits next to me and rolls his fingertips against the wooden surface of the table. "Why don't you trust us, Lama Dai?"

"*Khola*," the old man says, pointing toward the river. "Dangerous."

Bradley sighs and rubs his wispy beard. "I appreciate your concern, Lama Dai. It's early, and we're still getting used to each other. Know that you can trust us. David and I are seasoned vets. We've done lots of trekking."

Lama Dai nods and smiles, seemingly disinterested in continuing the conversation.

"*Dal bhat*?" the lama asks, finally.

My belly rumbles.

"*Lots*," Bradley says, rubbing his stomach. "*Lots* of *dal bhat*. *Very* hungry."

Lama Dai rises from his plastic chair and paces into the kitchen. Then he returns alongside the guesthouse owner, who proceeds to offer us each a plate of *dal bhat*. We've eaten *dal bhat* many times over the course of the last month, so I'm not surprised that's what's on the menu.

Bradley shakes his head at the owner's offer for silverware.

"*Atlehandso*," he says, and goes to work with his hands.

The guesthouse owner cracks a huge smile at the sight of two white boys eating with their hands and sticks around to chat with Lama Dai in Nepali.

As Bradley and I eat beneath the guesthouse awning by the dim glow of the lantern, we stare wide-eyed at Lama Dai. Despite being a skinny old man, he eats like his stomach is a bottomless pit. Handful after handful, he shoves enormous amounts of rice into his mouth at an impressive rate. As I work through my first and only plate, Lama Dai scarfs down his second and asks for thirds. Even Bradley seems impressed.

The *dal bhat's* predictable, same as always. As if everyone in the country conspired on how to make it. After a day with hardly any sustenance, I'm unbothered. I welcome what's familiar.

"Big day tomorrow." Bradley pushes his empty plate forward. "How do you feel about the trek, Lama Dai?"

"Sleep?"

Bradley and I laugh.

"Sure," Bradley says. "How many miles do you think we'll trek tomorrow?"

The lama shrugs. "Depends."

Bradley grins. "We'll find out tomorrow then, won't we? Which reminds me. You're welcome to join us for our morning meditation tomorrow, Lama Dai."

A confused look spreads across the old man's face.

"Meditation tomorrow morning? You know… meditation?" Bradley sits tall, crosses his legs, and shuts his eyes.

Lama Dai grins. "Ah! Meditation…"

"Yeah, that's it. How does five o'clock sound?"

"Seven?" Lama Dai asks.

Chapter 27

"Five." Bradley says, smiling. Like so many other things in Nepal, we've found ourselves in a negotiation.

Lama Dai grins. "Six."

Bradley and I laugh.

"Alright, six," Bradley says. "We'll see your ass in the morning!"

"Good night, Lama Dai," I say.

The old man nods and waves goodnight as we depart down the hallway.

I brush my teeth, change into my wool long johns, and plop into bed. It's chilly in the valley, but not nearly cold enough at this elevation to consider busting out my sleeping bag. The rose-patterned sheets will suffice.

I set my phone timer to an hour and sit up to meditate with Bradley. The jungle cicadas furiously chirp outside the guesthouse walls and the scent of burnt sage lingers. It's going to be challenging to keep this practice these next three weeks, but I have to try. After all, this is what I've been training for all this time.

Tomorrow, the real adventure begins. All that time spent in meditation centers and learning under Sajana has led to this. I must keep my practice going. I'll keep balancing and opening myself to the possibility of ultimate nirvana. I know it's possible. Now I just have to make it a reality.

My phone vibrates signaling the end of the meditation, and I realize I've been lost in thought for much of the last hour. It's probably a sign I just need sleep.

I lay down, but when Bradley starts snoring, I crack the window behind me. Just enough for the white noise of the river to pour into the room and flood my dreams. Beyond the river, I imagine a temple in the mountains, the sound of a faraway gong beckoning me closer.

CHAPTER 28
THE LEFT SIDE

I leave space at the end of my bed during our morning meditation, waiting for Lama Dai to shuffle into the room, but our door never opens. Either he forgot his promise, slept through his alarm, or had no clue what we were saying to him last night.

When our phones vibrate, Bradley and I stuff our things into our backpacks, slide on socks, and tie up our trail runners. This time, we're starting the trail wearing proper hiking shoes.

Bradley and I drag our packs to the front porch and sit across the table from Lama Dai. The old man quietly sips his tea then sets his cup down onto the saucer before him. Steam rises from the cup and disappears into thin air.

"Where were you this morning?" Bradley asks.

Lama Dai raises an eyebrow.

"Remember our promise? Morning meditation?"

"Ah… tomorrow."

Bradley laughs. "If you say so. Don't worry. If you forget, I'll remind you next time."

As Lama Dai takes another sip of tea and gazes out at the canyon wall, a part of me wonders if the guy even meditates at all. *He's a Tibetan lama—no doubt about that. But when does he make time for meditation?*

Chapter 28

Before long, the guesthouse owner swings by our table and places three pieces of fried bread in front of us. I stare blankly at the round brown disk.

Bradley picks his up, examines it from every angle, then gives it a sniff. "What's this, Dai?"

"Tibetan bread." Lama Dai snags a bottle of honey from across the table, drizzles it atop his fried loaf, then tears off a huge chunk with his teeth.

"What's in it?"

"Flour, water, sugar."

"Thought so." Bradley rips off a bite then drops it back onto the plate with a *thud*.

I try a bite myself. It's sweet and tasty and as empty of nutrition as one might expect a chewy slab of fried sugar dough to taste. *I know Ganesh gave us a good deal for this trek, but is this really our entire breakfast?* It's clear the days of our extravagant Pokhara breakfasts are far behind us.

"Is there any fruit around here, Lama Dai?" Bradley asks. "Maybe some village bananas?"

The lama turns his head and looks down the road. "I go see."

"Village bananas," Bradley repeats. "*Very* tasty."

Lama Dai sets off down the road.

It doesn't take me long to finish my piece of Tibetan bread. I then glance at Bradley's uneaten bread. "You fasting today?"

"We'll see about these bananas first. Anyways, I'm sure there's *dal bhat* up ahead."

I nod. "Mind if I eat yours?"

"Go ahead."

I rip off a huge chunk and set it onto my plate.

Bradley drinks from his water glass, then looks up at me. "What do you think of Lama Dai?"

"Not sure. He doesn't say much."

"No kidding," Bradley says. He sets down his glass. "You know what I think?"

"Huh?"

"I think he's worried about us. I have a feeling he'll want us to stick close for whatever reason."

"You think so?"

"I do. And I don't know about you, but I was hoping to get some alone time in on this trail. It might take some time for him to trust us. Hopefully, he'll relax after a few days and give us some slack."

"Sounds about right," I agree.

A few minutes later, Lama Dai returns to the table. "No banana."

"All good," Bradley says as he glances across the road. The sun peeks over the canyon wall and shines a dusty light onto the dirt path. "Should we get going?"

Bradley and I rise, throw on our backpacks, and step onto the road as Lama Dai gently tosses his tiny backpack over his shoulder.

"Hold on," Bradley says, looking at Lama Dai's feet. "Are you hiking in *those*?"

I look down. Lama Dai's still wearing those same athletic flip flops from the bus ride.

The lama smiles and gestures for us to lead.

"Good on you," Bradley says, turning up the road.

As I follow Bradley up the canyon trail, a rush of excitement swells inside me. It's been four years since I last embarked on a journey like this. My trekking poles click against the rock with every step, and my heart races imagining what lies ahead.

The path is wide, gradually inclining, and made of rock, gravel, and dust. We hug the mountain wall and take it toward the sky. It isn't long before we're high enough to view the river coursing through the valley and the jungle skirting the mountains on the other side.

Chapter 28

Then Lama Dai whistles and steps to the edge of the cliff. We scoot to the side, making room for the oncoming jeep. It barrels down the mountain, leaving the sound of crunched gravel in its wake. I offer prayer hands to the locals, who wave from inside the cabin and disappear around the bend.

I hike between the tire tracks while wishing they were animal tracks and allowing two more jeeps to pass by in the span of fifteen minutes. *Is this entire trail road walking?* I thought we'd be immersed in nature...

Soon after, a thundering blast and a loud cranking noise sweeps through the valley. I narrow my gaze to the distant cliffside. It seems like some villagers are chipping away at the stone with sledgehammers.

"Lama Dai," I ask, pointing to the specks harnessed against the wall and hanging thousands of feet up in the air. "What are they doing?"

Lama Dai glances up without breaking stride. "Jeep road."

I exhale. The last thing this valley needs is more roads and more vehicles.

If the jeeps and sledgehammers aren't enough to complain about, the sun exposure is brutal, and it seems like the mountain road stretches on for miles with hardly any change of scenery. Rock wall to the left, river to the right. The trail plays with my mind, rising and falling in elevation, following the bends of the mountain, but never shifting terrain. It leads us higher but never over a pass. It dips down but never falls to the river. Instead, the path stays forever suspended, exposed to the sun. I sweat profusely and the tops of my arms and hands begin to burn.

It's a nice enough view, but it's nothing like the Pacific Crest Trail. On that trek, it seemed like every bend offered something new and interesting.

I wish we had brought maps. I figured them unnecessary since Lama Dai knows the mountains.

"Lama Dai," I say. "How long does the trail stay like this? Jeeps and roads?"

"We walk left side," Lama Dai says.

"For how long?" Bradley asks.

Lama Dai scratches his head. "Hmm... five days."

My stomach drops. *Five more days of road walks and jeeps?* Hell, we might as well turn back now while we still have the chance.

Balance, I tell myself. *You're here.* All I can do is change my mindset and resign myself to the fate of this five-day road walk.

"The Left Side"

"*Pula,*" Lama Dai says, pointing ahead.

I look up and gulp. Ahead, the trail leads to a suspension bridge which spans hundreds of feet above the raging river.

I take my first shaky steps onto the walkway. Gusts of wind blow through the canyon, tossing my t-shirt, and the bridge wobbles and sways under my feet. I grasp my trekking poles tightly with one hand, grab the cable beside me

Chapter 28

with the other, and peer through the narrow gaps in the footbridge.

Nightmarish images flash before me. *The cables snap, I reach out for something—anything—but it's too late. I fall into space and every bone in my body snaps beneath the weight of my backpack as I crash into the rocky river. As my vision fades to black, the river pulls my lifeless body toward the village. Somewhere in a faraway village, a young girl with a soft imperceptible smile stands in the middle of a field.*

Someone grabs my shoulder.

"OK?" Lama Dai asks.

I shake my head and snap out of it.

"Good," I say nervously, picking up my pace again.

"*Bistaré*," Lama Dai says.

Slowly...

Crossing one of many suspension bridges

I fix my sight on the other side, trying to play it cool while lumbering forward with quivering legs. I'm surprised at how much confidence I've lost since the PCT. I must have crossed a hundred bridges on that hike.

When I reach the other side, I let out a deep exhale and wait for Bradley and Lama Dai, who spend time looking down into the raging river from the middle of the bridge. I nod as Bradley passes me and continues up the path. Lama Dai ushers me to continue in front of him, then sticks close behind.

Beyond the bridge, we continue walking for miles, now passing groups of villagers. Some carry nothing, others wear backpacks, and many haul packs so huge that carrying them is only possible with the help of a forehead strap. An elderly woman's veins protrude from her neck, but she shows no sign of complaint when she passes. She smiles softly, says *namaste,* and offers a few words in jest with Lama Dai ending in laughter. The locals really seem to like him.

As we pass more villagers carrying huge packs, I realize I've got it easy comparatively. And maybe those jeep roads make more sense than I had originally thought. Sure, blasting away chucks of the mountain seems rather unfortunate, but wider roads mean faster transportation, financial benefit, and an easier life for the villagers. *Buddhism, Hinduism, Tourism.*

Eight miles later, the sun reaches high noon, and the road levels off high above the river at a small village. Lama Dai inspects the guesthouse facades and removes his backpack beneath the shade of an awning.

Bradley and I peel off our shoes and socks, lay against our sleeping pads, and rest our legs up a wooden beam. As my legs go numb, I broaden my gaze onto the ceiling and wonder why I ever thought this would be a magical, worthwhile adventure.

For years, I've wanted another chance to immerse myself in nature. To re-experience something like the trail—an unforgettable place filled with trail magic, beautiful people, and amazing sights. But *this* trail isn't anything like that. There's no wisdom from the lama, beautiful vistas,

Chapter 28

or enlightenment. Only jeeps, sunburns, a quiet lama, and Bradley.

I just need to give it more time before things make sense, I reason. *Surely, things will improve.*

When the guesthouse owner brings out plates of *dal bhat*, we gather around the table to eat. Even though the rice and *dal* taste delicious after such a small breakfast, all I can think about is how I'm ready to call it quits and stay here for the night. Of course, such a thought is nothing more than a daydream. There's a lot of light left in the sky. We've hardly just begun.

"Lama Dai," Bradley says, chewing on a handful of mushed rice. "What's the name of the next village?"

"*Totopani*," he says.

Bradley's eyes grow large. "*Totopani?*" It takes him a second to finish chewing. "You hear that, David? Mean anything to you?"

I shake my head.

"*Pani* means water, right? Lama Dai, does *toto* mean hot?"

"*Toto?*" Lama Dai repeats. "Hot, yes."

"So, hot water?"

"Hot *springs*," Bradley says with a grin.

My eyes widen. Even though it's scorching outside, a nice warm soak would do well for my bones and morale.

The three of us wolf down our *dal bhat* (one plate for me, two for Bradley, and three for Lama Dai), then we head up the trail in heightened anticipation.

After another four miles of walking the Left Side, we arrive at Totopani. Bradley and I search the village high and low for signs of hot springs, but all the concrete pools are empty.

True Nature

The empty hot springs at Totopani

Bradley rubs his chin. "Lama Dai, no hot springs?"

Lama Dai looks at us with a far-off gaze then leads us to the far edge of town. There, water trickles from three tiny faucets into a stone basin. It's not a swimming hole, but it will have to do.

I unbuckle my pack and lumber toward the "spring" with sore legs like Sahor trotting over to his basin. I cup my hands beneath the spigot and splash handfuls of burning hot water onto my face, dousing myself in the smell of warm sulfur and clearing my face of dust. While Bradley plants his feet into a small corner of the basin with some depth to it, I also sit down to soak my feet. I dip in my toes, the searing-hot water wraps around my ankle, and I smile.

As the sky darkens and the night grows cold, we gather our belongings and make one last push into the next village.

"Dhoban," Lama Dai says a few miles later. To me, it's just another village. A place with guesthouses serving *dal bhat* and beds with rock-hard mattresses.

Chapter 28

Sure enough, Lama Dai leads us into an empty two-story guesthouse. He shows me and Bradley to our shared bedroom then vanishes to a room of his own. The rest of the evening unfolds in a predictable manner. I scarf down a plate of *dal bhat*, brush my teeth, then begin my hour meditation in the dark of our bedroom.

Thoughts plague my meditation. For some reason, I get the feeling that Bradley wants to be elsewhere. *Are these thoughts true or arising because I'm tired and grumpy after a long day's hike?* I decide to broach the subject.

I roll over and sit up. "Hey, Bradley."

"Yeah?"

"What are we going to do about the flow between us?"

Bradley lays down into bed. "I'm not sure there's much we can do."

My eyebrow raises. "Why not?"

"It's just—I've been thinking about the flow. Our spiritual partnership. About Sajana's teachings. And I've been questioning everything, including openness and balance. If you dive deep enough, none of it makes much sense."

I narrow my eyes. "How so?"

"Take balance, for example. Everyone's balance is different. Your balance is going to look different from mine, right?"

"Sure..."

"So what one person might consider imbalance for themselves, maybe that's exactly where I need to be. Which makes me think—what if imbalance can bring just as much growth as balance? Maybe the two aren't as separate as they seem."

I think on it. "There's a connection, but I'm not so sure seeking imbalance is the best way to go about life."

"I'm only saying it's a matter of perception. Either way, what you want isn't going to be what I want. We're different. What are we supposed to do about that?"

I sigh. This isn't how I imagined this conversation would go. "I'm... I'm not sure."

"Same here. Your version of enlightenment is different from mine. We can take different paths to get there. In fact, the more I follow my intuition, the more I find myself relating back to my old technique in new ways.

"I wouldn't say living with Sajana was all for nothing, though. I'm even more grateful for those lessons because now I realize there's nothing wrong with the technique—only my understanding of the technique and its teachings. It's always been there, same as it always has. It's *me* who's changed. I've been my own block and barrier. And with that removed, I can practice in a more balanced way."

"Interesting," I say. "For some reason, I'm even less connected to one specific practice and more confident in letting go of techniques. Do you think one is better than the other?"

"Let's test it. We can see where that leads."

Yeah, let's see where that leads. A race to enlightenment.

But first, I hope my hiker strength returns. And that the Left Side ends sooner than later.

CHAPTER 29
DONKEYS

I wake to the rooster's crow and a searing pain shooting down my legs. I'd forgotten the pain that comes from walking. Pain that takes days, weeks, and months to grow accustomed to.

Throughout our early morning meditation, I consider suggesting an early zero day—a day where a hiker hikes zero miles. After envisioning Bradley's reaction, I decide I'd better not. *Plus, what good would complaining do?*

As I roll out of bed, lace up my shoes, and slog toward the front porch, I remember Goma. Her legs paining, paining, and yet still she rises from the couch and follows the kettle's whistle to make milk tea.

Bradley, Lama Dai, and I eat slabs of Tibetan bread as the run rises. I don't mention the soreness in my legs, and no one mentions Lama Dai not showing up for meditation again. If he doesn't want to meditate, there's no reason to force him. Instead, we grab our backpacks and set up the trail.

Today's more of the same. The sun beats down on the valley, the trail weaves along the canyon wall, and we cross suspension bridges back and forth over the chasm. The river flows in the opposite direction, and the jungle crawls up the distant snow-capped mountains.

True Nature

There's hardly any space between the three of us. When Bradley tries pushing ahead, Lama Dai whistles for him to stop and stay close.

At least I had *some* space to myself at Sajana's house. Here, there's nowhere to run. Bradley and I walk yards away from each other, but it feels like we're miles apart. I can tell Bradley's frustrated with Lama Dai's distrust, too.

I know more conversation could help bridge our divide, but if this is my last trip with Bradley, I might as well start getting used to living on my own. If he doesn't want to fix things, then maybe I shouldn't either. Maybe our differences are irreconcilable.

The possibility of losing Bradley is a terribly unpleasant thought. He's my best friend, the only one who's been there for me on all our adventures. Considering I may never find my soulmate, this leaves me feeling alone in the deepest sense.

To take my mind off the situation, I try to recall my dreams from last night, dreams which were once so vivid in Pokhara, but nothing returns to me. Maybe yesterday's fifteen miles of trekking were too much for my body. Maybe my mind needed a rest from dreams.

The trail narrows, the tire tracks disappear, and we rise higher above the river. Just when it looks like jeeps are a thing of the past, a loud clicking of hooves approaches from ahead. Lama Dai whistles for us to step to the edge of the cliff, and a young man leading a long line of donkeys proceeds by. I take note of the supplies tied to the donkey's backs: huge bags of concrete, rice, and feed. Thirty-pound propane tanks, metal wiring, and planks. Supplies to build the roads and grow the villages.

No sooner does the procession pass before another donkey caravan pulls up from behind. *What is this—a trail for donkeys?*

We end up stuck behind this caravan for miles. The donkeys smell awful and leave behind impressive piles of

Chapter 29

excrement which we avoid like landmines. This section of the trail isn't much better than yesterday's jeep roads.

Lama Dai chats with the shirtless teenager shepherding the procession from behind as we walk. Much like Lama Dai, he has deeply tanned skin, a lean upper body, and large calves from years of trekking. He wears loose-fitting blue jeans, flip-flops, and a T-shirt tied around his waist.

Suddenly we come to abrupt stop, and the shirtless young man scans the line of donkeys. Spotting the culprit, he lets out a loud clicking noise, picks up a palm-sized rock, and hurls it as hard as he can at the idle donkey in the middle of the pack.

I clench my teeth as the jagged stone strikes the donkey's back with a hard thud. Luckily, these donkeys must have thick skin and coarse hair, because the animal seems totally unaffected and doesn't budge. Only when the young man strikes him with a second rock does the donkey begin to walk again. I shudder at the horrible treatment but try not to judge the boy. What do I know about leading donkey caravans?

We follow the donkey procession for miles, slowly trekking higher in elevation. Jeeps replaced by donkeys, the steps pass all the same. No matter how I slice it, donkey excrement or noisy engines, life presents unpleasurable situations.

I keep slogging forward, keeping pace with the caravan. Whenever the donkey in front of me slows down, I gently tap my trekking pole against his flank and try to imitate the whistle. If building those jeep roads means a small improvement for the lives of these donkeys, they'd better hurry up.

As the heat of the afternoon beats down into the valley, our newly formed caravan arrives at another village plateau. Bradley and I fill our water bottles from a spigot, then escape the sun by taking rest beneath a guesthouse awning. I chug water while laying atop my sit pad and watch the young men untie the ropes binding the large sacks atop the donkey's backs.

One of many donkey caravans

The bags fall to the dirt with heavy thuds. The unburdened donkeys whip their tails in joy and roll around in the dirt of the fields before lying in the shade of a large Banyan tree. The young men haul buckets of water taken the village spigots, pour them into troughs, then whistle loudly.

As the donkeys drink, the young men spread out bags of feed atop tarps beneath the sunlight, which dries the feed and prevents mold, then they summon the donkeys to feast with one final whistle.

Done with their work, the young men join us in the guesthouse dining hall for plates of *dal bhat*. I hunch over my plate and peer through the window at the donkeys lying beneath the shade of the trees. This is my life for the next three weeks. The routine of a Himalayan villager. Trekking from village to village beneath the elements, carrying supplies, eating *dal bhat*, trying to understand the language.

Chapter 29

I miss my old life, but there's something simple about this one, too. There must be more to learn here.

After finishing his third plate of *dal bhat*, Lama Dai dons his spectacles and unfolds a topographical map onto the table. Bradley and I glance at each other and start cracking up.

"You son of a gun," Bradley says while leaning over the map. "You've been hiding this from us this whole time?"

Lama Dai laughs and shrugs.

"What's the plan, Dai?" Bradley asks. "Where are we going?"

Lama Dai adjusts his glasses and places his finger along a thin red line. Slowly, he traces the line with his finger, a line that follows the river and traverses north across a mountainous terrain. Lama Dai then runs his finger along the line marked "Tsum Valley Trail," an offshoot of a trail that runs in a loop, which rejoins the "Manaslu Trail" where his finger stops.

I point to the Tsum Valley loop trail. "Why don't we just skip this part?"

Bradley furrows his brow. "Let's just go with what we paid for, brother."

"We could hike more of the Manaslu instead."

Before Bradley can respond, Lama Dai places his finger at the far end of the Tsum Valley trail. "*Mu Gumba.*"

"*Mu Gumba?*" I ask, staring at the map. "What's that?"

Lama Dai smiles. "Sky Monastery."

"Sky Monastery," Bradley repeats with a smile of his own. "Convincing enough for you?"

I bite my cheek from expressing a full smile as my eyes light up. *I can't believe it. That's what I've been waiting for! Sky Monastery. I knew this trek wasn't for nothing.*

Bradley points to another spot on the map. "And this—is this pass the highest point on the trail?"

Lama Dai nods firmly. "Larke Pass."

I gaze at Larke Pass. A spot on the map where the contour lines push so tightly up against one another that the mountains must be sky high.

"Alright!" I exclaim. That's the plan, then. First, *Mu Gumba* the Sky Monastery and then Larke Pass, the end of the Manaslu trail and the final climb of our trek. These are my best and last chances for finding enlightenment.

"Sounds like a plan," Bradley says.

As we all throw on our backpacks, I notice a renewed sense of purpose and strength flood my body. I now know where I need to be, and I'll do whatever it takes to get there.

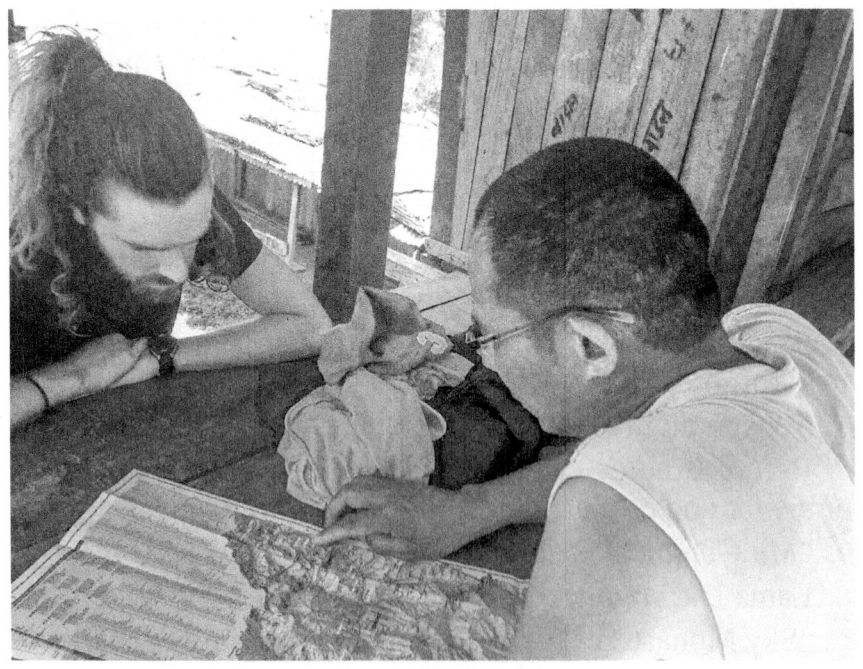

Lama Dai presenting the map of the Himalayas

We spend the evening cutting through the valley, crossing windy suspension bridges over the river and back again, trudging behind packs of donkeys, stopping briefly at a cold spring flowing from the mountainside.

Lama Dai lifts his plastic coke bottle beneath the spring, filling it to the brim. He sips directly from the spout with a

Chapter 29

gentle smile. Following his lead, I do the same. The water is cold and pure, without need for filtration, and it makes the heat of the day tolerable.

The sun descends behind the mountains, the trail flattens out, and we enter a sprawling village. It's the largest I've seen so far. There's a school, a sand volleyball court, and guesthouse after guesthouse, but hardly any people and still no fellow hikers anywhere. It's almost depressing at this point, and even a bit concerning.

Lama Dai leads us up the stone steps of a quiet guesthouse and into a two-bed bungalow before disappearing down the hall. Neither me nor Bradley discuss having to share a room, but our silence speaks volumes.

I try not to take Bradley's quietness personally. He said he wanted space on this trail, and if he doesn't want to talk, I'll let him have that. Maybe he's going through something he'd rather not speak about. Whatever the case, maybe it's none of my business. I'd better get used to the new normal.

As Bradley heads to the shower, I plop down into bed. I'd forgotten how challenging and miserable it can be to hike long-distance. Had my memory of the trail been flawed? Had I only remembered the pleasant experiences and overlooked the harsh realities that walking for twenty miles a day brings to the mind and body? Enlightenment requires solitude, but is solitude really what I want?

I miss my friends back home. I miss meeting new people. I miss speaking English with native English-speakers. That's one downside of traveling in a foreign country and not speaking the native language. Everyone in Nepal is kind and generous, but it's hard to connect deeply with others. It's not the end of the world, though. Solitude has its perks. The villages are quiet, the guesthouse owners attend to our needs, and the bathrooms are empty.

Bradley returns wearing his long johns. He nods, signaling my turn to shower.

I snag my camp towel and depart down the stone stairway in my Jesus sandals to find a small stone outhouse at the far end of the courtyard. It's pitch-black inside, so I flip on my headlamp and dangle the dim light onto a nearby hook.

I strip, turn the knob, and gasp. *Chiso*, freezing cold. I take deep breaths while rushing to clean my body of dirt and dust. Then I notice the water turning surprisingly warm. Hot water flows over my head and down my back. I close my eyes and allow my neck to fall limp.

Bradley's asleep by the time I return to the bedroom. Not a smudge stick in sight nor a whiff of sage smoke.

It must have been a long day for him, too.

I flick off my headlamp and settle into bed. I know my mood was horrible today, and meditation helps me face those feelings, but my legs are killing me, and I need to get some sleep. Missing one day of meditation isn't a big deal—right?

We're still three days from escaping the Left Side, days which will likely be repeats of today, but at least we're one day nearer to our final goal.

I shut my eyes and picture *Mu Gumba*—Sky Monastery—then Larke Pass, the highest and final pass of the trail. Something awaits me there… I just know it.

CHAPTER 30
TSUM VALLEY

Three miserable days pass along the Left Side, and it's morning when the path forks. Lama Dai whistles and points uphill. The path is much steeper compared to what we've trekked so far, made of nothing but loose rocks and scree. It looks rough, but at least it's change. And for that, I'll do anything.

I push to make up ground behind Bradley, sweating, slipping, and sliding up the scree. With every step, the weight of my pack pulls me down, reminding me of all this extra stuff I brought. Had I known we'd be sleeping and eating in guesthouses this entire trek and never once camping outside, I wouldn't have brought any of this deadweight. My sleeping bag, tent, cookware... I glance back at Lama Dai and his tiny backpack.

Yep, I'm an idiot.

Considering Bradley's pack is even larger than mine, I wonder if he's struggling as much as I am.

As we climb higher, I remember I've missed another two evening meditation sessions over the last three days. *Is missing these meditations affecting my mood? Or is this terrain really that challenging?*

Just as I'm wanting to throw in the towel, the climb levels off, and I notice a stone archway standing above me.

"Tsum Valley," Lama Dai says proudly.

As we pass beneath the archway, my mouth falls open. Suddenly, the path is no longer dry and dusty but rich and earthen. A shaded jungle canopy surrounds us, stretching far into the distance. A cool wind blows through the bows of the *sal* trees and whisks across my sunburnt face. Blackish-yellowish butterflies flutter through the canopy breeze, landing gently on moss-covered boulders to display their colors.

Relief pours over me and eases my mind as I walk in awe of the scene. Now *this* is more like it. After all the jeep roads, donkey caravans, endless sun-exposure, cliff-walking, and uphill climbing, I can hardly believe the dramatic change.

Tsum Valley, a change of scenery

As Bradley and I study the jungle, Lama Dai snaps a long piece of bamboo from the brush in one smooth motion. He grins with raised eyebrows and turns up the trail, his new staff pushing him forward. I glance at the trekking poles I lugged halfway around the world and sigh.

Chapter 30

Lama Dai leads at a considerably slower pace than me or Bradley, a pace that reminds me of our friend Tim from Pokhara. It's the same slow and confident stride of a man with nowhere to be anytime fast.

Lama Dai sporting his bamboo hiking staff

Around noon, we ascend above the jungle and reach a small guesthouse on the side of a hill. Lama Dai steps beneath the shade of the awning, leans his bamboo staff against the brick wall, and disappears inside the kitchen. By now, we know the drill.

Bradley and I unfold our sit-pads onto the shaded pavement and rest. From up here, the distant sound of the river is soft, replaced by sweeping winds and birdsong. We've climbed to higher heights, but I can still breathe easily. The elevation hasn't quite kicked in yet. We must still be below ten thousand feet.

The sun passes high noon, and the shade of the awning retreats. I lazily fish into my pack, draw my hat from the outside netting, and rest the bill on the crook of my nose.

Lama Dai shuffles from out the doorway, squats next to us on the pavement, and scrapes the end of his bamboo stick softly against the concrete.

Lama Dai perfecting his staff

Out of the blue, Lama Dai turns to me. "Villages before, Nepali. Villagers now, Tibetan."

It's the most English I've heard from him so far.

I glance over at Lama Dai. "Oh yeah?"

He nods, his gaze resting over the jungle. "Changing," he says, then he rises and disappears once again into the kitchen.

Changing? Yeah, I notice some changes, too: the jungle, the elevation, fewer guesthouses—but is that what he meant?

Villagers now, Tibetan, he'd said. He's excited about Tibet, but why?

I think on the idea a bit further. *Could there be other Tibetan lamas in the villages ahead? Ones who speak English? Ones I could talk to about enlightenment?*

Chapter 30

Maybe I'm getting ahead of myself. Reading too deeply into things.

Whatever's in the Tibetan villages, I put it aside. We have five days until we reach the monastery and another two weeks to climb to the highest pass. Until then, I need to take advantage of this time to rest. I pull the bill of my hat farther over my face and close my eyes.

A moment of rest

CHAPTER 31
BECKY

I wake to someone shaking my shoulder and the delicious aroma of rice and dal and cooked vegetables filling my nostrils.

"*Dal bhat,*" Lama Dai says.

I sit up and join Lama Dai and Bradley inside the cool, dark dining hall. A beautiful young woman wrapped in a red sari dress serves us plates of *dal bhat* from a cauldron. The *dal bhat* comes and goes, and it's time to begin again.

"*Pani* ahead?" Bradley asks, throwing his backpack over his shoulder.

"Yes, *pani,*" Lama Dai says. "*Chiso pani.*"

"That's what I like to hear," Bradley says as he forges onward.

With all the cold water ahead, there's no reason to subject myself to extra weight, so I leave my water bottles empty and head up the trail.

But it turns out there's no water anywhere. Instead, we ascend a seemingly endless rock stairway. I run my tongue across my cracked lips and swallow down dust. My mouth is as dry as the earth beneath my feet. I look up to the sun and shield my eyes, glimpsing the shadow of a hawk circling me from overhead. It's fine—I'll live. I've been here before on the trail, having hiked miles without water in

Chapter 31

the desert. Water will come eventually, but that doesn't keep me from getting frustrated at Lama Dai. I slog up each step, telling myself I'm building metal fortitude and that these chicken legs need this training for the days ahead.

A day of stair-stepping up mountains

It isn't until hours later that we reach a straw hut with a water hose. Bradley and I throw off our backpacks and chug bottle after bottle. As we recover in the shade, Lama Dai walks into the hut and returns moments later.

"Nepali chocolate," he says with a smile, placing a small piece of candy into each of our hands.

Bradley and I unwrap our "chocolates" and chuckle. It's a cough drop.

"Thanks, Dai," Bradley laughs.

I pop it into my mouth and feel a cool relief starting at the back of my throat. It's hard to stay mad at someone with a gesture like that.

"Next village close," Lama Dai says.

This time, he's right. We push through the forest until nightfall, approaching a large cliffside lodge. While the outside of the structure presents a finished product, the hallway is too dark to see anything. We flip on our headlamps. Beams of light shoot out onto the walls made of unfinished wooden planks and drywall. Lama Dai ushers us to the last room on the right. We flip the light switch back and forth, but nothing happens.

"*Dal bhat* soon," Lama Dai says.

"Sounds good, Dai," Bradley replies, unpacking his backpack. "We'll shower up and see you in the dining hall."

Lama Dai nods and departs into the darkness.

"Mind if I go first?" I ask Bradley.

"Go for it."

As Bradley meditates atop the bed, I strip down to my shorts, grab my camp towel and long johns, and step down the dark hallway, following the dim, white glow of my headlamp. In the space beyond this wide circle of light, the hall is pitch-black.

I make my way forward until something suddenly slams into the side of my head. I nearly stumble backward. Pain pulses through the side of my skull. I push against the feeling with my hand as if to dam the floodgates of incoming sensations.

"Sorry!" she says in a British accent. "Are you okay? These stupid doors just fling right open. I didn't know anyone else was here! Did I get your face?"

I rub the lump on my head and stand up straight, slowly regaining my composure. A dull pain throbs through my brain.

"I'm fine, no worries," I say, trying to offer a smile.

Then I readjust my headlamp and look in the direction of her voice. My light merges with the light of another headlamp shining back at me, which sits atop the face of a

Chapter 31

brunette woman about my age. The pain in my head begins to recede.

She wears a tight thermal top that reveals the shape of her breasts, athletic shorts slipped over her black long johns, long wool socks riding up her calves, and a pair of worn-down hiking shoes. Her hair is wet as if from a recent shower. I stand in silence, not knowing what to say.

"I should have been more careful," she says. She dims her headlamp slightly and points it to the side so as not to shine it into my face. "Are you sure you're okay? Do you want me to take a quick look?"

"It's really no problem. I'll be fine, don't worry."

Then she looks down at me and giggles.

I follow her eyes, shining my headlamp across my half-naked body. I blush. "I was just looking for the umm—is the shower around here?"

"It's the last door on the right at the end of the hall."

"Thanks."

"Say, what's your name?"

"David." We shake hands. "And you?"

"Becky."

Her eyes are green, the same hue as Hannah's.

"Good to meet you, David. Enjoy your shower. Maybe I'll see you around later?"

"Yeah... I'll be here."

Becky smiles then disappears down the hall.

The bathroom is even darker than the hallway, but at least it's operational. I hang my headlamp and camp towel on the head of a nail, turn on the showerhead, and step beneath the cold water. As I scrub my body of dirt and sweat, I think about Becky. Finally, another English speaker on the trail, and a woman at that!

Before Sajana, I think the last English-speaking woman I spoke to was Nina from Hostel Yog or our book-reading hotelier in Kathmandu's tourist district. At least a month had

True Nature

passed since then, and I can't help but feel excited at the prospect of getting to know her.

I towel off, don my long johns, and walk down the hall. As I pass the other rooms, cold air seeps through the cracks of the unsealed doorways. I wonder which door is hers, but it's hard to tell. They're all closed shut.

Back in our room, Bradley's already gone.

"*Dal bhat* soon," Lama Dai had said.

I throw on shorts over my long johns, stuff my arms into my puffy jacket, slide my feet into wool socks and trail runners, then walk across the lawn toward the main lodge. There, Bradley and Lama Dai sit in candlelight around a large table, slowly shoveling handfuls of *dal bhat* into their mouths. I sit next to them and begin doing the same.

"Did you meet her?" Bradley asks.

I finish chewing while nodding. "Briefly."

"She sounded nice."

"Yeah."

"You should get to know her."

"The thought came to mind, but I don't want to force anything. If it happens, it happens, you know? Are you not interested?"

"Nah, that's all you. Too tired."

After a quiet *dal bhat* dinner, the three of us walk the lawn back to our living quarters, planning to go right to sleep. Then I see her sitting at the edge of the cliffside, staring out across the valley.

Bradley must notice me hesitate and stop in my tracks because he smiles and laughs. "Go for it, bro."

I roll my eyes. "I'll see you back in the room."

She seems to hear my footsteps in the grass as I approach and turns around.

"Mind if I join you? I ask.

"Not at all."

Chapter 31

I sit on the grass next to her, lean back against one of the boulders, and gaze out at the valley shrouded in the glow of a full moon. Crickets chirp, and bright speckles of stars scatter about the skies.

"What a view," she says, nodding toward the moonlit valley.

"Yeah, it is."

"How was your shower?"

"Freezing, but better than nothing."

"It had been a few days, huh?"

I blush. "You could tell?"

"Just a bit."

I scratch my head and feign a smile. "It seems like I brought everything but deodorant on this trek. I've been wanting to swim in the river, but our guide doesn't trust us."

Becky nods, leaning down toward the dark chasm. "He has his reasons."

"How so?"

"Not for distrusting you, specifically. About the river, I mean. Last year, an Israeli couple were swept away. A search party tried looking for them, but they never found the bodies. Happens every year."

I nod. I hadn't considered that before.

"Sorry to be so grim," she laughs. There's a moment of silence, making even more space for the symphony of cicadas, and then she asks, "How's your trek been?"

"We're still alive."

She laughs. "That's good."

"How about yours?"

"I'm not here for the trekking."

I tilt my head slightly. "No?"

"Nope. I live here."

"In this guesthouse?"

True Nature

"Not *here*, silly." She giggles. "My village is a few days away. I just like to get out sometimes. This spot's my absolute favorite."

"I can see why," I say, gazing out at the moon above.

"It's a bit off the beaten path and higher up than the other villages along this trail, but relatively easy to get to. It's one of my favorite views, especially at night. There's something special about the nighttime in these mountains. I just love the way the moon glistens off the snow on the distant peaks and illuminates the valley. It's especially pleasant because there's not many people around right now."

"Yeah… why is that?"

"You haven't heard?"

I shake my head. "I've been trying to figure that out."

"Everyone's out hunting *Yarsagumba* right now."

"*Yarsagumba*? Is that like… the Chupacabra?"

She giggles again. "They're mushrooms, dummy. *Cordyceps*. You know, the long brown things sticking up out of the ground? They're everywhere this time of year. You might see them in season along the trail if you haven't already, but they're mainly in the northern jungle hills and the alpine pastures. That's where the villagers are right now."

"Why? What's so special about *yarsagumba*?"

"For one, they're basically dead caterpillars."

My eyebrow raises. "What the heck? The mushrooms are dead caterpillars? Freaky."

Becky smiles. "If you think that's crazy, just wait until you hear how they're made."

"How's that?"

"Basically, mushrooms attack the larva of underground caterpillars, killing the insect, and filling their body cavity with mycelium. Before long, the mushroom grows out of their foreheads and pops up out of the ground."

"That's insane."

Chapter 31

"Yep. They come packaged in all sorts of trendy ways: teas, pills, powders—you name it, they make it. Thanks to the demand in Chinese and American markets, you wouldn't believe the price on these things. A single mushroom can go for upward of ten-thousand rupees these days. Most expensive insect-herb in the world."

"Pretty damn pricey."

She nods. "So you can imagine why the villagers take off to the hills for a while. If they find a good haul, they can rake in about a thousand dollars a week. Not bad, if you ask me. If I needed the money, I'd be searching jungle alpines, too."

"You don't need the money?" I ask.

She shakes her head. "You really don't need much to live out here."

"Yeah, you really don't," I say, again reminded of all the extra stuff I brought. "So you said you lived in a village around here?"

"For the last seven years."

"Woah." As someone who's only been trekking for a week with more than my fair share of complaining, I pause to think about the weight of living this life for so many years. After a few moments, I ask, "What brought you here?"

"It's kind of a long story."

"I've got time."

She laughs. "I guess I do too."

Then she shuffles to sit up and brushes the dirt and grass and dew off the back of her bright-red puffy jacket.

"I'm a linguist. I came here on project to preserve some of the smaller local dialects in this region. Languages tend to die off when no one uses them. Words disappear. It's my job to make sure we keep those words. Every little word gives us insight into the way we think about the world. Words connect us to the past, ground us in the present, and guide us into the future. They tie us together and connect us.

Words can bind us together and tear us apart. That's the power of language."

Her head tilts and she shrugs. "That's not to say some things can't be put into words, though. Like images and feelings and sounds for instance."

She smiles brightly and gazes into my eyes. "You can try your hardest to come up with just the right words to describe an experience—let's say, about what it's like to love another person. But no matter how precise your words, they fall short of the real thing. The actual experience becomes lost in translation. Words can point the way, but everyone has to discover for themselves what love means. Does that make sense? I know, I'm rambling. My work isn't the most interesting, but I find meaning it in."

"As you should! That sounds really fascinating."

She sighs and looks down across the valley. "It's been dreadful lately, though. This country really hasn't been the same ever since the earthquake."

I raise my eyebrow. "Earthquake?"

"No one's told you about that either?"

I shake my head.

She tilts hers and looks at me quizzically. "And you've been here for how long?"

"In Nepal? About a month."

She smiles, but the smile soon flattens.

"It all happened about four years ago," she says in a more serious tone. "Maybe you heard about it on the news back then. Maybe it got lost in memory—an inevitable biproduct of the twenty-four-hour news cycle. Scientists measured the earthquake's magnitude at an 8.1, devastating much of the country, especially the communities near its epicenter. Kathmandu and many surrounding cities got hit hard. You've seen it in the city, haven't you? Everything under construction, buildings cracked and broken, half-erected.

Chapter 31

"Some of that construction is business as usual—simple improvements and renovations generated by the tourism sector—but much of it is rebuilding what used to be. Things still aren't back to where they were. They may never be the same. The cities were hit bad, but out here in the mountains and villages, they saw the worst of it."

Now that she mentions it, I'd been wondering about the construction in the city and why everything looks like it's crumbling and falling apart. "That sounds terrible. Were you here when it happened?"

"I was mid-flight to the UK to visit my family for the first time in years when the first earthquake hit. I remember walking through the airport when the first news reports started coming through. I booked my return flight to Kathmandu for the very next day."

"You went back?"

"As soon as I could. People were in trouble—people I knew." I notice a tear run down her cheek. She wipes it away with the sleeve of her puffy jacket and blinks.

"We don't have to talk about this if you don't want to," I say.

She sniffs. "No, it's okay. It's good for me to talk about it." And so she continues, but her voices still trembles: "When I finally got back, I couldn't believe it. The city was hit hard, and the village… so much was destroyed. Homes, infrastructure, roadways. Thousands of people died. Men, women, children, buried beneath the rubble from landslides and fallen buildings. Some, I knew. A few of these villages were wiped clean off the map. It was just… awful."

She buries her head into her hands and tears run down her cheeks. Unsure of what to do or say, I wait as she wipes her face dry and finishing sniffling.

"I'm sorry," I say.

"Thanks. It's been years since it happened. I thought I was over it, but I guess some things stay with you for a while. It was just so horrible. I'm still processing. I really didn't know what to make of it at first. I lost a lot of hope that day. When we least expect it, nature can take back everything in a heartbeat. Sometimes I think it's helping us. Sometimes I think it's against us. And other times I'm not sure it even cares."

I nod. "I wish I knew."

She pulls at one of her ears and looks at me. "Isn't that strange, though? The day I leave, the only day I've left in the last seven years, was the very same day the earthquake came? I mean, what's that supposed to mean?"

I shrug. "I'm not sure. But maybe if it didn't happen, you'd never have flown back."

"Yeah, maybe you're right. And when I came back, there was hardly time to grieve, because that's when the second earthquake hit. This one was 7.2 in magnitude, they said. It wasn't as strong as the first, but it was the most unbelievable thing I've ever experienced in my life. The earth was literally in waves. I saw a tractor lift off the ground like a ball thrown from a trampoline. Thankfully, it didn't last long. The worst of the damage had already been done."

I nod, no words coming to mind.

"Like I said, I stayed to help. We slept in tents for months and rebuilt from the ground up. We didn't have much, but when you go through something like that—death and destruction and pain and suffering—you start to notice what's important. You start to pay attention. You become resilient. At least the people living here, that is. Most of the people I know back home in the UK, they'd leave after something like that. Fly out of the country. Hire someone else to rebuild. Wait until the hard work's done. Come back once things get comfy again.

"Not these people. They stick around. They adapt and make the best of things. They grieve, but they don't complain. I guess I've learned to see the whole thing as a blessing. Everyone came together. Rich and poor from cities and villages. But I've gone on for long enough, excuse me."

"No, don't apologize. Thank you for sharing with me."

Chapter 31

"Thanks for listening. I guess it's been a while since I've spoken fluent English to someone."

"Me too."

For a time, instead of speaking, we listen to the loud clicking of cicada wings mixing with the whistling wind, a wind which courses through the valley, rushes through the bows of the jungle trees, and carries with it a deep sense of serenity. The faint sound of the river raging far below rises to meet my ears. A dusty moonlight envelopes us all.

"Why are you hiking the trail?" she asks after a long silence.

I shrug. "We got a good deal."

She laughs. "You must be crazier than I thought. Hardly any tourists trek during monsoon season."

"I heard that, but we haven't seen any rain yet."

"Yeah, something feels different this year. Weather hasn't been acting quite right. It very well could be all that pollution going on in the city, but who knows. The monsoons come every year. You can guarantee that."

If that's the case, I hope they can wait. Given how crazy the rains were in Pokhara and Kathmandu, I can only imagine how bad they get up here.

"Well, not much we can do about it now."

"Nope," she replies. "You're stuck here now. It's just that usually the tourists come in the winter. They prefer the scenery they see on postcards—that magical layer of snow blanketing the rooftops of the guesthouses. Snowflakes wisping through the air. A soft crunch beneath their feet while mushing up the trail. It really gives them that 'Himalayan experience' they're imagining. Makes for some flashy social media photos, too."

She giggles, a noticeable levity arising in her smile once again. "I'm not saying the snow isn't beautiful. It really transforms the place. But if you've lived here long enough, you realize snow isn't what makes the Himalayas special. The snow falls, things get cold, and then it melts. It's just another part of the larger process at work, no more magical than the sun or the rain.

"Each has its own beauty, I suppose. But most people like the winter snow up here. That, combined with the current monsoon season, is why I find it interesting you've come here during this time."

I shrug. *Sometimes I wonder why I've come here, too.* "We didn't really come for the beauty."

"Then what did you come for?"

"I used to think I was looking for something specific, but now I'm not so sure anymore. Maybe I've been missing the point."

"If you haven't noticed *this* yet," she waves her hand across the valley, "then you really are missing out. This place grows more and more beautiful the higher you climb."

The cicadas roar into an overwhelming crescendo. Then another burst of cold wind sweeps over the cliff. I dig my fingertips into the grass and dirt as it sweeps downriver into the canyon, settling the insect's song.

"Whatever you're looking for," Becky continues. "I'm sure you'll find out soon enough. Just like the *yarsagumba*, if you look hard enough for something, you start to notice things you didn't before. Maybe you won't find any *yarsagumba*, but you'll notice the rich smell of the dirt, the flowers. Anyway, I'm hiking back to the city tomorrow just to be safe. You're going to keep heading up the trail?"

"Yep," I say.

"How much longer are you hiking for?"

"We have at least a couple more weeks left."

Becky bites her lower lip. "I haven't seen a weather report, but you're cutting it close. Either way, it seems you have a good group with you. Just be safe. And get some rest."

"Thanks, I'll need it. My legs are killing me. Must be getting old."

Chapter 31

"Shut up," she says. "You're not *that* old. How old are you, anyways?"

I think on it for a moment. "Twenty-nine." I say it with the surprised realization that I've forgotten my own birthday. "As of today, actually."

"What? Today's your birthday?"

"I guess it slipped my mind until now. We've been so busy. And my head's been elsewhere. Maybe the *yarsagumba* got to me, gonna pop out my forehead any day now."

"You're silly," she says, laughing. "Oh, that reminds me. Here, follow me."

As Becky stands from the cliff's edge, I follow her up the lawn and into the lodge.

CHAPTER 32
SKY MONASTERY

Becky flicks on her headlamp, stands on her tiptoes, and pulls down one of the jars on the shelf.

"Here, take two. They always keep extras for the guests."

"Thanks," I say, stuffing two pieces of Nepali chocolate into my pocket.

"Don't mention it."

"Is this another reason why you like to come here?" I ask while holding up one of the chocolates.

She smiles and pops one into her mouth. "Mhm." She moves the candy to the side of her mouth and glances out the door into the night. "It's getting late. I should probably get some sleep."

"Yeah, same."

"Wanna walk back?"

"Sure."

We flick on our headlamps and make our way across the lawn and into the lodge. I hang a right, and Becky turns left.

"It was great talking to you, David," she whispers.

"You too, Becky. It was a pleasure."

We hug, and she turns around.

"See you in the morning?" she asks.

"Yep. I'll be here."

Chapter 32

She smiles, then heads down the hallway and disappears into the darkness.

When I crawl into bed, I think of Becky. She has her reasons for being here, but what about me? I thought I was searching for enlightenment, but now, I'm not sure.

Before I shut my eyes, I flip on the faint red light of my headlamp, reach into my pocket, and unwrap one of the small golden packages.

* * *

I wake the next morning to rain slamming against the bedroom window. As I open the shutters, the sun is nowhere to be seen. My heart stops. *Oh, no. Is this...?*

There's a knock at the door and Lama Dai appears at the doorway.

"Lama Dai, monsoon?" I ask.

The lama sits at the edge my bed and shakes his head. "Little rain."

"Little?" Bradley asks, his face scrunched into a scowl. "It's storming like crazy out there, Dai."

"Breakfast soon." Lama Dai smiles. "Tibetan bread."

"You really think we're hiking out today, Dai?" I ask.

The lama closes his eyes. I get the sense that he's sensing something, tuning in, and stretching his perception across the valley. "One hour."

"One hour until we hike?" Bradley asks.

Lama Dai nods, lifts himself up, and disappears through the doorway.

"I guess that settles it," Bradley says.

As Bradley slips on his trail runners and grabs his backpack, I sigh. Please, keep raining. If the rain continues, we can stay here. I can rest my legs. I can lay in bed, unmoved for the rest of the day.

Busy with my desperate requests to the rain gods, I'm unbothered to meditate. Come to think of it, I haven't fulfilled my second hour of prescribed meditation for days. I've been too tired at night to give that extra effort. I'd come all this way, kept my practice for years, and now all of a sudden, I'd stopped cold turkey.

Remembering Lama Dai's call to eat breakfast, I reluctantly pack up my things, put on my rain jacket, and sprint into the downpour. Raindrops throttle my jacket as I cross the lawn, and my shoes splash on the soaked ground, all the way up to the front steps of the guesthouse porch.

Inside, Bradley and Lama Dai sit in the darkness of the main cabin. Warm slabs of Tibetan bread sit steaming on the plates before them.

I settle down, chew my bread, and gaze through the open doorway at the rain. A thick mass of clouds blankets the skies, hardly offering any morning light at all.

No shot this rain ends in an hour. This is the kind of rain goes on for days.

As my Tibetan bread gets nibbled away, the dark clouds outside the doorway disperse, and the sun illuminates the mountains. Lama Dai stands. He grabs his backpack and his bamboo staff from the doorway, and he heads out to the trail.

I check my watch. One hour on the dot. I guess Ganesh was right. Lama Dai does know the mountains. Much better than I do.

As I strap on my backpack, I consider checking the guesthouse one last time to say goodbye to Becky but think better of it. If she's here, she knows we're leaving. And if she's gone, she left without saying goodbye.

I step outside and follow Bradley and Lama Dai up the muddy trail beneath the sunshine. Some people enter our lives just as quickly as they leave. But that doesn't make them any less special.

Chapter 32

* * *

Three more days of trekking remain between us and *Mu Gumba*, the Sky Monastery. Days that proceed in very much the same manner. The morning rain falls, mud sticks to the bottoms of my shoes, and never has the earth beneath my feet risen so close to the sun.

Our climbs above the jungle leave us exposed to the sun without any shade, and the tops of my hands and arms and the backs of my calves develop a torturous burn. I'd expected cold temperatures at higher elevations, but the ice and snow must be an even higher climb.

Of course, I didn't pack sunscreen. My attitude toward sunscreen was about the same as deodorant. Most products were packed with toxic chemicals. Plus, I went without it for six months on the PCT, so three weeks in the Himalayas wouldn't kill me. Aloe vera would be nice, though. That's for sure. Or if you could convince me of a non-toxic brand, I might reconsider. Until then, I have to be resourceful.

I throw off my backpack and opt for a long-sleeve pullover and rain pants. The added clothes help keep the sun off, but different problems arise. The clothes are like an oven, and I sweat profusely and bake in my long sleeves. To make matters worse, the moisture causes my baggy pant legs to rub together with every step, producing a horribly annoying swishing sound. Thankfully, whenever the terrain levels off and the path cuts through a wide-open plain, the occasional breeze blows through the fields of the valley, reminding me that everything's impermanent.

When dusk spreads through the mountains, the day's hiking is done. Lama Dai flicks on his headlamp and leads us door-to-door of the village homes in search of shelter. We try knocking and continue with no responses.

As we trot through the dark and empty valley, we pass beside stone walls and crop fields spanning the distance. A cold wind blows through the fields, cicadas stir, and my stomach growls. It isn't until we spot a small lantern in the distance that we find a place to stay.

* * *

The next morning after our meditation, Bradley and I wake and head to the guesthouse kitchen for breakfast. There, the smell of warm sugar bread wafts through the room. A piece of dough pops and sizzles in a frying pan. Lama Dai stands over a counter flattening dough with a rolling pin. Fewer and fewer villagers and guesthouse owners means Lama Dai cooks our meals now. We eat Tibetan bread, then Lama Dai hands us each another piece to-go.

"No village for stopping today," he says. *"Mu Gumba."*

Finally, today's the day. I slide the bread into my food-sealed bag, tuck it into the mesh of my backpack, and pass through the doorway into the dawn.

It's a cloudless day as we take the arrow-straight dirt path from the village. Judging by the rush of cool wind blowing through the paddy fields, I can already tell we're higher in elevation than the days before. I walk one foot in front of the other between Bradley and Lama Dai, trudging into the remote wilderness between towering Himalayan mountains.

We come to a fork in the road beside a pile of rocks and walk to the right of them. Lama Dai whistles loudly and gestures for us to come back and walk around the left side.

"Why the left side, Dai?" I ask.

Lama Dai points at the stones.

I bend down, noticing markings and symbols etched into the rocks.

"Om Mani Padme Hum," he says.

I run my thumb across the smooth indentions. It's a familiar phrase, indeed, and things start to make sense. It's not just a pile of rocks. They're symbolic, treated exactly like the

Chapter 32

stupas and shrines in the city roads—you always go left, a sign of honor and respect to the symbolic nature of Buddha.

It's clear we're approaching somewhere deemed especially sacred by the locals, because these rock piles keep popping up every couple miles. We also pass ornate stupas, shrines, and massive doorways, the insides of which contain colorfully-painted depictions of Tibetan lore related to the Buddha. It's remarkable artwork, signs that remind me of my own aspirations, and of how each stride is one step closer to *Mu Gumba*. Lama Dai was right—this section of the trail is different, changing. Despite the pain of walking, I notice a smile stretching itself across my face.

Sanskrit etched into the stone shrines along the path

Around noon, the path dips down gradually to meet a calm glacial river. Bradley unbuckles his pack and strips down to his shorts. I look behind me across the plains, but Lama Dai's gone from sight. He must have stopped to take a leak.

Before Lama Dai can tell us otherwise, I throw off my pack, shoes, and shirt, and jump in. The water is freezing, and

I re-emerge with a loud gasp. I quickly swim out and stretch in the sunlit grass. I set my gaze upon the clouds and think about nothing for some time while my body pulses and trembles from the cold. It's the most relaxed I've felt in ages.

When Lama Dai appears over the hill, Bradley and I get dressed and wash our socks in the river before strapping them—soaking wet—to the top of our packs. No amount of squeezing fully rids them of dirt, but knowing they'll feel soft and new when dry is worth forgoing them for the time being. We fit our bare feet into our shoes and begin the march forward again, fueled by bites of leftover Tibetan bread.

Finally, a chance to bathe in a Himalayan river

The trail shoots up from plains to jungle then again rises into the mountains. As the afternoon passes, a herd of yak lift their heads then trample away up into the mountains. A troop of monkeys sit idly in the grass, picking at the dirt. Distant waterfalls descend from cliffs so high up that the water has

Chapter 32

nowhere to land, so it disappears into a mist. It's magical, but I'm focused on what lies ahead.

Even as the daylight fades away behind the mountains and the first shades of darkness descend upon the valley, I can still see through the blue veil and make out a temple perched high atop the distant foothills surrounded by clouds.

Lama Dai whistles from behind and points to the walled fortress. That must be it.

Mu Gumba. Sky Monastery.

Lama Dai takes the lead and forges an uphill route. Our steps crunch the overgrown shrubs and bushes scattered about the ground. A biting wind whips across my face, an air colder than any I've experienced thus far.

I balance my pack against a boulder, pull out my beanie and down jacket, and notice my wet socks are already frozen stiff. I exhale and glance ahead into the clouds while fitting into my cold weather clothes. Then I toss my pack over my shoulder and continue upward behind the others.

Heading off-trail and into the clouds

Where the hill meets the mountain, the shrubs surrender to a stone stairway carved into the mountainside. I grasp my trekking poles in one hand, press my other palm against the rock wall, and ascend into the narrow corridor.

The steps beneath our feet unfold higher into the sky, carrying us into an ever-thickening cloudy mist. I breathe heavily and try to lighten my footsteps by pressing my weight against the tops of my knees. Occasionally, I reach out to run my fingertips along the cool and jagged surface of the walls beside me.

Just as the sun sinks into the sky and a sliver of moon appears overhead in the last remaining daylight, we arrive at an ominous red door held by slabs of rock on all sides. In a surreal way, it seems to float in the sky.

Lama Dai pounds five forceful knocks into the red door. Each blow erupts through the sky, tears into the clouds, and reverberates down the stairway. A flock of wild dove roosted above the doorway flap and fly away.

With my backpack still strapped to my back, I lean against the wall beside me and stare at the rows of Tibetan prayer flags soaring in the wind, trying to touch the setting sun.

The door opens inward and reveals an old man with a round belly who greets us with a gentle nod. His long gray beard dips and rises with the bow of his head, and it flaps and flits over his round belly and priestly robes.

His robes are the same maroon as Lama Dai's vest, and they contrast brilliantly against the green-beaded necklace dangling over his chest. My necklace matches his exactly.

When we pass through the stone entry, he closes the door behind us and slowly turns up the stairway. We take this as an invitation to follow.

Chapter 32

One of the iconic red doors of Mu Gumba

Beneath the last of the day's light, we follow the round-bellied man as his robes drift over the remaining cobblestone steps. We pass through a wide courtyard circled by ancient rock huts. In the distance, more stairways lead to homes, which crawl up the mountainside. At the far end of the courtyard, a large prominent temple watches over the misty village.

We stare in awe at the complex as a cold wind swirls around us. Leaves blow across the plaza. Serenity fills the air, reminiscent of Ulleri village. I'm amazed anyone lives this high up in the mountains, so far away from society, so dedicated to a spiritual path.

This is the place I've been looking for. This is where one achieves enlightenment.

As I soak in the atmosphere, two figures appear in the distance: A robed lama and a little girl with long brown hair carefully descend the temple's front steps. With one hand, the little girl holds the lama's hand; under her other arm, she carries a small stuffed animal. When they get closer, I can make out it's a stuffed monkey.

When the little girl gets near enough to see us, she clings to the leg of the old man and clutches her monkey tightly. The old man then smiles warmly, takes the hand of the young girl, and bows to us. We return the gesture. After a small conversation between the robed lama and Lama Dai, the robed lama turns around, and we follow him toward the temple.

The temple is large and set against the mountain. Lama Dai places his backpack beside the wide double doors at the front of the temple, slips off his sandals, and disappears inside. We follow suit, slowly shuffling out of the cold.

The hall is dark and silent. Flickering candlelight at the far ends of the room illuminates golden shrines and colorfully painted walls. The air coming into my nostrils is cool and thin. The round-bellied lama gestures to the three cushions at the back of the hall, perfectly positioned in the center of the room.

Our steps creak against the wooden floorboards as we make our way forward. When I settle down onto my cushion, butterflies rush into my stomach. This place is enchanting. *A place worthy of pursuit.*

Then a loud bell clangs throughout the village. The sound rushes into the hall and resonates for some time. When it finally dies out, two doors at the back of the temple creak open. More robed lamas proceed into the temple. Their figures float through the distant passageways, their coverings drift across the wooden floor. The candlelight casts their long and thin shadows upon the decorative walls. I count six in total. One by one, they sit on pews and face each other in rows lining the center aisle. The lamas clear their throats and open the books on the podiums before them. I close my eyes, and it begins.

The chant from the first monk is deep and grumbling:

"*Om Mani Padme Om. Om Mani Padme Om.*"

Another raspy voice joins him in canon:

Chapter 32

"Om Mani Padme Om."

Then another, and another, and another—until all six voices swirl throughout the hall.

As I try to meditate, I notice that each lama sounds different. Each has their own unique tone. A certain vibrato. A specific quality. And each plays their own part in the chanting. No lama tries to be like another, and each projects his own voice without any worry of the others. They work together, and the result is musical.

It makes me think about how I'd been so wrapped up in Bradley's way of chanting, but these lamas could care less about correcting each other. Why can't I be more like them? Someone who focuses on myself and plays my own part. One voice among many contributing to the same goal…

Just as my mind begins to slip away and sink into the sounds, the chanting stops. I hear fumbling, but I keep my eyes shut so as not to disturb my deepening meditation.

From the silence erupts the sounds of drums beating, horns blasting, and symbols crashing. The noises shake up my mind, drown out my thoughts, and pull me in deeper. The vibrations feel as if they're massaging my insides. And no longer does my mind try to make sense of anything. There are no puzzle pieces to assemble. I offer no resistance to the discomfort. No grasping for pleasure. Instead, I allow everything to remain exactly as it is. Loud, annoying, clashing. And in turn, there's peace. A quiet in the chaos.

I surrender to the sounds and lose track of time. In this timeless space between thought, the questions no longer demand answers. *This space is where it resides. The space that allows all sensation. A choiceless awareness no matter what phenomena arises. The space where the witness itself falls away and merges with all things.*

Suddenly, the music stops. The books slam shut. The lamas shuffle out of the temple. Bradley and Lama Dai stand and walk outside.

True Nature

As a serene quiet returns to the temple, I remain seated. Deep down, I know this isn't enlightenment. This, indeed, is something. But this isn't it.

I feel shaken up. I stumble out of the hall, dizzy and confused.

CHAPTER 33
THE FALL

When I wake up in the morning, I find myself curled inside my sleeping bag atop a stiff mattress in a dark, stone-walled room. Bradley's already sitting up and meditating in the bed across the room.

What happened last night?

I'm unable to recall specifics. Vague scenes flash before my eyes: a *dal bhat* dinner in a dimly lit kitchen. A stone stairway leading into the foothills. Cliffside structures made of rock. Crawling into this sleeping bag.

I must have been exhausted after last night's events, or my mind must have blocked out the remaining details—a desperate attempt to forget my disappointment. To erase this temple in the sky from my memory. The spot where everything was supposed to click and didn't.

I sit up to meditate but can't focus. Images from the night prior flicker before my mind, interspersed with scenes from the days before it. Everything's turning into a blur on this trip.

Instead of sticking out the meditation, I lay back down and wait for Bradley's meditation to end. Then I pack up and depart through the doorway behind him.

It's a misty morning in the foothills of *Mu Gumba*. A thick fog surrounds the edges of the village, obscuring my vision. I head down the stone stairway into the foggy village.

Yes, last night's coming back to me now. This was the path I walked. I remember this dining hall, too. The stone floor, the wooden table, the large cookpots of rice and *dal* now traded for the scent of sugar bread.

Lama Dai, Bradley, and I eat our Tibetan bread in the kitchen and carry on. Fully disheartened by last night's *Mu Gumba* experience, I slump down the mountain. The trail returns us to the fields, to the jungle, and eventually, to the Manaslu Trail. Our final days push toward Larke Pass.

For years, I'd thought the enlightened ones escaped society and lived in faraway mountains and caves. But now I'd met those people—the villagers, the lamas in the mountains. They were different, but still human. Just like Lama Dai. Just like Sajana. They seemed content, but that had nothing to do their environment. It was the state of mind they cultivated within themselves.

Leaving the walls of Mu Gumba, Sky Monastery

Did I delude myself into believing I'd uncover something special, spectacular, and life-changing on this hike?

Chapter 33

Maybe—but that's no way to think. Not right now. Not when I still have two weeks left and Larke Pass remains. It's the highest point on the trail, so it has to happen then and there, or it won't happen at all.

* * *

The days in the Himalayas zip past one after the next like motorbikes through the city roads. The sun rises, travels its prescribed path across the sky, then sets. We trek through ever-changing vistas and awe-inspiring landscapes, steep ascents and descents of valleys, long stretches of green bluffs and pristine pastures, dense jungle canopies and spacious mountains.

Relief visits me when stumbling across a cold spring or an empty guesthouse in an empty village, which are fewer and farther between with hardly any people. By the time the trees and mountains cast their longest shadows across the valley, we've hiked fifteen to twenty miles—miles filled with pain and frustration, but also purpose and progress.

This trail seems like a well-kept secret, my chance for solitude. With my sights set on Larke Pass, I keep silent and either hike slowly behind or far ahead of the group, stretching the boundaries of Lama Dai's comfort and guidance. At times, it feels like pouting, but this is what I need to process, think, and be. It allows me space, more than enough space to think deeply, look inwardly, and become lost in the fantasies of my mind.

I daydream about friends, soulmates, air conditioning, Wi-Fi, writing, and enlightenment. With so many potential reasons for my unhappiness, I sit atop a rock and take inventory of what's been floating around in my head.

For two weeks, we've been at this trail without a day of rest. It's been four years since I've hiked so consistently and for this many miles, and I'm worn to the bone. The body adapts, but the adaptations I built from the trail took months.

That same endurance and strength won't reconstitute during this three-week stint.

Not only is my body exhausted, but my mind wears thin, too. I haven't meditated in days, being too tired to sit at the end of such a long day. *How did I expect to reach enlightenment without a practice? How have I led myself so far off-course?*

While thoughts of enlightenment and relationships consume my mind, towering mountains and ominous glacial lakes surround me at every turn. Beauty that goes mostly unseen.

Trekking higher

Chapter 33

Empty villages

Incredible views

True Nature

With only three days left and sixty miles of trekking remaining on the hike, Lama Dai says we will soon reach Larke Pass at over 15,000 feet in elevation. That moment nears as we trek toward the sun at a snail's pace.

The atmospheric pressure forces shallow breathing, and fatigue spreads through my body. My breaths send puffs of smoke into the air. I look around at the snowcapped mountains. We must be close.

Just as I can sense us approaching our final goal, a raging headache consumes my brain. It's crushing—the worst I've ever experienced. I narrow my field of vision to three steps in front of me onto the rocky trail and breathe to the rhythm of my steps.

Every so often, I glance up to orient myself to the world, trying to focus my attention on anything but the pain inside me. Thankfully, the affliction passes a few miles later.

High mountain outposts

Chapter 33

Darkness covers the snow-patched earth as we reach an outpost high in the mountains. The shelters scattered about the plateau have bolted doors and no windows, necessary precautions to stave off the freezing wind and snow at this altitude.

Bradley and I set down our belongings for the night. My head throbs, fatigue sets in, and nausea twists me into submission. The combined effort slowly strikes me down. I throw my sleeping bag atop the plywood bed, curl up, and bury my head in my hands.

What have I done to deserve this? Why now? I endured high altitudes numerous times on the trail, so why would this altitude be any different?

When the steel door to our shanty opens, a cold gust of wind sweeps through the room. Lama Dai sits at the foot of my bed.

"Sick?"

"Fine. Everything's fine. I'm good."

He places the back of his hand against my forehead and shakes his head.

"*Beesonay*," he says, then walks out into the cold and closes me inside.

Rest. If only that was possible for me right now...

An eternity passes, my stomach churns, and I shiver inside my mummy sleeping bag. Time thickens and every moment stretches on.

The next time the door opens, Lama Dai says *dal bhat* is ready. I push myself out of bed, lace up my trail runners, and follow Lama Dai and Bradley through biting winds and patches of snow to a distant outpost. Bradley glances up from his plate of *dal bhat* and nods.

I sit before mine, but I couldn't be less enthused. My appetite is non-existent. I try one bite and feel my stomach churn. So I fold my arms against the table and rest my head.

"*Beesonay*," I say to Bradley and Lama Dai, then I stumble out of the kitchen. Instead of returning to the shelter, I trudge through the snow to a distant outhouse. The moment I step inside, I purge.

After everything leaves me, I stagger to our bedroom outpost and huddle inside my sleeping bag. I shiver and sweat as my world twists out of control. My body is both feverish and freezing cold. I press the bottoms of my palms against my closed eyes, but nothing helps. I try bringing attention to my breath, but nothing changes. I lean into the pain, but the pain only intensifies.

Suddenly, the door opens again. A cold floods the room like opening a freezer door. Lama Dai sits at the edge of my bed and hands me a pill bottle. I turn on my headlamp.

"Zolamide," reads the label. "Used to treat altitude sickness."

While I typically refrain from medication, instead wanting my body to face the pain, I'm desperate to feel better. I take two pills, swallow them down, then hand back the bottle.

As the door shuts, everything fades into darkness. Shadows and shapes dance in the nothingness behind my eyelids, capturing me in this inescapable moment. I keep my breath going, trying to hold on. Never have I felt so close to our destination and yet so far from enlightenment.

David… drink, eat, rest. You are weak. Things may not end up as you wanted them.

I know, but how do I get better?

Balance.

I wrap my arms around my chest and squeeze. My quickening heartrate and breath soften for a noticeable moment.

I don't know how much time passes until the steel door opens once again to the cold world outside, but this time, Bradley enters and crawls into bed. Lama Dai instructs me to sit up and hands me a warm bowl.

Chapter 33

I force myself to sit up and take a whiff. Ginger garlic soup. I take one spoonful. It's easier on my stomach compared to the *dal bhat*, but I still can't stomach anything more than a couple measly bites.

"If sickness stays, we go back," Lama Dai says. "Stay at lower village."

"No, I'll get better soon," I insist. "We keep going."

Lama Dai looks at me longingly and sighs. "*Beesonay.*"

Then he opens and closes the silver rectangle at the other end of the room.

I set the bowl on the floorboards and close my eyes.

"Are you going to eat that?" Bradley asks.

Bradley. When was the last time I'd heard from him? I know the smell bothers him, but he'll have to wait it out. It's nothing compared to the smell of sage smoke.

"Yeah, just leave it. I'll finish it when I wake up."

Bradley sighs. "We have an early morning tomorrow. The final ascent. Lama Dai said the winds over the pass are brutal past ten o'clock. We have to get up early and push."

"Yeah," I grunt. "I'll be ready."

Then I shut my eyes and pray. *Please, get better. We can't backtrack now, not after we've come this far, not because of me.*

The plea feels unfamiliar… I can't remember the last time I prayed.

* * *

I wake to a completely dark outpost bedroom in what must be the middle of the night because Bradley's fast asleep. Famished, I reach for my headlamp, adjust the warm, red light to its lowest setting, and find my soup on the floorboards.

One bite at a time, I spoon-feed myself the cold soup in the dim red light, letting each bite rest in my stomach before

True Nature

introducing the next. Like this, I'm able to devour the rest of the soup. Then I set the bowl back onto the floor, lay back into bed, curl up, and close my eyes again.

I must have managed some sleep because my eyes flicker open to a cold, crisp wind swirling into the room from the open door. The sunrise must not have come yet because the room stays completely dark.

Lama Dai presses his hand against my forehead. "Sick?"

I take note of my condition.

"No sickness," I say, genuinely surprised. My headache has almost entirely dulled along with my nausea. I'm not completely unconcerned, but there's enough in me to make the final climb. "Better. Ready to trek."

Lama Dai peers at me for a long while. Finally, he nods and hands me a piece of Tibetan bread. I take my first bite while packing up, then discretely stuff the remainder into my empty food bag at the top of my backpack.

Bradley rises from bed, and we layer ourselves with all the clothes we can fit onto our bodies in preparation for the ascent: gloves, beanies, down jackets, rain pants, wool socks, and trail runners. It's almost our entire clothes bags. Finally, I'm getting some use out of this weight. Then we shoulder our backpacks and step outside into the dark morning fog.

An unsettling chill surrounds the outpost grounds. The altitude is thick and palpable, and I can hardly see the peaks hidden behind the clouds. With one last turn, I look back at the silver door. Then the three of us set up the rocky trail higher into the mountains, leaving the snowy outposts behind in the fog.

Slowly and steadily, I push forward behind Bradley and Lama Dai, taking cautious steps atop a rocky path. And then it happens. My sickness returns to me like a poison spreading through my body. Shortness of breath, headache, weakness, fatigue—everything rushes back to me all at once.

Chapter 33

Lama Dai trekking into the clouds

I stop mid-climb and steadily suck in air, conscious of the stories told to me about careless hikers vomiting blood and ending up in the hospital from ascending too quickly.

That won't be me, I tell myself. *I won't let that happen. I know what my body needs. I know when to turn back. Just slow down, you can make it.*

We hike through the early morning, each summit leading to another plateau. Glacial mountains surround us on all sides and patches of snow line the trail. Down below, glacial streams and lakes sprawl across the valley.

When I catch up to the group at the next lake, I lay down to rest and close my eyes.

Lama Dai springs to his feet and shakes my shoulder. "No sleep on mountain."

I sit up as Lama Dai gazes intensely into my eyes. "Sick?"

I shake my aching head, rise to my feet, and usher him in front of me. "No, all good. Ready to hike."

He peers at me suspiciously, then he turns around and continues up the trail. Bradley follows close behind him.

As we walk, my pace slows and my headache pulses and pounds against my skull. An invisible force tries pulling me beneath the earth. I lean against my trekking poles with all my weight, trying to stay standing and make ground.

Nevertheless, I fall farther behind Bradley and Lama Dai, losing their shadowy silhouettes to the thickening fog. Thankfully, the path has trail markers—little poles marked with yellow tape sticking up from the ground every fifty yards. They're here for a reason, omens to follow.

I nearly laugh at myself for starting to sound like Bradley, but I can't because of the fatigue. *Just follow the poles to keep up. They're your last hope. Everything will be fine.*

Suddenly, a sea of dark clouds crawls across the sky and a shower of snowflakes drifts down around me. The snow is beautiful, shimmering like diamonds, dancing slowly and magically to the ground, splashing my face like cold kisses. The flakes are so large and fall so slowly that I can almost see their complex crystalline geometry before they hit the ground. Still, I'm unable to enjoy anything given my worsening condition.

Then the flurry picks up. Snowflakes spin and twist all around me, blanketing the ground in powder. The inches pile up, faster and faster. A snowy curtain stands before me in every direction.

I look up. *Where did the trail markers go?*

My heart pounds as I turn in circles, realizing I'm unable to see into the distance. I've lost the trail entirely.

"Dai!" I yell into the snowfall. "Bradley!"

I try again, straining my ears and waiting. Still nothing.

I've been avoiding their voices for so long, craving isolation.

Chapter 33

But now I'd give anything to hear them.

If only I could hear one more time the voice of the man screaming from his Pokhara rooftop, the middle-aged woman yelling from her balcony, the racket of the Ulleri village band.

With the storm worsening, there's no time to waste. I have to keep going.

I slog with heavy legs across the snowy rocks, dragging my feet through the powder. I stumble forward aimlessly between the shadowy mountain ranges that I can make out through the flurry. My consciousness starts to waver and fade, my vision blurs, and my backpack feels heavier than ever before.

Maybe this is it. How it all ends. No enlightenment, no soulmate. They were all distant mirages. Lofty dreams and hollow shells. Doors leading to dark hallways and empty, lifeless rooms.

But none of those things matter anymore. Right now, I just want to feel like myself again. I want everything I used to have. I want to keep on living.

As I stumble forward, the icy touch of a necklace presses against my chest. The mala beads. I clutch the necklace. *Where did I go wrong?* All I could think about at Sajana's house was trekking the Himalayas. And yet here I am, wishing to be back at the house again.

Had my life always been like this? Dream after dream fulfilled in unseen ways but always wanting more? A deep sadness rises from my chest, knowing how little I appreciated my life.

Just as I'm about to fall to my knees, as the air in my lungs begins to dwindle, the winds die down long enough to glimpse what looks like a distant cave carved into the mountainside.

My heart skips a beat, and a surge of energy returns to me.

True Nature

I drag my feet through the snow and stagger toward the hollow, my breath quickening. Even though it's in my sights, it feels miles away. The snowstorm gathers speed and swirls around me. With every step, I remember Goma following the kettle's whistle into the kitchen. Sahor lumbering to his food bowl. Tim strolling through the city streets. Sajana seeing Buddhas and light everywhere. Lama Dai trudging up the mountainside in his flip flops. Nowhere to be anytime fast.

As pain fills my head and my heartbeat slows, I stumble inside the cave and collapse against the wall.

CHAPTER 34
THE CAVE

It's dark. A pitch-black of a kind I've never experienced. The air is so cold and so thin.

And I'm alone. Finally, alone.

Am I dead?

Not yet. That much is clear. I'm trapped. Suspended. Waiting for the floor the give way. Sinking down into an endless depth. Caught between two worlds. A waiting room to a place I can't yet comprehend. And in the frigid silence, I shiver.

For so long, I thought there was something missing. I tried to get somewhere and obtain something. I thought that truth had to be profound and complex. Something bright and shiny and new to be sought after and found. I'd gone on a search for that special moment where everything clicked and fell perfectly into place.

I sense the cold creeping up my fingertips, seeping into my shoes, grasping my toes.

I called that moment enlightenment. I'd invented a story about what it looks like and how it feels to attain it. It was a brilliant state of perfection. A state where the voice inside me no longer spoke so loudly. Where the witness of this voice no longer judged and reacted. Where I forever rid myself of faults and flaws, able to meet the demands of every moment with complete and utter awareness and equanimity, transcendent to suffering because my experience was finally free of it. I dreamt of an idealized version of myself necessary for my contentment.

The cold travels up my legs and through my arms. My bones are turning to icicles. My face is numb.

I tried to arrive at a destination. I tried meditation techniques. I tried changing my environment. I tried swapping material desires for immaterial ones. Ultimately, I deceived myself.

My headache pulses and throbs in the darkness. The rocks of the cave dig into my polyester outerwear and press into my back like needles puncturing new pathways for the icy-cold to spread.

The more I reached for perfect states and a perfect self, the more I suffered, and the farther I felt from enlightenment.

The shivering is uncontrollable. My jaw tightens, my teeth chatter. The sound of enamel striking enamel like a jackhammer fills my head. My heartbeat is slowing and softening. The world grows darker. There's no use in fighting it.

All those false stories, ideas, delusions, and expectations became like an invisible veil slipped over my consciousness. They influenced my reality, caused unnecessary suffering, and bled into my friendships, my relationships—every part of my life.

My blood is thickening and slowing. It's freezing. What remains of me rushes toward the very core of my being. Just let it happen. There's no use in resisting.

It was difficult to love others for who they were because I didn't fully love myself. It was difficult accepting others' faults because I didn't fully accept my own. Requiring others' perfection and enlightenment of myself was a coping strategy for my perception of an imperfect world, a self-sabotaging mechanism I used to avoid connection, commitment, and heartbreak.

Chapter 34

An icy grasp travels up my spine, seeps into my ribcage, and fills my lungs. It feels like I'm breathing in knives.

If no one was perfect—if I wasn't perfect—then I could use this belief as an excuse to avoid commitment. I couldn't fail what I never attempted. I feared loving imperfection because settling for anything less meant giving my personal approval to something faulted. And yet this very reasoning is why my relationships fractured and fell apart. All along, I was avoiding the pain.

Everything's falling apart. Accept it. Lean into the pain.

I was so far from the reality. Enlightenment has nothing to do with attainment or perfection. Even those awake remain imperfect. They have flaws and weaknesses. They make mistakes.

No one escapes this cold. No one escapes the end. No one escapes nature.

I don't want to be perfect anymore. Life isn't about ridding myself of unpleasant experiences—that's partly what it means to be human. There was no need to impose. Change was already unfolding. Everything tied together at the deepest level.

May I accept my imperfections. May I let go of identifying so tightly to ideas about myself. May I let go of identifying to thought itself.

Let go of myself. Let go of self. Let the self be as it is.

In my search for a special meditative moment, I'd missed something. I'd missed… my life. The support, gifts, and blessings that surrounded me. I fell into the exact traps I'd tried to avoid. Is it too late to re-examine the source from which I derive my sense of meaning?

I'd forgotten what it means to love and how lucky I am to be here—if only for these last few moments.

If I have more time—if I'm given any more time after this—I don't want to mislead or delude myself anymore. I don't need to fight myself. I don't have to. I can step outside myself, redirect attention, change perspectives, the way

True Nature

I relate to phenomena, view everything objectively, observe it all as it is… listen, notice, and allow myself to be taught… I can experience who I really am.

I can allow. Allow the cold to take over. Allow the darkness to flow over me.

All this thinking only caused more problems.

So just be here. Where it's so cold, it's almost warm.

Accept it. Allow the wants and desires.

Don't resist. It's burning. These clothes need to come off.

I want to live in the real world. To be imperfect. To be.

I can't move. Everything's losing feeling. Balance.

And the more I grow aware of these stories, the harder it is to delude myself.

Open yourself. My face burns.

Slowly, the delusion fades away.

Along with everything else. A searing hot cold spreads all over my body.

Into the present moment.

I feel sleepy, tired.

Maybe, this is where enlightenment resided all along.

I'm so sorry… I wish I had known what I know now. I didn't mean to hold onto what was supposed to happen. About how my life might turn out. About how my life should be…

And one more breath leaves my lips.

CHAPTER 35
ALIVE

"David!" Bradley yells. "Wake up! Can you hear me?"

"Awake," Lama Dai says.

Their voices sound drowned out as if coming from deep underwater.

After a long gasp, my eyes flutter open. Familiar faces take shape before me as I blink hard. I try to stand.

"Easy, easy, easy," Bradley says.

The air remains thin and difficult to breathe, but warmth covers my entire body. Even my sickness has passed. I'm alive—but how?

"*Pani*," Lama Dai says, holding a plastic coke bottle to my cracked lips.

I allow the cold water to flow down my throat and cough from trying to drink so quickly.

As I come to my senses, I notice a small fire crackling behind them. Slowly and steadily, Dai and Bradley carry me over. I reach my hands to the pit and stare into the twisting flames, remembering everything.

"You okay?" Bradley asks.

I glance outside the cave. The storm has died down. "Yeah…"

Bradley exhales deeply. "Thank God, man. You scared the shit out of me." He kneels beside the fire and stares, too. "I know this is rough, but we have to go as soon as possible. Lama Dai says the monsoon could come back at any minute."

I take a deep breath, scoot closer to the flames, and allow feeling to return to my body. Thankfully, the fire warms me up. My body puts itself back together.

"Alright," I say.

Bradley reaches out his hand and I feel myself pulled to my feet. My legs feel weak, like I've been bedridden for days, and my joints snap back into place. As I start to lift my backpack, Lama Dai grabs the straps.

"I carry."

I sigh and reach for his, but he takes both backpacks in his hands. I watch as he skillfully fastens his backpack atop mine with a clever interlocking of his backpack's straps before throwing them both over his shoulder and onto his back. An impressive feat.

"*Pani*?" he asks me.

I shake my head.

At that, Lama Dai pours the remaining water from his plastic coke bottle onto the fire, extinguishing the flames. Then he hands me my trekking poles and walks into the light.

I follow Lama Dai and Bradley outside, planting the steel tips of my poles into a familiar snowy terrain. This time, only a few snowflakes fall around me and splash against my puffy jacket.

As my eyes adjust, the surrounding mountains take shape, and everything comes into focus. There's a distant wooden sign set against a pile of boulders. Hundreds of Tibetan prayer flags tied between the huge rocks flap in the wind. This must be the top of the pass.

I walk over to the largest boulder and collapse on top of it. This place was supposed to spark my enlightenment. I laugh

Chapter 35

a tired and exhausted laugh, and my heart swells. This moment is all that matters.

Larke Pass

Lama Dai looks up at the patch of dark clouds creeping into view.

"We go," he says, then he nods toward the valley. I take it as a sign that he wants me to lead.

I trek across the rocky pass with careful strides through the saddle in the mountain. Beyond it, we reach a steep descent into the valley. My first steps onto the loose rock and scree send me sliding down the mountain, but I lean back and dig my feet and poles into the rocks to keep from toppling over.

Lama Dai slides behind me and grabs my shirt. "*Bistare*."

Slowly.

I take my time sliding down the mountainside scree with weak, shaky legs and blurry eyesight. Thankfully, the hiking is a thousand times easier without a backpack. I look back at

Lama Dai and smile as he surfs the scree with both of our packs.

Lama Dai keeping a close eye and carrying my pack

The snowpack on either side of the rocky trail melts away as we descend. By the time we reach the bottom of the valley, the sun hangs high in the blue sky, and we come to the outskirts of a tiny village.

Bradley and Lama Dai situate themselves on the guesthouse porch, and the bright light of the sun sparks a piercing headache and nausea once again. I spot a nearby enclosure and stumble beneath the tent.

I welcome the darkness beneath the thick shade of the tarp. Without thought, I drop my poles and spread myself across the floor. A chicken roosted in the corner pops up and marches out the vestibule entrance, leaving me alone.

I close my eyes.

Hannah strokes my chest with her fingertips. Ganesh shakes my hand and grins. Sajana lays her hands upon my shoulders.

Chapter 35

Lama Dai sits quietly beside me on the bus. Bradley meditates on the rooftop.

The next time I wake, Lama Dai enters through the tent flap and sets a bowl of ramen before me. By the time I roll over and sit up, he's already gone. I grasp the bowl and take a whiff. The slightest smell of the noodles makes me realize I'm ravenously hungry. I slurp up every bit of the warm savory soup, which slides easily down my throat. Then I lay back down and find myself drawn into a deep sleep.

I wake again to someone opening the tent's vestibule door. This time it's Bradley.

"How ya feelin', bud?" he asks.

I scan my body for a moment. "A lot better than before."

"You had us worried."

I nod. "How'd you guys find me?"

"You've got Dai to thank for that. He told me we should backtrack and then found your footprints in the snow. You were already at the top. You just wandered a bit off-track. I have to say, you gave us a pretty good scare—you'd nearly turned into a popsicle by the time we got to you.

"Thankfully, the cave had enough dry sticks and logs for us to get a fire going. Some of the villagers must have spent time in there before. And it turns out one of the few things Dai packed in that little backpack of his was fire-starter. Pretty lucky, huh?"

I shake my head. "An omen."

The ends of Bradley's lips curl upward. Then he gazes at one of the tarp walls for some time. "I really thought we were going to lose you there for a minute..."

As a tear falls down his cheek, my heart warms. For the longest time, I've wanted him to change. I felt uncomfortable with who he was. I wished he was someone different. Someone who behaved and thought like I do. He thinks differently—but all our different thoughts, beliefs, ideals, and techniques—they're subject to change. Thoughts aren't what make us who we are and the differences I perceive in someone doesn't make me separate from them. We're something much deeper, threaded together, and connected by a shared essence.

"You know," I say, finally. "I've had this feeling that this might be our last big adventure together. I haven't wanted to talk about it. I didn't want to fight or entertain the thought of losing your friendship. I've wanted to hold onto what's familiar. To have someone there with me through thick and thin, every step of the way, all the way to the end. And you are... but it might not look the way I expect. It's just that—"

"Look," Bradley says. "Who knows what happens after this? We'll just take things one moment at a time and accept whatever comes our way. We aren't separate, just like Sajana said. No matter what path we choose, we'll always be connected."

I nod and take in a long breath before exhaling. "You're a good friend, Bradley."

"Any time, brother." Bradley rises to his feet. "Plus, I don't think I could get rid of you even if I tried."

I crack up laughing. "We're tied together."

Bradley nods. "Ready to finish this thing?"

This time, I push myself up and follow him out the tent's vestibule door. Lama Dai's resting on the guesthouse porch hunched over his map.

Lama Dai looks up and smiles. "Sick?"

I shake my head. "Better."

"Tonight," he says. "Wi-Fi, hot shower."

Bradley and I laugh. That would be nice. Some time spent relaxing and sleeping off what remains of this fatigue. And when all of this is over, getting back to my ordinary life. That's what I'm looking forward to the most. A mundane existence that I can grow to love, to make special in my own way without the need for theatrics or pushing myself to the edge of death. A simple, boring, and beautiful life filled with appreciation for whatever time I have left.

Chapter 35

Lama Dai snags my backpack and the three of us make our way downhill, leaving behind the towering glacial mountain peaks and returning to the valley's thick jungle.

"You know what?" Bradley asks suddenly. "This trek has really got me thinking."

"About what?"

"Maybe I am ready for a relationship."

I smile. "It's time, is it?"

Bradley wobbles his head. "I've been so focused on meditation these past few years. But there's so much you can learn about yourself through another person. I figure I could stay open to the idea."

"I'm sure she's out there somewhere."

Bradley laughs. "Just staying open, that's all."

For a moment, I think about Hannah. I'd put so much pressure on myself by subscribing to the idea of a soulmate, but a fruitful relationship isn't rooted in idealism or perfection, nor must it always start as a blazing bonfire. It can start slow, like a tiny flame, and be built from the ground up. It's something that requires compromise, sacrifice, and navigating difficult conversations. With enough attention, awareness, and trust, I know the fire within my heart will grow slowly over time and spread to others—possibly even a special someone. It's the kind of love where my happiness doesn't depend on another person.

Late that afternoon, we emerge from the canopy to reach a pink-painted guesthouse with a large courtyard at the foot of a great forest. We indulge in the hot outdoor showers, charge our phones, eat a *dal bhat* dinner, meditate for an hour, and lay on our beds. I roll over and bury my head into the pillow.

"Feel better soon, brother," Bradley says to me.

"Will do," I reply. "Goodnight."

"Night."

CHAPTER 36
FINAL DAY

After waking from a deep sleep, I feel reborn. I dreamt many dreams last night, but none of them involved lying next to Hannah on the Japanese futon that stormy night.

We meet Lama Dai in the courtyard and discuss the trek over a plate of Tibetan bread. There, Lama Dai says it's best we take a bus at the next village and end our hike. I'm hesitant to end the hike a couple days early, but as the day goes on, the trail's mostly road-walking anyway. Additional rest will do my body and mind some good.

The final miles are bittersweet. Instead of our usual pioneering pace, we walk slowly and silently. Whenever the trail leads us beside green bluffs, we stop and gaze at distant waterfalls and listen to the wind. With the miles running thin, there's nowhere to be. Hiking through the Himalayas and living in Nepal has been naturally spectacular, incredibly beautiful, and challenging beyond belief. It's difficult leaving comfort behind, but I emerge from nature with an improved wellbeing, lighter in mind, stronger in body, and connected to all. I may not have found enlightenment, but I rediscovered the things worth living for. If I'm to die tomorrow, I've already lived a life worth living.

Chapter 36

Bradley and Lama Dai road-walking our last miles

Me and Lama Dai, nowhere to be

True Nature

We reach a dirt road in the early afternoon heat and wait in the shade of a bus stop, watching the shadows of the nearby jungle creep across the rocky terrain. When a bus finally pulls up, the three of us climb aboard and take a bumpy drive down the mountains.

Lama Dai looks out the window, and I follow his gaze at the passing the jungle. This trek was so unlike the Pacific Crest Trail, but maybe that's what I needed. With so many unmet desires and expectations, I was forced to look inward, practice presence, and find balance.

Parts of my life may not turn out how I envision them, but instead of attaching myself to specific visions, I have the option to ground myself in the ever-changing sensory experience of nature—sensations that pierce through the illusions of perfection, loneliness, and despair.

I'm grateful for every step of this adventure. For Bradley, who led me to Sajana. For Sajana, who led me to balance. For Lama Dai, who led me through the mountains. And for all of them who led me to myself and reminded me of what truly matters.

The bus rumbles up the road and shakes up my thoughts. I'd gotten meditation so wrong that I laugh at myself to avoid the embarrassment. Meditation isn't just confined to sitting. It's continuous, unending, and teaches me how to live. Cultivating a still mind when seated is useful, but carrying that stillness into life's chaotic moments requires opening and balance.

The mind will continue to replay made-up scenarios and imagined situations that prevent me from seeing the reality. Thoughts about loneliness, unworthiness, and expectations will keep arising. Unwanted thoughts are part of the raw data of experience. Such thoughts, sensations, vibrations, and temperatures will keep crashing over me in waves. The peaks and valleys might seem to drag on. Earthquakes may seem like they're here to stay. But nothing is forever.

Chapter 36

Everything is impermanent, coming and going, changing like the wind and water and earth.

So why cling or push away? It's all here for me. No matter what arises, sunshine or storm, it teaches me about myself, the nature of reality, and reminds me to return home.

I don't need to get rid of suffering—suffering can be a necessary catalyst for change. Suffering and change are intertwined, embedded into the fabric of reality and nature. All my suffering, struggles, and failures brought me here, and I wouldn't be who I am today without them. It takes going out of balance to learn what it means to balance. It takes closing down to know what it means to open in a healthy way. I'll need suffering if I wish to experience change, and the two will remain intertwined until I don't need to suffer anymore. And the less I resist suffering, the more it dissolves.

CHAPTER 37
BESISHAHAR

Three hours later, as the sun begins to set, we arrive at a small city called Besishahar. The streets are filled with the familiar bustling noises of the city. Horns, engines, and motorbikes fly by, their headlights illuminating the darkening streets. It's a stark contrast to the music of the jungles, plains, and mountains.

Lama Dai puts us up in a cheap hotel in the heart of the city. It's no Hostel Yog, but it does the job. Bradley and I split a small twin bedroom on the second floor. When it's my turn to shower, I scrub off the last remaining dirt and dust from my body then change back into my hiking clothes. Apart from washing my socks in the river once or twice, we've gone this whole trek without laundry. I imagine myself hanging up freshly cleaned shorts and T-shirts atop the rooftop clothesline at the Pokhara house, gazing out to the very mountains we've spent the last three weeks trekking.

I splay myself onto bed, plug my phone into an outlet, and turn on the old box television in the corner of the room. We flip through the channels, stumbling onto an English-speaking sports program replaying soccer and cricket highlights. We leave it on just to hear the English before turning it off again.

Around that time, Lama Dai knocks on our door and says it's time for dinner. A few locals eating in the downstairs

Chapter 37

dining hall acknowledge our presence with nods and we're ushered to a table in the corner. For the first time in what seems like forever, each of us study a menu and order something other than *dal bhat*. I end up choosing a mushroom pizza, Bradley gets a plate of vegetables and *momos*, and Lama Dai orders fried rice.

The pizza tastes a bit bland and chewy, but I don't care. I enjoy every bite of something that's not *dal bhat*.

After stuffing ourselves full, we walk the busy streets beneath a night sky, listen to the passing motorbikes, and study the shops facades. The nearby construction reminds me not of a broken city but of an earthquake that happened years ago, whose effects still echo into the present, of a place building upon itself, of change and impermanence.

To my surprise, Lama Dai joins me and Bradley in our bedroom to meditate for one last time together. There's nowhere to go, nothing to do. With no agenda or goal in mind, there's so much to explore and nothing is off-limits.

My witnessing softens. I surrender effort and let go of tips, tricks, and techniques. The less I do, the more benefit I receive. I work effortlessly in ways that I feel I'm best progressing. I stop running and reaching. I grow curious and witness my experience as if for the first time.

I still my body and send signals for it to relax. The tension in my face, neck, and shoulders eases. This is my past leaving me. My breath is like the wind. It's everywhere—in my nostrils, face, neck, shoulders, chest, back, and stomach. Sometimes, it's heavy and intentional. Other times, it falls shallow and sails away like a ship over the horizon, so faint that it practically disappears. I allow my breath to be as it is. When discomfort arises, I lean in not with masochism but with curiosity.

This practice is subject to change, dependent upon circumstance, and custom-tailored to fit the needs of the moment. It softens the rigid areas of my life. It frees me to stay flexible and adaptable. I let go of and return to prescriptions, tools, techniques, and lineages. I show love and compassion, listen to my heart, and follow what's best for my life.

This practice invites me to shine a light into the dark corners of my mind. To clear out the old forgotten rooms. To bring about something new and promising. And to keep facing the tides with courage, not in the hopes of a future when discomfort and existential angst disappears, but because that's what it means to live in my true nature.

* * *

We sleep until morning, pack up, and wait outside the hotel. I squat roadside, awaiting the arrival of our bus to Pokhara, and stare at the blades of grass bursting from the cracks in the concrete. Nature grows even in the most urban landscapes, following us into the city. I imagine Sajana's voice:

"Hard times are part of the process," she very well might have said. "But do you see how resilient nature is? How even in the city the grass grows between the cracks of the sidewalks? How the vines climb up the walls? How the hillside temples are covered in so much of moss and trees? Such is your inner nature, too. No matter how difficult life becomes, you can always grow. There is nothing on the outside which can stop your nature from unfolding."

I smile, wondering when I'll see her again.

When our bus to Pokhara finally arrives, Lama Dai stays standing on the sidewalk. Apparently, he's taking a different bus to visit his family in some other faraway town.

Bradley and I turn to thank him with a tight embrace.

"*Dhanyabhat*, Dai," I say to him.

Lama Dai smiles. He may not speak much English, but some things can only be felt.

After exchanging contact details, I step onto the bus and plop down in one of the window seats near the front. To my surprise, Bradley takes the seat beside me.

Chapter 37

"Mind if I join you?" Bradley asks.

I smile. "All yours."

As our bus pulls forward, I breathe a deep breath and soak in the scenery streaming past my window. From there, we rattle up the dusty red road, a road leading away from the Himalayas and toward the concrete jungles of man and motorcycle.

EPILOGUE

Bradley and I spent three memorable months living with Sajana and her family in Nepal. I'll always remember living in the Pokhara house, taking trips into nature, and hiking in the Himalayas as a special turning point in life. Thank you to the many beautiful and influential people we met along the way. Not included in this book were many more wonderful people, adventures, and experiences in Nepal. To Sajana, Shiva, Amit, Goma, Devindra, the entire family, and so many others: thank you for your kindness.

Me, Sarod, Nanu, Devinda, Shiva, Goma, & Bradley

Epilogue

Sajana remains with her family in Nepal where she supports a local orphanage and travels the world with the help of her non-profit organization, Universal Love. Details can be found at the website universallove.world.

After our trip to Nepal, Bradley and I embarked on one more adventure together: living for three months in Australia with Richard Walker, our old hiking buddy from the trail. We served in his coffee shop, embraced the local community, and spent time walking the whitest sands in the world (or so claims the Hyam's Beach marketing department).

Once our visas expired in October of 2019, we returned home to the States. I currently live in Dallas practicing movement, meditation, and writing. Meanwhile, Bradley is homesteading land in Georgia and growing a fruit forest.

I hope that you find peace, meaning, and gratitude in this moment.

ACKNOWLEDGEMENTS

This book took effort, not just on my behalf, but from many others, too. A special thanks goes to Brianna Boes for guiding me with an exceptional manuscript review, and to Ben Wolf for his pinpointed professional line edits.

When this book was in its final stages, I enlisted the help of many friends and family members for alpha and beta reading. Thank you to Bradley Lovell, Jacob Glenn, Robinson Erhardt, Carol Weaver, Cody Holbrook, Etienne Bognar, Malcolm MacDuffie, Jonny Martin, Reg Spittle, and Michael Aldape. Words can't express how deeply I appreciate your generosity.

A beautiful book would be nothing without a beautiful cover. Once again, I'm grateful to Kett McKenna for creating this brilliant cover art. Please consider supporting his work by hiring him yourself and finding him on Instagram (@kettdoesart).

To my parents, John and Charla Smart: Thank you for everything. I love you, mom and dad.

A final acknowledgement to my dear friend Bradley. Thank you, brother.

FINAL REQUEST

If you enjoyed the story, **it would mean a lot to me if you considered writing an honest review on Amazon or wherever you read your books (Goodreads, iBooks, etc.).** Reviews are critical to the success of any indie author's book. Thank you for your consideration in crafting a short review.

If you'd like to read more of my work, my thru-hiking memoir The Trail Provides is available on Amazon and Audible today. **I also keep a blog, which you can follow to at www.thinkingwithdavid.com.**

I look forward to hearing from you, and I wish you well today and always.

Love,
David

BOOKS BY DAVID SMART

The Trail Provides: A Boy's Memoir of Thru-Hiking the Pacific Crest Trail

True Nature: The Wise Woman in Nepal and Searching the Himalayas for Enlightenment

Now available on Amazon or directly from me at:
www.thinkingwithdavid.com

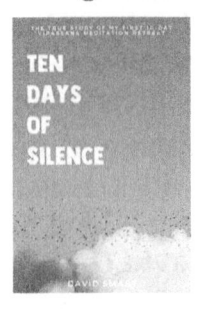

Subscribe to my blog and receive a free eBook, Ten Days of Silence.

www.thinkingwithdavid.com/newsletter

STAY UPDATED

Want to stay updated on when I release new books?

* Follow my blog at https://thinkingwithdavid.com
* Follow my instagram@stay.in.alive

Thank you for reading. I hope you enjoy the continued adventures.

Wishing you well today.

Love,
David

Printed in Great Britain
by Amazon